# The Love Queen of Malabar

*Memoir of a Friendship with Kamala Das*

Merrily Weisbord

―――――

McGill-Queen's University Press

Montreal & Kingston • London • Ithaca

ISBN 978-0-7735-3791-0
Legal deposit fourth quarter 2010
Bibliothèque nationale du Québec

Printed in Canada on acid-free paper that is 100% ancient forest free
(100% post-consumer recycled), processed chlorine free

Published simultaneously in India and the Indian subcontinent by Research Press.

McGill-Queen's University Press acknowledges the support of the Canada Council for the Arts for
our publishing program. We also acknowledge the financial support of the Government of Canada
through the Canada Book Fund for our publishing activities.


Library and Archives Canada Cataloguing in Publication

Weisbord, Merrily
The love queen of Malabar : memoir of a friendship with Kamala Das / Merrily Weisbord.

Includes bibliographical references.
ISBN 978-0-7735-3791-0

1. Kamala Surayya, 1934–2009. 2. Kamala Surayya, 1934–2009–Friends and associates.
3. Weisbord, Merrily. 4. Women authors, India–20th century–Biography.
5. Authors, Malayalam–20th century–Biography.
I. Title.

PR9499.3.D35Z93 2010          828'.91409          C2010-903734-0

Photograph on page 18 by Angie Kaye; page 30, unknown; page 67, Guy Borremans; page 95, Stephen
Legari; pages 216 and 226, Elizabeth Klinck; pages 229 and 248, K.C. George; page 261, David Schaffer.
Photographs on page 148 courtesy T.P. Nandakumar, chief editor, *Crime Fortnightly*, Group Publishing Co (Pvt) Ltd, Calicut, Kerala, India; pages 162–3, *Chandrika Malayalam Daily*, 29 February 2000;
page 258, *Mathrubhumi Daily*, 8 March 2005. Early photographs of Kamala, mother, and family
courtesy of Kamala Das and Nalapat Sulochana. All other photographs by the author.

Quotations from "Morning at Apollo Pier," "An Introduction," "Composition," "The Old Playhouse,"
"Blood," "A Requiem for My Father," "Loud Posters," "Anamalai Poems," "Forest Fire," "A Phone Call
in the Morning," "The Freaks," "The Sunshine Cat," "Jaisurya," "Tomorrow," "Radha," "Grey Hound,"
"Substitute," "The Millionaires at Marine Drive," "Herons," "Convicts," "A Widow's Lament," "For
Auntie Katie," "Gina," "My Grandmother's House," "Next to Indira Gandhi," "The Inheritance," "The
Siesta," "The Swamp," "Terror," "The Dance of the Eunuchs," "Palam," are taken from *Only the Soul
Knows How to Sing: Selections from Kamala Das* (Kottayam, Kerala: DC Books 1996).


This book was designed and typeset by studio oneonone in Minion 10.5/16.

For Kamala Das, long may she reign.

# Contents

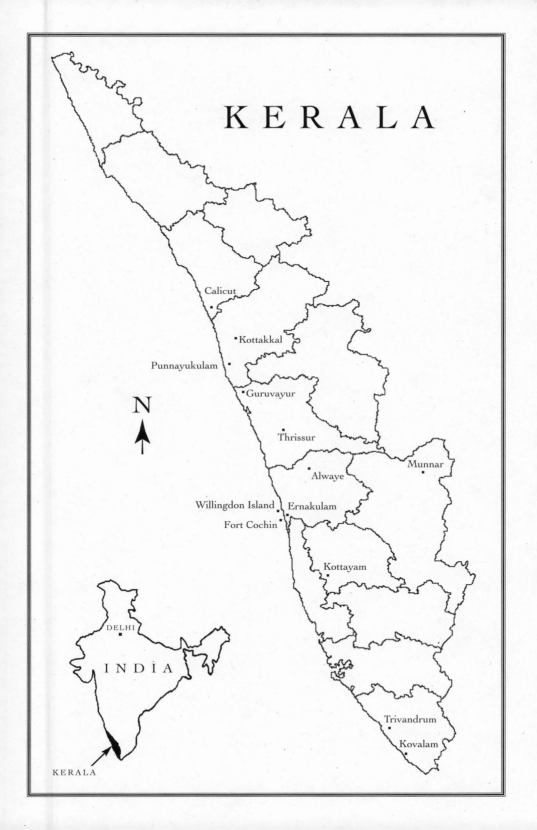

KERALA

N

Calicut

Kottakkal

Punnayukulam

Guruvayur

Thrissur

Munnar

Alwaye

Willingdon Island
Ernakulam

Fort Cochin

Kottayam

DELHI

INDIA

KERALA

Trivandrum

Kovalam

# ONE

# Cochin, Munnar, Kovalam, South India
# 1995

when I walked in
I feared that you might hear my heartbeats thump

# 1

# The Stranger and I

Perhaps every new place has to humble you with its nature, customs, history, bacteria, something that exhausts, confounds, or lays you low. In South India, it is the heat – the oppressive, overbearing heat. Moisture dries briefly after a shower, which is perhaps your third or fourth, and enfolds anew. Heat presses in like an unwelcome, cloying lover.

"When are we moving?" my friend Angie asks when I stir. She's ready for action, a documentary film director, fresh off the plane from England. I am half here in India, half dreamily in Nepal where I was recently trekking in the Arun Valley hills.

"Should we phone ahead?" Angie asks.

"What schedule do you envisage?" she nudges. "How do you plan to proceed with Kamala Das?"

At the mention of Kamala Das, I snap awake, alert as a tiger with her cub. Beloved, notorious Kamala Das, India's honoured writer and great contemporary love poet, read by millions, revered and reviled, is largely unknown in the West and to me, and feelings about our meeting are too delicate to share. I have seen pictures of her, a dark-haired beauty with eyes a lover could swim in, and have read accolades to her courage in life and art. Her gorgeous poetry enchants me, and her ground-breaking autobiography transports me to another world. She was the first Hindu woman to write frankly about sexual desire and would not back down when attacked. "I fling arrows at the uncivilized brutal norms of life for women in Kerala," she challenged, "I tweak the noses of puritans" – a response that inspires me.

Angie's questioning make me nervous. Standing on a lime-green marble floor in an eighteenth-century palace off the Malabar Coast, I am on unfamiliar turf with no parameters to gauge what happens next. Kamala Das is the reason I have flown into this South Indian heat, and I have no plan except to proceed spontaneously with all my antennae quivering.

It's been a month since I left Canada, running away from a memoir I wrote for over a year. I'd been writing professionally for decades, and was using the memoir to survive an uncommunicative phase with my companion, talking myself through on the page. Then one day my companion patted my head lovingly, and I didn't feel anything because I was typing angrily about the day before. When I realized that the memoir had become more real than life itself, I abandoned it. I saw then that I was free and alone in a way I hadn't been for years – my kids living independently and my companion consumed by his work. I longed to fly out of myself and into a larger world. I felt that if I stayed put, comfort and familiarity would close around me like a shell. Writing a travel book seemed the perfect escape, and Kerala, a small tropical state on India's southwest coast, beckoned.

Brochures promised waving palms, sandy beaches, canals and backwaters, stunning mountains, exquisite cuisine, and generous hospitality. Centuries ago, Phoenicians, Greeks, Romans, Arabs, Chinese, Dutch, and finally British traded in Malabar, the Spice Coast of India. Jews had lived in Kerala since the first century AD, Muslims claimed a mosque from the time of Mohammed, and Christians believed the Apostle Thomas converted Kerala Hindus in 52 AD.

Not only was Kerala beautiful and cosmopolitan but it had the lowest infant mortality and highest literacy in South East Asia. Kerala Nayars were matrilineal, and in a country where female fetuses were aborted, Kerala was the only state in India to have more women than men.

I lingered over pictures of the wildflowers and wildlife on the seaward slopes of the Western Ghats, and photos of the wild, blue-green Arabian Sea. Kerala was the destination I hoped for, but I didn't want to write a superficial travel book, and I couldn't imagine a way to journey more deeply into another culture. And then, in my foot-high research file, like a siren calling, was Kamala Das and a poem so beautiful it made my body tingle.

Welcome me, lying down, dear love,
And remain so,
I shall shut the window
for, upward floats the leper's tremolo …

And when I read her autobiography, *My Story*, I saw that Kamala Das was also writing to comprehend, remember, reinvent, and transcend her life, a life so fascinatingly different from mine that her need to write was all I could truly fathom.

I was intensely drawn to her as are millions of others, to her vulnerable longing for someone to love, "like alms looking for a begging bowl," and to her great, wild hunger "to take in with greed like a forest fire that consumes all that comes my way," a fire I could feel igniting in me. Even though Kamala Das was a grand celebrity, short-listed for a Nobel Prize, her confessional tone encouraged me to think I could know her. I wanted to smell the wind from the Arabian Sea as she described it, walk the Malabar Coast, taste a Nayar feast, see the poet whose sensual love poems stirred the heart of modern India. Above all, I wanted to know the woman who could cry out –

… Rob me, destiny, if you must,
Rob me of my sustenance, but do not, I beg
Of you, do not take away my thirst …

I had never dared to publish a memoir as personal as *My Story*, but I too wrote intimately about my life. When Kamala Das revealed why she wrote, I sensed she was a kindred spirit and began to dream of meeting her.

I went quite far in this Kamala/Merrily fantasy. My idea was that I could visit Kamala and learn about her life, through her. And, if the idea pleased her, she could visit me with the same intentions. I started to believe that if she and I were in each other's countries and in each other's lives, we could travel beyond cultural stereotypes, perhaps into friendship. I could go to Kerala and see Kamala's world through her eyes, and she could come to Canada and do the same with mine.

The only trouble was, Kamala didn't know I existed.

Angie and I take the ferry from Bolgatty Island to mainland Ernakulam, and an auto rickshaw to an efficient, downtown hotel near Kamala's apartment. We unpack, and Angie watches bemused as I hesitate, obfuscate, and circle the phone. I am on edge and concerned about bringing a friend, whom I invited for company and support on this fledgling, sans-family journey, to my first encounter with Kamala Das. When I realize I don't have to include Angie, I get up my nerve and make the call.

A Malayalam speaker answers, and I ask for Kamala Das.

"Hello, Kamala, it's Merrily."

"Where are you?" she asks.

"In Cochin."

"Just come over. I will not take my nap. I am not stirring today. Come any time. I am very informal."

"How are you?"

"Fine, considering."

"Uh ... considering?"

"The world we live in, Merrily," she says.

In Canada, after having read all Kamala's available work, I faxed her name to Ellen Coon, a colleague researching a film on development models in Kerala. Ellen wrote back within days:

> Yesterday I met Kamala Das in her fine, high-ceilinged old bungalow
> painted terra-cotta and turquoise. She is queenly, grandiose and aggrieved.
> She wears white saris, her hair is graying, wavy, worn loose and she is quite
> fair. I got the impression she makes revealing personal pronouncements in
> order to conceal herself and is used to being slobbered over without being
> nourished.
>
> She is hurting right now because her husband died two months ago. She
> invites you Merrily to come and live with her for a month.

I had faxed Ellen saying Kamala was someone I "discovered" in my reading – a *possibility*, an *idea*. And now, too suddenly, she was accessible. I would need time to go gently to her world from mine ... "I see birds rising over sentry stalks of bare, black maple. Lichen fluorescent against the rain-stained rock. I have, alternately, a great growing power and a frightened mortal aloneness."

Ellen helped me begin the necessary correspondence.

Dear Kamala Das,

Even though you don't know who I am, you have been in my mind for over a year. I have been thinking about us both – professional writers, with children, husbands in my case, husband in yours, a predilection for questions of desire, unconventional within the bounds of our own cultures. I had planned to write you, formally as befits my respect for your work, and suggest we meet. My idea was that I could visit you and learn about your life and your culture through you, and you could visit me with the same intentions, if the idea pleases you. I thought then we could create a joint memoir. I thought such a memoir might cut through the layers pasted over our respective cultures.

It is amazing to find you are real. Not my construct. You live, breathe, suffer. And you invite me to visit. I feel like I was performing a shadow play and the screen disappeared to reveal me gesticulating in the light of day.

I would receive three subsequent letters from Kamala Das. This was the first:

Ellen this afternoon gave me your letter. I gulped it down hurriedly and later reread it at night facing it as though I was facing you.

Yes, we must meet. But I do not know when. After my husband's death writing for a living has become distasteful to me. But there is no other activity that I can live on. From my eighteenth year I have spent half the night constructing stories that were saleable. Now I am exhausted, weary. I want to be normal, ordinary. I want to be able to sleep the night away. Talent perhaps is only an abnormality, a sixth finger.

You must visit me. My home shall be your home. My sons have grown out of their need for me. When my husband was alive I could feel useful, washing him and giving him his medicines. I have so much of gentleness within me but none to offer it to ...

Kamala's letter arrived when I had hurt my back on a cross-Canada book tour for *Our Future Selves*, my book on sexuality and aging, and was beset by problems troubling my children that I was powerless to fix. Yet Kamala's warmth and vulnerability reached out and drew me to her. I felt I could go to her and she would welcome me. I tried to touch, intrigue, distract her, from a distance.

What a pleasure to hear from you. I hope someone has made you smile since you wrote to me.

I was away for a few days and am now back in my home on this granite shield called the Laurentian Mountains. I have summered here, 40 miles north of Montreal, since my deluded paternal grandfather bought this land to farm. Four years ago, my youngest child turned fifteen and I left our city home and came here to write. I'd had children to care for since I was nineteen. Finally, I could continue where I left off.

I tell you this so you will perhaps understand why I am so happy to know you. I am not you, nor do I pretend to be. But you are caught up in concerns I share – the way writing-for-money leeches energy, the conundrum of adult children, how we express love and create intimacy. To these questions, now the air you breathe, I would add my personal interest in who I am and how I grew.

Your letter filled me with joy. I am so happy you exist.

Soon after, on my birthday, I received a fax and a birthday poem, from Kamala.

Your second letter was as cherishable as the first. It reminded me once again of clear skies and of the feeling of being wanted. Although miserably inadequate as the traditional Indian wife, I loved him more than all and wanted his arms around me whenever I felt insecure. Now I feel that I am rudderless. Even boatless. I shall have to swim. The question that comes up so often since his death is: Where are you swimming to? Is it worth the swim?

I am sick and weary with artifice and the foolish talk of the wealthy. I need to rest. I need to stop thinking. I need to clear out the glands of the mind before I can fill them again with healing thoughts.

The birthday poem she sent me reads:

Our passions,
like paper flowers,
tremble at window sills,
cursed with immortality
in a gaudy, gaudy world ...

# 2

# An Introduction

I hail an auto rickshaw and direct the driver to Kamala's apartment in Ernakulam. The rickshaw negotiates extreme traffic on the main thoroughfare, MG (Mahatma Gandhi) Road, and turns into a rutted side street. It careens around motorbikes and potholes and drops me facing the smudged plate-glass window of Astro Vision Computerized Astrology. There is a beauty parlour next door, and I think at least I could say, "You don't have to go far for a pedicure," because the building, although inhabited by doctors and lawyers, is utterly charmless cement. I am scrolling through the directory when a woman spots me and takes me to Kamala's apartment. The door is opened by a maid. I take off my shoes, place them near the entrance, and look up to face a large apartment, a little child, someone in the background, in the shadows, coming forward.

> … I am Indian, very brown, born in
> Malabar, I speak three languages, write in
> Two, dream in one …

Kamala holds me at arm's length. I see a round, nut-brown face, luxuriant dark hair, full lips, diamond nose-stud, and pools of black behind thick glasses, taking me in. On the phone I had confessed my nervousness, and she said, "It's like an arranged marriage, each hoping the other will treat them with the kindness due." She studies me leisurely at a distance, and with a slow smile deflects her face teasingly away from my eyes. And then we embrace, a heartfelt, on my part, acknowledgment of the talent and courage of this enigmatic, attractive woman.

Then, immediately, I am swept away – through an improvised receiving room where nothing matches. "No frills, spartan," Kamala says, leading me past an ornate antique daybed, a modern little kitchen table, a life-size painting of a nude ("I've done a series"), to a concrete kitchen to meet the vegetarian cook. Then she hustles me quickly out of the apartment to beat the inevitable influx of writers, supplicants, admirers, friends.

I trail in her wake, soaking in sound-bites of her current life – her long fast after her husband died "hoping for a painless, blameless end," her son's insistence that she move to Cochin to live nearby, her founding of a legal organization that defends abandoned women and investigates mysterious female deaths, her responsibilities as patron of the writer's workshop and mentor to the young women who come for support "and curl around and cling like creepers." Visitors arrive constantly unannounced: "What can you do?"

We hurry downstairs, and as soon as we step outside, Kamala's old white Ambassador, India's roly-poly touring car, cruises into position. The driver stops at the entrance and opens the back door. Kamala is inching along the back seat when a clean-cut young man darts from the shadows, notepad in hand.

"Interview, Amma [Mother]."

"Please, another time."

Undeterred, the journalist moves closer. "Amma," he persists, "do you agree with poet Giri's comment that feminism is a bunk?"

Kamala translates the Malayalam, asking what I'd answer, but the journalist's head is though the window and I am busy manœuvring around his backside. Anyway, his goading has worked.

"That is his opinion," she says to me, "good poet but not a great thinker." Then an angry stream of Malayalam, hands flying, as she gestures the journalist away.

But he's holding fast to the door. "And those women you are defending who say they were raped. How do you know they are not prostitutes? Do you have proof?"

Kamala retreats into a corner, wrapping herself in her shawl. "If you were to say my mother is a prostitute, I have no evidence to say she is not," she retorts in Malayalam.

The young man releases the car door and scribbles furiously.

Kamala rolls up her tinted window and turns to me. "My mother is eighty-five years old, a celebrated poet, the last word in respectability, they adore her."

We begin to move, and the young man runs alongside the car like a news hound in a 1940s movie. Kamala sighs, upset at herself. "Tomorrow they'll print that. I shouldn't let myself be provoked over last week's controversy."

"Doesn't it tire you?" I ask.

"Who else would do it?"

"Yes," I say, "British writer Geoffrey Moorhouse described you as the South's most famous living writer after Narayan."

"Narayan would be pleased, " she says.

That early afternoon in Cochin, all I know about Kamala Das is what I've culled from articles and readings available in Canada. It's enough to appreciate being with her, but not enough to explain the star treatment that I just saw, extraordinary for a writer.

My research notes read:

Kamala Das is an upper-caste Nayar.

The traditional cosmetics of the Nayar woman: dab of turmeric on the cheeks, sandal-line on the forehead, collyrium in the eye, betel in the mouth.

Kamala's great-grandmother was the daughter of the Raja of Punnathore Kota, her mother the daughter of the Chittanjur Kunjunni Raja.

Kamala spoke English in Calcutta, and Malayalam, the South Dravidian official language of Kerala, with her grandmother in Malabar.

She was married off at fifteen and has three sons.

In 1984 she was short-listed for the Nobel Prize for Literature along with Marguerite Yourcenar, Doris Lessing, and Nadine Gordimer.

Poet Balan Chullikkad calls Kamala Das "the first feminist emotional revolutionary of our time."

The Indian tabloid press calls her "The Love Queen of Malabar."

Kamala sails into the Renaissance Room of Ernakulam's Avenue Regent Hotel, me in her wake, dazzled by her unpredictable utterances. She veers right to the corner banquette and sits with her back against the wall, surveying the scene. "When I was younger, I wanted to possess what I loved," she says, hands grabbing and enclosing a hypothetical being, "but there is freedom in letting go." She points across the starched white tablecloth to an extravagant buffet across the room. "I don't have to take home the silver trays to enjoy my lunch."

By mutual consent, a tape recorder whirs on the table between us, as it has from the moment we met, and I'm grateful I can review the array of topics it registers during that first lunch: an introduction to her mother, the distinguished Malayalam poetess who lost her memory and is being helped by the five-thousand-year-old healing system of Ayurveda, said to cure chronic diseases like rheumatism and arthritis; an introduction to the Hindu god Krishna, Kamala's true beloved; and a discourse on the joys of no longer being a sex object but an Amma, Mother, a woman of substance – "not devalued for losing that erotic image as American women are, lifting up the breasts, lifting up the behind. I have climbed the rungs of a woman's dignity from Chechi [Elder Sister] to Amma, and become stronger. Now I can speak on platforms and ask questions society has to answer. Now the soul takes over. The body was everything, now the body is just a witness.

"Merrily, eat something," she says. "Are you not going to eat something?"

The buffet is laden with regional specialties cooked in coconut milk and unfamiliar sauces. I take bits, lots of familiar pineapple, so I don't appear befuddled, but I am too keyed up to taste. I am trying to take it all in – Kamala's young women visitors as "creepers," her relief at no longer having "to feed the hungers of the body," memories as "light luggage." The metaphors jolt my mind. My mind heaves, and inside I laugh with joy.

"Do you like spicy food?" I ask, to say something.

"My husband used to be fond of such things. That's another kind of life, when my husband was alive. We lived in a huge place, five servants …"

We are interrupted by an elegant, older Malayali in leg-revealing *mundu* (a sarong-type garment, worn by men and women in Kerala) and western silk shirt, introduced as B.A. Raja Krishnan, a wealthy industrialist with a string of newspapers and magazines.

"How many publications?" Kamala inquires.

"Nine."

"You want to see his office?" she asks me.

In a blink, I am to be picked up, taken somewhere (I should reserve the day), going boating. "It's not a bad program, Merrily," she says. "They can interview you, put you on the cover." He takes my number, I take his, we'll be in touch.

"I used to write for his paper. I had columns simultaneously in four journals," Kamala says.

"You must have worked hard."

"Very hard. Because my husband came from a feudal background, one of the wealthiest joint families in South Malabar. Until the day he died, I kept him well, and every night he would remind me, 'Okay, Kamala, go up and start typing.' While the family slept, I'd work in my room till about three, sleep a few hours, get up and bring his tray. When he was dying, he said, 'Thank you, you made my life,' in front of everybody, in the front of the doctors. 'For what?' I asked. 'For love,' he said, 'for looking after me.' So it was a complete marriage, made perfect by his realization of how I had worked."

Kamala's bell-like articulation and the music of her voice captivate me. But I am having trouble reconciling what she's saying now with what she wrote about her husband twenty years ago, at age thirty-seven, in *My Story*.

She said then that she was given in an arranged marriage to K. Madhava Das, an older relative, when she was fifteen. He raped her on their wedding night, "again and again he hurt me," and she became "one more relative to submit to his clumsy fondling." She left her privileged city life and ancestral home and lands to live with him in what she describes as a claustrophobic, matchbox house in a low-class colony, and "at night, he took me several times, with a vengeance."

On her birthday, her husband came home with his boyfriend. "[They] shoved me out of the bedroom and locked themselves in. I stood for awhile wondering what two men could possibly do together to get some physical rapture, but after some time, my pride made me move away. I went to my son and lay near him. I felt then a revulsion for my womanliness. The weight of my breasts seemed to be crushing me. My private part was only a wound, the soul's wound showing through."

Decades later, she published a much-anthologized poem – about another man.

… It was not to gather knowledge
of yet another man that I came to you but to learn
what I was and by learning, to learn to grow …

And yet Kamala is telling me that her husband's deathbed words made her marriage perfect and complete.

"You didn't resent working for him?" I ask.

"I liked working for him because he would praise me. I come from a matriarchal society. Matriarchs are expected to look after husbands. And there was some feeling that I was protected. He was giving me some kind of emotional shelter."

I keep eye contact, not wanting to stem the flow, and check the tape recorder discreetly, trying not to miss a word. I haven't yet read Kamala's poem "Composition":

... I must let my mind striptease
I must extrude
autobiography.

Or "Loud Posters":

I am today a creature turned inside
Out. To spread myself across wide highways
Of your thoughts, stranger, like a loud poster
Was always my desire ...

I think her candour is just for me.

"Forty-three years of married life with a man I married at fifteen. So you see, it grows on you. I don't resent, I don't regret. All the grief inflicted upon me by my husband paid dividends. All the struggles proved useful later. Poetry came oozing out like blood out of injuries. How could I have written so much of poetry if he hadn't made me cry? All the anguish, you weed something out of it."

Kamala calls for hot water with cumin seeds for the digestion, and I stir the pineapple bits on my plate. Then she rises, dons her dark glasses, and waves to B.A. Raja Krishnan. I look wistfully at the groaning buffet table as I walk her to the elevator. She invites me to the house the next day, touches my arm, ruffles my hair.

I walk the few blocks back to the hotel trying to make sense of Kamala – shunned by her husband yet defending him, chased by the journalist yet welcoming me, churning out columns, oozing poetry – disconnected, unfathomable glimpses, flying loose.

# 3

## Love in Another Country

I shut off the air conditioner and open the window, mistakenly thinking Angie has lit a mosquito coil. At 3 AM, I feel a bite, jump up, squish the bloody bug, slather the bite, and reread the malaria booklet from the American clinic in Nepal: seal all windows, air condition at all times, tuck mosquito nets tightly around the bed, use coils and Deet, do not use perfume, which attracts insects. Reeking of essential oils from the Fort Cochin wharf, I slam down the window, start the AC, consider a blood test, make plans for palliative care.

Day dawns calmer. I scurry to the market at Broadway and merge with a turmeric, peacock, bottle-green surge of dark-skinned, saried women with beautiful, thick, black hair. We stride energetically past stalls of vibrant, fresh produce, a feast of colours without the exoticism of Katmandu's mix of Sherpas, Tibetans, Kumals, and orange-robed Sadhus seated bolt upright in the back of a rickshaw en route to Shivaratri. Cochin is bustling into modernity. Its major port, Willingdon Island, houses massive storage sheds, wharves, and the HQ of Southern Naval Command. And its commercial heart, mainland Ernakulam, is planning an international airport. Fort Cochin guidebooks may feature Kathakali dance, backwater tours, Chinese fishing nets, habourfront hotels, a church dating from 1503, a palace from 1555, and a synagogue from 1568, but in the flood of humanity on Broadway in downtown Ernakulam, I am the only foreigner I see.

I hurry to meet Kamala whom I've invited for lunch and am five minutes late, at which she says brusquely, "The hostess is later than the guest." She doesn't remove her dark glasses and instead of talking to me, suggests I interview the chef. This is not as disconcerting as it could be, because K.C. Joseph knows his "mother food" – pumpkin simmered with toasted coconut, okra in yogurt sauce and mustard seeds, fish poached in coconut milk, seasoned dal, *dosa* (sourdough crepes), *idli* (rice dumplings), *sambar* (legume and vegetable stew), Black Pearl Spot fresh-water fried fish, chicken minced curry, red pumpkin and broad bean curry, rice noodles with a seasoned coconut sauce, mango, pineapple and lime pickles. I return, salivating, and Kamala announces curtly that a journalist and a lawyer are waiting at home for her. She seems distant, not at all like yesterday, and I don't know why.

"So what shall we do, wait until Angie comes?" she asks tersely.

At first I am taken aback by her change of mood. Then, I realize that the problem may not be me, but the associations evoked by Angie's clipped English accent at our first meeting, when she appeared briefly to photograph us. Kamala grew up under the Raj and attended a school for "whites," one of only six brown-skinned children allowed in. In *My Story*, she describes the day the governor's wife arrived and the Indian children were stashed away in the hall behind the bathrooms. Kamala peeked out and saw a pink-cheeked little girl with blond ringlets reciting a poem to the august lady. It was a poem Kamala had written, and the other girl took the accolades for herself.

"No, no, we'll start," I gulp.

"Tomorrow my sister has invited you to her grandchild's naming ceremony, and I will pick you up at 9:30. Afterwards there's a lovely feast, sweet curry, pungent curry, hot curry, like an orchestra. You've not seen a naming ceremony."

"I've been to a Newari wedding feast in Nepal, and the bride looked so sad."

"She's sad to leave her parents' home forever."

"Were you sad?"

"Not I. I was too young. I was excited about the new clothes, jewellery. I was not sad at my wedding. But on the wedding night I was sad, shocked, grieved. I did not expect such things. I had not even dreamt such physical brutalities would take place. Someone should have taught me the facts of life. Then I wouldn't have hated sex so much."

"I know your first sexual experience was very violent," I say, assuming Kamala means the sex on her wedding night. She is India's greatest living love poet. She writes familiarly about desire, love affairs, lust. "Often sex is often not very good at the beginning," I commiserate. "I didn't really enjoy it until I was about thirty-five."

"Do you have a husband now?" she asks, changing the subject.

"I am living with a man I've been with for seventeen years."

"Did he have a former wife?"

"Never a formal wife. Actually, I have not married him, and I don't think I will. We share our homes."

There is a pause as something I take for granted clicks in Kamala's mind.

"He sleeps in your room?" she asks, to verify.

I'm not sure how to respond. If I tell the truth, I may lose her. Yet, if I don't, I will never know what she makes of it, or me.

"Yes. Sometimes we live in different houses, but when we are together we sleep in the same room. I feel protected, yet not smothered."

"You feel protected." Kamala repeats, emphasizing a feeling she understands. "What does he do?"

"He's a film producer."

Kamala segues smoothly onto the safer ground of filmmaking. Australian, British, Dutch, Indian filmmakers have made documentaries on her life. The last five-day shoot, she believes, killed her husband with its shouting, wires, gadgets, people swarming for days, even into the prayer room, giving him no rest.

"You know, the mistress gets a huge flat, central AC, gets a car, driver, two servants thrown in," Kamala says, looping back to describe a "mistress" of her acquaintance. " I really think wives should envy the mistress. What can the wife get at the most?"

"I'm hardly a mistress after seventeen years. What would you call my relationship?"

"I think it is a kind of friendship. Exploitative friendship."

I ask her if she could choose to live with someone without being married, and she says no one would tolerate it. I mention the recent articles about college students living together, and she says that they're so young, there isn't that grand passion that would take their cohabitation beyond the ordinary: rather, it's as ordinary as friction.

"You have to bring quality to every action. Otherwise, you just live together and you sleep together and you think it is a marvellous thing because you're free to live without marriage. How does it exalt you? It can be very depressing. You don't want to think that you don't hold or own a thing. You don't own his buttons, you can't, you don't own his hairbrush, it doesn't belong to you at all."

Angie arrives in the middle of this, and trying to include her makes it harder for us talk. Kamala glances toward her but can't help talking to me. Angie is itching to speak but remains silent.

"You said yesterday you thought love was no longer possession," I remind Kamala. "But now you're saying that it is a lesser relationship if you don't own anything."

"Because I'm analyzing again. That's how we grow, we have to contradict ourselves sometimes."

"But that's an interesting question you've asked: what do I have?"

"What do you have? You have nothing, nothing at all, absolutely nothing. At least if a shabby surname is thrown at us, at least that you have. Nothing else. In my marriage, what did I get from my husband? He sold all my jewellery, sold the flat I had, took an overdraft. But then I still had this, I was the wife."

I take this opportunity to excuse myself and go to the buffet to fill my plate because I definitely need time to think things through. I don't know why marriage is so important to Kamala. Or what she means by the words – wife? love? sex? love-making? – and what experiences have formed the meanings I don't yet understand.

My mother and father were so devoted to each other they seemed square to me. I had sex at sixteen; shotgun marriage at nineteen; the idealized, open arrangement of Jean-Paul Sartre and Simone de Beauvoir as my relationship model at university; divorce at twenty-one; remarriage at twenty-four. Jane Mansfield, Playboy bunnies, Sylvia Plath, Twiggy, Margaret Atwood, Dianne di

Prima, Gertrude Stein, single parenthood, women friends; and now an evolving, decades-long whatchamacallit.

"It's taken me seventeen years to figure out what I think I have," I say to Kamala when I return. "I think I am as important to Arnie as he is to me, which means Arnie loves me and is profoundly committed to me, even without legal sanction. But, for you, living with someone doesn't seem to be an option."

"I am ten years older, so I understand things in another way. It's very difficult for me because I get up, go to the bathroom, put the lights on, maybe write something. I don't want something living in my room from dusk to morning."

"Do you want anything a man has to offer?"

"It's a very tricky question. It's very strange that in the aging process one does have such hungers, because we are reminded. If you are not reminded, you don't miss it."

"But what if you are reminded?"

"Who's going to do the reminding?" she asks.

Meanwhile, I am acutely conscious of Angie sitting uncomfortably across the table. As she tells me later, she is consumed by the question of what, if anything, of her husband belongs to her and is stifling a burning desire to talk. Kamala is hiding behind dark glasses, peeking at Angie but talking only to me. Once again I feel torn between responsibility to my travelling companion and responsibility to the delicately evolving intimacy with Kamala. I see new worry lines on my face reflected in the mirror behind Kamala. I smile and look like a gargoyle.

"The heat feels like a sauna, or hot flashes," I say when I walk Kamala to the elevator.

She answers quickly. "In fact, there's a kind of cleansing that only heat can do. Like boiling water cleanses all impurities. So I suppose, we all have to be cleansed too, by the heat, by the absolute heat." She stops and looks directly at me. "I think you will like India, Merrily. Don't plan too much."

On the street I buy flowers to send to Kamala with a note promising to meet alone next time. I think of her lying on the bed, curled up on her side, reading my note, and wonder if this will help or cause more misunderstanding. Kamala is cuddly, fecund with intellect, experience, humour, seemingly open and totally unreadable. I despair of knowing her, yet our exchanges enthral me. On the other hand, I have just read the English translation of her Malayalam story "The Sign of the Lion," and I see how bitingly cruel and intellectually snobbish she can be. I think I am much kinder. I should worry what she will write about me. I wonder if she *is* writing. She said she didn't care what people thought of her, and I said it was wonderful not to care if people like you or think you're smart.

"Yes," she replied, "what you care about is your own response."

I agreed. But I care what she thinks. I am not crazy with care. I am intrigued.

I arrive at Kamala's apartment with trepidation the next day and rejoice in the warmth of her greeting. Our rapport revives as we inch through noisy Ernakulam traffic toward her sister's home in Kaloor, a leafy suburb of quiet, narrow streets and expensive homes on the outskirts of the city. Kamala is wearing a formal sari, a form of protective colouring, she confides, for familial occasions. Yet no sooner do we enter the driveway than her sister, Sulu, and brother-in-law, Unni, are there to receive us. Kamala collects herself, and we enter a spacious, two-storey bungalow built with Unni's Tata Tea manager's salary and rubber factory revenue.

The interior is cool and so is Kamala. I notice her restraint, an almost haughty politeness, and wish she were more relaxed. Then I remember that after my second marriage I decided there was no sense interfering with or trying to change the relationships of my husbands with their mothers, a principle I think applies to all hard-wired family relationships. Kamala said she feared her "cold and autocratic father" and was wary of her sister. She also said that in 1984, when she lost her voice, money, and spirit in an independent election bid, Sulu rescued her – took her to the Anamalai mountains, nursed her, and gave her a tape recorder to talk out her despair. In the mornings, Sulu sent a secretary to transcribe the poems Kamala was too exhausted to write.

At times I feel that I hide behind my dreams
as the mountain does, behind the winter's mist ...

Upstairs, we join twelve others, all relatives, for the naming ceremony. Kamala lounges on the carved Malabari swing, and I am seated beside her brother and sister-in-law on a velvet-upholstered sofa. Sulu's son, Arun, recently graduated from

an American university, sits on the marble chip floor straining to cross his legs.
As eldest son and titular head of the Nayar matrilineal family, he has pride of
place between his sister – the baby's mother – and the baby's father. Arun opens
his arms, cradles the twenty-eight-day-old newborn, and ties a single, natural,
unwoven thread around the infant's waist. He whispers a name three times into
his nephew's right ear, then left, and passes the child to father and mother for
their whispered blessings. The baby has dark, collyrium-ringed eyes. He's all eyes.
And now he's named.

Sulu fetches an early family photo album while Kamala rests in the bedroom.
"Mother was a poet, on a different plane. Father was strong, like a banyan tree,"
she says, pointing:

Father in sepia, thin, dark, first Indian managing director of a British luxury
car company under the Raj, dwarfed by his English predecessor.

Mother in white homespun khadi, distracted, willowy.

Kamala as a child, round, placid.

Father later, silver-haired, managing editor of *Mathrubhumi* (The Mother-
land), one of Kerala's highest circulation Malayalam dailies, on a post-indepen-
dence junket to England. He is laughing with actress Kamala Kumari, seemingly
taller, stronger, more comfortable in his skin.

Father, I ask you now without fear
Did you want me …
Did I disappoint you much
With my skin as dark as yours …

"He protected me," says the fair-skinned, younger daughter. "I didn't even
know how to buy a train ticket myself."

Sulu leaves to supervise the feast, and Kamala leads me downstairs to meet
her mother, Kerala's most revered poet. Through the doorway of a spotless,
monastic room, I see eighty-five-year-old Balamani Amma perched on the edge
of her bed, cheekbones pronounced, white khadi cloaking her spectral frame.
Kamala dismisses the attendant and sits beside her mother, stroking her sinewy
hand. I greet the famous poet respectfully. She's so thin she's an essence. She nods
to me and smiles in a strangely comforting way.

"My mother is a highly respected person," Kamala tells me, "She is a scholar with access to classical mythology, fed on the *Vedas* and the *Upanishads*, all the scriptures, and she incorporated messages from them into her poetry. She was considered distinguished because she took knowledge from teachers and books rather than being a total original. So, therefore, in contrast, my poetry seemed very clumsy. I didn't have any spiritual message to give."

Kamala smiles and murmurs to her mother as she muses about their different paths. As a girl, her mother was trained to speak quietly, in hushed tones that couldn't be heard in the men's quarters. As a woman, she was trained to be chaste, faithful, and not show any signs of desire, which was considered wanton. When she began writing, she imitated the forms of the classics she knew and wrote according to the prescribed themes for women's writing: "God, her children, and domestic bliss. Nothing else," Kamala says.

"That's all she thought about?" I ask, looking at Balamani Amma, who is leaning toward me with a kind, social smile.

"That was the only tradition I could find," Kamala says. "Indian women writers lacked a literary tradition. Of course, there was the oral tradition. Janabai, Mahadevi Akka, and Mirabai all went around singing in praise of God, all beyond scandal."

Kamala's reference to women poet saints makes me think of the scandals swirling around her for disobeying the prescriptions of her society and for writing about men as living gods. When she first discovered love, a friend warned her to put the name Krishna in all her love poetry so no one would judge her harshly. And she didn't.

"Since all my mother did was write, I emulated her," Kamala says, looking at her mother. "But having watched mother, grandmother, great-grandmother, great-aunt suffer with a silence that did not protect them at all, I determined to write honestly. All the pain unexpressed and all the sad stories left untold made me write recklessly and in protest."

She lingers beside her mother, gently patting her hand and facilitating the encounter with the foreign guest. Balamani Amma lived with Kamala for fourteen years after Kamala's father died. When Kamala too was widowed, Sulu took over their mother's care.

"Mother was silent. She never wrote freely, frankly," Kamala says, putting her finger across her lips to mimic silencing. "We must speak."

A delicious, traditional Kerala treat of puffy Kerala rice, mixed with coconut mango curry, pungent with herbs and spices, drips from my inept fingers. When we first met, Kamala described me as a feminist in her Malayalam column. "Merrily who spends hours in my house with her recorder has learned to eat rice, Erissery, fried vegetables, curd, pickles, dosa, chutney using her fingers. She does not eat idlis. I keep a fork with a red handle on the left of the plate for her. But she does not use it. Just like I used a fork and spoon when I was abroad, this woman from Canada uses her fingers to eat in India."

But today, at the naming ceremony, I am no longer a feminist. "Merrily is a sociologist, " she informs her relatives.

# 4

## Esoteric Exotica

To escape the heat, Angie and I hire a car to drive us to the old Raj hill station of Munnar. We wend our way along spectacular roads draped with mauve jacaranda and edged with dark green tea, up four thousand feet to Tata Tea's ninety-year-old High Range Club. A turbaned, liveried waiter delivers tea and snacks to the verandah of our cottage above the club. Tropical rain washes the air cool. Water trickles deliciously from the eaves. Beside bushes of brilliant fuchsia bougainvillea, I open my arms, lift my face to the rain, and embrace a familiar climactic zone. Then I shower and think about Kamala. There is so much unanswered, so much that is culturally unfamiliar.

I assemble the notes and tapes I've made, and the articles and books about and by Kamala unavailable in Montreal and bought in Cochin. As a non-fiction writer, I take my raw material from Kamala and anything connected to her. As a poet, Kamala is her own raw material. It will be hard for us to switch roles – for her to be Boswell, the diarist, and for me to be Johnson, the principal character. For me, discovering others is second nature, and I interview and document like a bloodhound on the trail or a retriever chasing a stick. For Kamala, the inward journey is more natural, and her writing moves others to experience what she feels. She also worries that a book project will upset the healing simplicity of her life, by giving her quiescent ego a stage on which to gyrate and make a mess. "Now, the stage is empty, it's good. I have to switch myself off for peace."

I asked her how she was able to find this peace now.

"I am switched off, really switched off. But then of course you came, and the switch is on. Part of me lives. But I am seeing it only as a kind of friendship between two women who are sensitive. I am not seeing it as a venture. Whether this book gets written or not, something sweet has come out of it. I trust you. That's more beautiful than the book or the publicity that the book might receive. That Merrily came and met me and somehow, wonder of wonders, I met her."

Her words bring me close and also keep me at bay. I am happy to be part of her lives, and confused and concerned about the part that's "switched off."

"But Kamala, you are in some other state that I have to understand so I won't worry about you."

"I don't know," she answers. "Maybe you are in an enviable state. There is more life in the state you are in, some mobility. In my state, there is nothing. Tides don't rise at all. But whether I write about it or not, I think this is what I was aiming at from the beginning, when I was restless, when I wanted to be loved."

Angie and I wait until dinner to explore the High Range Club. We enter a dark, wood-panelled bar with leather armchairs, fireplace, stuffed animal heads, all pre-1940s including the "Men Only" sign. We follow scarred, brown rugs past the billiards room and the Edwardian clock stuck at 10:15. Large windows overlook wide verandahs, rows of parked cream-coloured Ambassadors, and Tata Tea and Harrison Tea Factory cricketers hard at play. We stop in the dining room and sit on plastic folding chairs, eating glutinous vegetable soup served on signature china and a starched white table cloth, giggling with disbelief.

"Raj time warp," says Angie. "Nothing like this left in Britain."

In a dark den near the dining room, we meet the managers' saried, bejewelled wives killing time before the post-match dinner party and Men's Only billiards and drinks. They are watching, or not watching, a scratchy TV, and greet us irritably.

"Kamala Das has funny ideas, especially for us," pronounces a company lady when I mention Kamala's name.

"Water will be very cold," says another when asked about swimming in nearby Deviculam Lake. "Temperature will go down. Suddenly you will get a heart attack."

Back in the cottage, Angie begins reading Kamala's autobiography, *My Story*, and can't put it down. She likes the crisp sentences, short sections, the emotions written in blood. She reads selections aloud to illustrate how Kamala's husband made her suffer. She cannot understand why Kamala says she loved him.

In the evenings, my husband took me for walks but my legs used to hurt, hungry that I was and weak with vomitings. I was not much of a companion for him. Any sign of kindness from people made me weep like a child. He grew weary of my temperament very soon and one day suggested that I go home to my grandmother for rest. I disliked the idea, for seeing him and sleeping near him had become precious to me.

"This is after the disastrous wedding night," Angie says, "after he raped her and had sex with a boy in their bedroom. Why did she love him? The beginning is all about loneliness. Maybe that had something to do with it."

I have no answer for her. I don't know what Kamala means when she speaks about love, or even what the phrase "love affair" means to her. It is enough that her writing moves me for a brief moment toward ecstasy.

I lay in his white arms drowsily aware that he was only water, only a pale green pond glimmering in the sun. In him I swam, all broken with longing, in his robust blood I floated, drying on my tears.

It doesn't parse and I don't care. I don't care to analyze it. Kamala's baroque, extravagant woman's longings and sensual incantations make my heart lurch, opulent reminders of the niggardliness of my own spare prose. Yet I wonder if there is any relationship between the inspiration for the poems and the feelings they inspire in me.

Did Kamala ever enjoy sex? If not, what was she looking for?

The cool night air is a sensual treat, and I snuggle into an actual blanket, wondering if Kamala's notorious affairs are a non-genital lusting to melt into the godhead, or if they have a sexual dimension, or if my preoccupation with this question is culturally determined and irrelevant. I think of Arnie and me, and of Kamala and her husband – her pleasure in giving, her pride in nursing him, and her fulfillment in his last grateful words. I think I should take better care of Arnie. I drift back into the dreamy shade of an ancient, moss-covered tree and feel a liberating release from possessiveness, an unexpected sexual letting go.

The next morning I receive a fax from Arnie with such playful, over-the-top allusions to our lovemaking that it makes me laugh. I wonder what Kamala would make of the letter. Her writings on love and longing are a defining part of her and of how she is perceived. But her wanton public image conflicts with what she's said in our discussions. It occurs to me that showing her the fax may further our talk.

"Do you want to read it?" I ask as soon as we meet again.

Her eyes gleam, hand reaches out. "Of course I want to know. I am curious."

She reads intently, holding the flimsy paper like a worm or a snake. And returns it with a moue.

"What?" I laugh. "What are you thinking?"

"My God, what an appetite. I doubt if any other woman in India ever received such a fax. I hope he won't drive you mad."

"Do you think anyone will understand its secret words?"

"I can understand. Tell him not to be a glutton in love."

This disapproving reaction is not what I anticipated. Kamala would obviously be affronted by receiving such a fax.

"I asked him to send me a love letter," I protest, trying to protect Arnie.

"How old is this gentleman?"

"Fifty-six."

"He's not slowing down?"

"I haven't seen him for two months. He has lots of time to –"

"To plan the campaign."

More like he had time to miss me. Love-glutton Arnie planning a sexual campaign to drive me mad was not the first image that came to mind.

"Will you be embarrassed to meet Arnie now? Did I do the wrong thing?" I ask.

"Very childish man. Not mature. Send a fax, 'Please grow up, Arnie.'"

"Life is so serious, Kamala. It's fun to play sometimes."

"It must have cost some dollars."

"To send this fax?"

"All those things. Inner thigh. Outer thigh."

"Is the frivolity bothering you? We laugh sometimes when we make love. Is lovemaking here so serious?"

"Gloomy, like a gloomy game that has to be played. Gloom, gloom, and more gloom."

I tuck the fax away like an unseemly bra strap. I wanted to know more about Kamala's feelings about sexuality and expected the fax would precipitate something. But I couldn't have imagined the conversation I just provoked, nor much of anything that is happening – lunches in the luxury of the Avenue Regent, conversations on Kamala's bed and on the ornate settee where her grandfather, the raja, used to sleep, my laughter, her slow smile.

Yesterday I asked Kamala to come to Canada, and she said an American gallery owner had offered to bring her to California to paint.

"She will get my paintings. What will you get?" she asks.

"We'll get a book out of it."

Someday soon I should attempt to describe to Kamala what I think I'm doing. In Munnar I began a list of usual documentary research: interview Kamala's sister, lover, son, feminist admirer; find bibliographic and audiovisual sources; clarify dates. I asked Kamala for a reference to a researcher, and she asked why.

"To collect material, arrange interviews, find the documentary films made on you," I said.

"You can't find them here."

"To make a list."

"Merrily, maybe you should study someone else, another writer. Let's just enjoy."

I heed the warning and dump the secondary sources, realizing that nothing in this project is usual. With Kamala, a question starts a riff, a rap, a cascade of memories, connections, metaphorical allusions, storytelling. I am learning to submerge and go with the flow, a process of revelation unlike anything I've known before. Angie is busy exploring the backwaters and shops of Cochin, and Kamala and I are developing a rhythm. We meet in the morning, relax into each other's company, and Kamala gives generously of her time, trying to be very fair, "to be as much as I can" for her Canadian visitor.

"There have been other writers coming with prying questions that were ugly. The intent behind the questions was also ugly. Mostly I am relaxed with you, and for that I am grateful."

I am also grateful – to enter Kamala's presence and be allowed into her life. It's only my absolute interest in her that keeps me in Cochin in April. I awake in the heat, oppressed by the heat, with questions. There is so much unresolved, but seeing Kamala calms me. I listen, talk, record, return to the hotel, cross-reference conversations with her writings, and attend again as Kamala casts her spell.

"Some people say for reasons of obscenity you should ban Kamala Das because she talks about sex, the lovemaking," she tells me. "But when I talk about lovemaking, I'm thinking of Radha and Sri Krishna sporting – how Radha's anklets used to jingle when he was on her, and the smell of her hair, how the flowers were crushed under them. If I visualize Krishna, the God of all Hindus, sporting with his girls, how can I think of sex as something unclean?

"For me, sex meant something beautiful, something sacred. When I was thirteen or fourteen, I read of sex in the *Gitagovinda*, a prayer book. I danced to the Gitagovinda as a girl, and at those moments I became Radha dancing in front of Krishna. Radha was older than Krishna and married, yet Hindus consider the love between them to be the most perfect love. In certain chapters, songs describe their lovemaking. How Radha once mounted him, and her thighs became tense, and she could not go on because suddenly the muscles became taut. In one song, Krishna calls to her from the forest glade:

Set your golden anklet on my bed like the sun …
Throbbing breasts aching for loving embrace are hard to touch.
Rest these vessels on my chest! Quench love's burning fire!
Offer your lip's nectar to revive a dying slave, Radha!

"My grandmother was a devotee of Krishna. She didn't ask me not to touch that book. She thought, 'Well, that's a prayer book, it's about God. It's sung every-day on the steps of the temple before the evening service.' So I never had the feeling that sex was obscene or shameful. If Krishna, my God, could perform that, I thought, what is wrong? If God figures in a love story, then a love story is sacred. It's not profane."

I can't help reminding Kamala that despite this early acculturation, in later years she came up against something not quite so beautiful.

"Sex?" she asks, confusing me, because I thought we were talking about sex.

"Well, the way you were treated by your husband was not as beautiful," I answer.

"That's probably the reason I kept writing about beautiful love. Because I didn't get it in real life. My husband was a homosexual, you know."

I did – from her autobiography and from previous allusions.

"He made me be nice to his boss."

And Kamala tells me about her "love affair" with her husband's boss when she was barely thirty and he, a distinguished member of the Indian Civil Service, was old enough to be her father. She says she imagined herself as a character in a Graham Greene novel so she wouldn't feel cheap being nice to him, and willed herself to be fond of this corpulent old man who "trembled like jelly taken out suddenly and talked like he had pebbles in his mouth." And yet, she says that she grew to admire her husband's superior, "a true Brahmin, of the priestly class." And that slowly, unexpectedly, she found in him the tenderness she'd lost when she was taken from her grandmother as a girl.

"He was the only one that bothered to educate me," she says gratefully. "He felt he could, and he did so beautifully." He bought her books by Stefan Zweig and short stories by Japanese authors. He taught her Sanskrit and beamed when she chanted her first Sanskrit stanza. He chanted mantras, made her laugh, and courted her with education, conversation, and fun. "You have spelled 'bureaucrat' wrong," he teased, "but you have spelled a bureaucrat."

Her lover's tenderness assuaged the loss and emptiness of her marriage. She was unbelievably happy, and alone in the dark rooms of her home she sensed his presence and sang for joy. She says her love was as simple and childlike as unquestioning devotion. "For the first time since childhood, I forgot my loneliness … He and I used to get up early. All the rest would be sleeping. So there would be a phone call in the morning.

Just voices in the morning, you
and I.

"I would walk up to the Taj Mahal Hotel where he was staying. 'Uncle is waiting for you,' the desk clerk said. I would go up to his room. Through our window we could hear the nasal cry of the lepers on the pavement below. He would ask me to shut the door because he couldn't bear the sound.

Welcome me, lying down, dear love
And remain so,
I shall shut the window
For, upward floats the leper's tremolo …

"After about three o'clock he would open the door, switch off the AC, and open the windows. We liked to see the sea. The Taj Mahal faced Apollo Pier and the sea, grey and white like a pigeon's wing.

It is morning now at Apollo Pier.
There is a choppy sea …

"I would walk to the hotel smelling the birds, because the rich people scattered grain for them and there were pigeons on the pavement. I would walk, seeing all that, knowing there was a man waiting upstairs for me. I would go into his warm bed wanting him to

... hold me, hold me once again,
Kiss the words to death in my mouth, plunder
Memories ...
Love me, love me, love me till I die ...

"And yet, there wasn't anything. When he held me close, which wasn't very often, I knew his body was a male body, but I shied away."

She sat on the floor, put her face against his knee, and he touched her bare arm, stroked her hair, petted her. "At that time I had lustrous hair, he loved that. Even in front of others, visitors, children, he would still stroke my head. How dignified he made this love."

Sometimes, when they were alone, she lay near him and he tickled and kissed her toes and laid his head on her stomach. "'I will never exploit you, Aami, you are so innocent,' he would say."

I ask Kamala when her lover first saw the poems dedicated to him, her most famous love poems. She says it was in 1965, when *Summer in Calcutta* was first published. He caught the next plane and came to her. "Forgive me if I have ever hurt you with words," he said. "This is the richest experience of my life. You have made something out of me."

Kamala sees that I am glowing in the reflected glory of the moment. "From top to bottom he gazed on me, then he said, 'Come to me,' and he held me. I thought then, 'I've returned home.' The security of him reminded me of my grandmother."

Kamala tells me she was deeply in love, and soon this large, soft man was obsessed with her too. "At first he had said, 'I don't know what I must feel for you, but I am afraid to use the word "love," I am a family man.' But how could he resist such poems from a very young woman who was also good-looking in those days? The poems were like a bird singing to entice its mate, to conquer him and get his love. The intensity increased with each poem until finally he fell, and what a fall. Being an emotional person, he could respond to poetry."

They would meet every three months, and afterwards they would drive to the airport, stopping at a guest house or a club, walking together to the plane, and holding hands until he had to leave.

> Walk away from me into the lonely night
> With my fingerprints on you, my darling, go …

"It was love, both sides, love. It's beautiful when you love each other, you know, taking leave,

> … while like blood
> Running out
> And death beginning, this day of ours is helplessly ending.

Finally, when her scholarly lover was "really trapped in the maze of my poetry, in my emotions," Kamala found him limiting. "I wanted to be free. It wasn't enough finding a man, learning everything about him, quickening to his responses. I wanted to quicken to myself, listen to my own inner voices, so different from his. I wanted to know the meaning of growing up, having these feelings, thoughts, sensations. What was to be the purpose of my life? Surely not just embracing a man, whispering to him. It's a strange alchemy. There is this all-consuming passion, and suddenly there's nothing at all. What you are clasping is only a death head."

Most of Kamala's finest love poems are about this man, "the only distinguished man I got involved with, someone who treated me properly. It was good to hold a man and love him and to know that he loved you. That was the greatest ecstasy I have known."

She thinks if her gentle lover had married her, her life might have been different, "but I don't think the poetry would have been better." Her husband's boss is old now, near death, and she says he calls her still. "You are the only beautiful memory I have," he says.

We finish the morning talk and I realize, without understanding, that Kamala has described her most significant love affair, the affair that inspired her most intense, erotic poetry, and that this love affair was never consummated. In naked genital terms, she and "the greatest love" of her life never had penetrative sex. I am confronting this peculiar revelation when Kamala, for whom it is not news, says, "The publication of *Summer in Calcutta* made my reputation, made me a poet."

Suddenly she was an artistic celebrity, with liberty beyond that of a middle-class housewife. Other poets flocked to her home to welcome her, and she walked through the Delhi winter in a black cardigan with pearl buttons and a skirt – "I didn't wear a sari at all." Preaching a new morality, she publicly declared marriage without love meaningless, and sanctioned infidelity for women in love-less marriages. She advocated the return to a social order that allowed women to have more than one husband, and she strolled with men along the sea in Bombay, hair scandalously loose, youth blazing like a summer sun, flaunting her unconventionality.

"The women of Nalapat House, my ancestral home, had all been frigid, saying prayers from morning to night. I had crossed the first tides, and I had got into the deep sea in my search beyond."

In her mind, love was associated with tragedy and beauty, not crude marital duty, and she yearned to be Anna Karenina, Madame Bovary, or Juliet for a love-crossed Romeo. Suitors regaled her with words of love, but she soon learned what they meant was only lust.

... all the hands,
The great brown thieving hands groped, beneath my
Clothes, their fire was that of an arsonist's,
Warmth was not their aim ...

She tells me that for the first time cynicism seeped into her thoughts. It seemed that men loved her poetry and her image more than they loved her. With every pelvic thrust they hoped to hear, in skilful verse, the range of her response. It hurt her, and like a windup toy mimicking emotion, she became increasingly reckless. To forget her noble lover, she fell in and out of "traps of desire," spinning, unbalanced.

I leave Kamala leaning cross-legged against the back of the settee, playing with her grandchild Nayanthara's hair. Braving the 104 degree Cochin heat, I walk to Favorite Tailor, a tiny cement shop with six pedal sewing machines, pay a listless girl for hemming my mundus, return to the hotel, shower, and remember how recklessly I behaved when my husband left me. I too lived madly then, raging with desire to live and love fully, wild with pent-up force. I was at the height of my powers and my beauty, as was Kamala, described to me by the writer and filmmaker Suresh Kohli as "buxom like a South Indian film star, with a perfect figure and face." Kohli, who sat at Kamala's feet in the 1970s as she recited in her famed Bombay salon, told me that writing *My Story* and being a Nayar woman enhanced Kamala's bold, taboo sex appeal, "because sexually starved Indian men were fascinated with the voluptuous South Indian women they'd seen in frescos, temple art, art books, films, and Nayar women were distinguished from the rest of the South as being sultry, the coastal factor adding a little salt, coupled with them having long hair covering their entire backs, and being from a polyandrous society."

I stop dressing to squish two biting ants like the ones that kept me awake last night, and remember Kohli calling Kamala "the rebel Indian poet, landmark Indian poet after independence, firebrand writer in her native Malayalam." Yet his analysis of her appeal casts her as sexually exotic, like the characterization of Jewish women by some French-Canadian men.

I turn the fan on high and let the AC blow on my naked back, wondering why "exotic" is a concept I try to avoid. I flirt with it, it tempts me because it is so seductive. But though some Indian men may see Kamala as the alluring "other," I identify with the force of her longing and the recklessness of her desire.

I head back to Kamala's after a little rest and within minutes of walking, I'm drenched again. But now I don't really care. I remind her that she's left me in free fall after the account of her first love affair, and ask what happened next.

"I was coming out of a shop and I collided with a wicked, powerful politician whose picture I had seen," she tells me. "Later, he called me and invited me for tea. I knew this man hired assassins, hobnobbed with international smugglers, and

killed without remorse. He was 'the richest the strongest the deadliest i lit one thousand and one lamps at our snake shrine praying for a mate such as he.' I was clean, active, at my strongest. I knew how respectable men loved, and I thought an evil man would be exciting 'for I would then unpeel his soul and taste the sweetness of love.' The old man who was my guru, who taught me Sanskrit, said, 'I cannot think of you stooping this low.' And I answered, 'Why does the mud lark roll itself in mud? You have to forgive me. I'm a writer. I have to experiment.'"

Drunk with excitement, hoping to be ravished and physically aroused, "to impregnate his heart," Kamala entered the mirrored bedroom of the man she called the lion, and observed his lust and his roar, "like a wounded lion," when he climaxed; "he rubs oil on me he puts me in his bathtub i cower before his incurious stare the warm water grazing my harbours his eyelids droop he is about to fall asleep." Once, dozing after sex, she felt his hand against her cheek and heard him secretly whispering her name, an exceptional tenderness, "the supreme moment" of the affair. Finally, she concluded "the wicked mate like birds, no time for the preliminaries, you get no ecstasy at all," and she wrote off the experiment with the lion:

... like frankensteins brutal toy i shall rise one day i shall stalk out of his bed
i shall walk along the marine drive he will then become just another man
just another season and the summer then will burn to ashes in his garden.

Kamala's experimentation is behaviour I recognize, having believed in my twenties that the fastest way to know someone was to sleep with him. As a single parent attending university, working, and trying to write, this seemed the most expedient and stimulating drama possible, given my limited time and resources. Later, like Kamala, I processed the experiences through writing. But my promiscuous sexual behaviour was only mildly disreputable in 1960s and '70s North America, while Kamala's subversive, relatively innocent behaviour was exponentially more transgressive in India. She says she "unshackled" herself from orthodox, puritanical morality, and I ask her how she did it.

She tells me she had been cheated out of a normal life, so she had to create a persona through whom she could celebrate life. "She was the one I wanted to be and could not, so I thought I have to do the things expected of her – loving intensely, meeting her lover. I detached myself from this body and watched this persona move towards this lover, observing myself in the role of lover, the role of a woman loved, as though I was another person. Then, I began to make it real. She and I merged into one, and it became easier for me because then it wasn't as if I was fantasizing, I only wrote what happened. It was real."

Kamala says she went to others for healing and couldn't have survived her life without the euphoria of those days, "the way they burned like the gulmohur tree, everything in bloom, everything burning, and you walk into that place." She says she wrote with more vitality when she was in love, staying awake all night "because I didn't want those moments to be lost."

I nod my understanding of that impulse to write things down.

"But then I knew I had to get out and be Kamala Das again, because my existence was at stake." She waves her hand as if to dispel her turbulent past with its emotionally draining love affairs. "Now and then take a holy dip in the waters of love, but then you come out for air.

"And now, for twenty years I've been a celibate," she concludes. "So now I will not pounce upon a man and try to hack at his parts. There is no such hunger, no greed at all for the flesh. I don't want to waste vitality. When I turned to celibacy in 1975, I became a true writer. Those following three or four years, I wrote hundreds of stories. It's enough. It's more than enough."

We are seated at the small table in the receiving room, and I sense Kamala has confided as much and more than is comfortable at this stage of our friendship. She tells me, "I can be at ease with you, be myself," and calls me "disarming" for not concealing things like Arnie's fax. "I hadn't thought a woman from another country would be so free with me." Yet when I first came, Kamala told her readers I asked her to collaborate on a book on feminism, saying, "I did not want to deny being one and confuse her. I was ready to play the role. When I play a role, I grow into it" – which gives me pause.

Of course I am not fully myself either. All my senses are hyper-aware, sometimes on high alert, and I am very careful not to offend. We are each in our own way storing what seem like clues to knowing the other, and talking at cross-purposes, especially in our tentative explorations of female identity. The feelings we have about our womanhood reveal intimate aspects of our upbringing, our writing, ourselves, and unravelling and comparing how we navigate our choices is part of the fascination of our friendship. Yet, although Kamala tries to talk openly to me, what she takes for granted will take more time and learning for me to comprehend. Even now I have a lot to digest. I still can't understand how she could take such good care of a husband who abused her badly. Or what a "love affair" means to her.

"Kamala, do you have patience for my many questions?" I ask.

"Yes, but I may not be able to answer all. They may perplex me," she says honestly.

"Because I am still confused when you speak about a love affair. Is that different from sexual desire?"

"At least for me. Sex gets thrown into it sometimes, probably when I was young and someone was sexually impatient, like a bribe. In those days, I traded sex for love. By presenting the body, I thought I might get the mind as well. I wanted emotion to ride in him. Emotion that would suit mine, because I had such a rush of emotion."

"In North America a love affair means it involves sex. What does love affair mean to you?" I ask baldly.

"Love a person, go out for walks, eat together, have lunch at the hotel, hold hands – that type of thing."

"Did you ever enjoy sex with anybody?"

The question visibly unnerves her. I seem to have asked something coarse, or dangerous. She hesitates uncertainly and looks upset. Finally she says, "Maybe once or twice."

The confession is so shocking it literally takes her aback. Kamala Das writes openly about love, longing, desire, but has never publicly admitted to *sexual* pleasure. She jerks away from the microphone and retreats to the far wall.

"There you have it," she says defiantly.

"At least you had it once or twice."

"It came as an unpleasant surprise to me when I could enjoy it with someone," she says inexplicably.

"An unpleasant surprise?"

"It surprised me that I could have enjoyed it. It is something that an orthodox Hindu woman could never dream of – getting fun out of it."

Had I properly considered this response, I might have questioned why the "Love Queen of Malabar" so readily identified with Hindu orthodoxy. But I am too taken by a seemingly revelatory cultural insight.

"But Kamala, that's how our cultures are so different. In my culture, since the '60s, women are supposed to enjoy sex."

"Not in ours. A woman can never admit she enjoys it. It is a cross, the marital bed is a cross. We are not supposed to show lust. You're just a body, and the lord and master uses that body. You hand your body to him so he'll feel soothed, he feels it's his birthright. You sleep on your husband's bed, you don't call it yours, his bed, his home. I learned from that convention, but I can't do that anymore. I want my bed to be mine."

# 5

## Lines Addressed to a Devadasi

I wake in the hotel covered in a fine mist of myself. Outside, traffic belches into the 98 degree, pre-monsoon street.

I leave the hotel in a skirt and white kurta, hoping the kurta won't stick to my body, holding the newspaper like a shield in front of my breasts. Hugging what is left of the sidewalk, I walk along the whizzing street – auto rickshaws, cars, trucks, six-way traffic – thinking I will use my friend Ellen's trick of crossing beside locals who know what they're doing. I look for people to cross with and find, unlike in Nepal, they're scared too. They scurry, look behind and over their shoulders, jump, hop, run between cars and horns. I chose a man, close my mind, and step out beside him into the traffic, playing it by ear, improvising for my life.

I find Kamala in her bedroom, resting because her ECG is not good. By-pass surgery is recommended, but she says, "We all have a cross and we get used to it, and then we are sentimental about it." I try to help by pre-selecting poems for an anthology proposed by Macmillan India, and eventually find a book containing selections from her five poetry collections, only two of which she actually owns. When I think of organizing her professional life, I feel overwhelmed. Yesterday I watched her open two Malayalam fan letters, see the closely written script, and release the pages from her long, slender fingers like doves. To read, she must remove her glasses and bring the text within inches of her face. She scans words like an ultrasound machine, looking deep into their bones.

I didn't wake with any burning questions this morning, rather a familiar, mundane list of things to do: arrangements and obligations for Kamala. It's not because I can't still learn from or be surprised by our conversations, but because I see her needs too blatantly. I don't feel comfortable setting myself up at the table with my recorder, watching her give and give to others, and I am taking too. I will write the publisher for royalties, ask novelist Varma how he found his stenographer, arrange to send a Dictaphone machine from Canada, and read Kamala her poems so she can choose for the anthology. Her situation reminds me of Dorothy Livesay and Martha Gellhorn, other older women writers I've known with no one to help manage their personal and professional lives. No wives. No female lovers like those of Marguerite Yourcenar and Gertrude Stein. The phone rings incessantly, and Kamala reaches for every call. The answering machine is not working because her granddaughter broke it. I asked the driver to take it to the repair shop, but it's still here.

I work at Kamala's small wooden writing desk, a tablet that lifts to close and lowers to make a table, now piled with unopened correspondence addressed to Kamala Das, Poetry Editor, *Femina Magazine*. Kamala wafts sleepily into the room, hair flowing, wearing the loose housedress she favours, entering like a Hollywood geisha with quiet, swishing movements. She lifts her head when she sees me and reaches out, almost touching my hair, almost touching my back, never quite connecting unless I say something perfectly apropos, or outrageously incorrect, when she flicks her wrist against my thigh and leans back with a full-lipped, satisfied smile.

"You're working so hard for me," she says.

"Yes. Because your life could be so much easier if you had three things: a secretary, a stenographer, and a Dictaphone machine. Look at this pile of unopened mail."

"It's poems for *Femina*. I don't open them because it depresses me to read bad poetry. But I'll have to, they pay me two thousand rupees a month."

"But someone could read them to you. I could read them to you." I am standing facing her, looking like a puppy who ran for a stick she couldn't find. "I'm trying to get you organized, take care of business, but you don't seem to care."

She looks at me and takes my face gently between her hands. Her back is to the large window overlooking the street and I am facing it. I must be sharply etched by daylight. She is almost in silhouette, thick glasses obscuring her eyes, her face dark, round, softly smiling.

"Imagine you are the earth and there are streams running over you," she says. "Those unanswered letters, the publishers that don't pay me, those are the streams. Life is the river underneath. In India, there's a river that has disappeared called the Saraswati River. They say if you keep your ear to the ground, you can hear it. That is what I am doing, keeping my ear to the river that has gone underground. The publishers, the unanswered letters – what does this matter to someone who is going to die?"

Her words release me. Who am I to tell Kamala what to do? She has her ear to the ground listening for the underground river while I row away, straining my muscles, not yet ready to face the other shore.

"I never had this peace before," she says. "I used to care about my husband's health. Now I have no responsibilities. I don't have a care in the world.

"I wear floppy things. I lie down."

Knowing we are soon to leave India, Angie urges me to accompany her to the seashore, and we board the four-and-a-half-hour express train to Trivandrum. We arrive in the dark and drive straight through the old capital, past paddy fields, to our chosen Kovalam hotel with balconies overlooking a private beach. When we awake, the beach is empty, surf low. I wear a bathing suit, and for the first time in South Asia, sea water cools and caresses my boldly exposed skin. Then, I walk to a cabin on the hill and on a raised table overlooking the beach, a beautiful black-haired Malayali in a gold and red sari powders and waxes my legs. She lays down a cloth strip and rips the hair away in one sure stroke, dexterously plucking out the strays with threads stretched taut between her fingers and teeth. Without embarrassment, she waxes the inside of my upper thigh and the outside of my vagina and anus, "the bikini line," telling me to turn on my stomach for the back of my legs. I lie on her table looking out at the sea, as sounds of the surf and her Malayalam pop mix with the anticipation of seeing Arnie, and the sensation of her silk sari on my skin, my foot against her stomach, her arms pressing against me as she positions herself to pull hairs from the back of my thigh with fingers and teeth.

In a dreamy haze of anticipation and arousal, I open the doors to my balcony and read Kamala's "The Dance of the Eunuchs," a poem that suits my mood.

It was hot, so hot, before the eunuchs came
To dance, wide skirts going round and round, cymbals
Richly clashing, and anklets jingling, jingling,
Jingling. Beneath the fiery gulmohur, with

Long braids flying, dark eyes flashing, they danced and
They danced, oh, they danced till they bled … There were green
Tattoos on their cheeks, jasmines in their hair, some
Were dark and some were almost fair …

In the hot afternoon lull I visualize Kamala against the pillows of her high fretted daybed, *pallu* (end of the sari) flowing in a river of colour across her breast and shoulder, sari draped in painter's folds over her crossed legs.

She is saying her husband "hacked" at her parts, that an old man attempted to rape her, and her husband's young friend tricked her onto a dark, deserted building site. "And he made me lean against the wall and he kissed me. It was slurping mouth kiss, mouth to mouth, all his spittle going into my mouth, and I was disgusted, I felt like vomiting."

When I remind her of the ecstasy of her love affairs, she says dismissively, "I don't understand how those petty men, little creatures, could cause such storms in me. I am thinking now that it was only my passion that transformed them into these rich, legendary figures. It wasn't anything to do with them."

"Yet you fell deeply in love."

"It was like becoming an aesthete, nothing else mattered. It was like the worship of God because if I fell in love with a man, I worshipped him."

She finds it odd that I don't understand how profoundly emotional and spiritually satisfying a love affair can be without sexual intimacy. That I don't seem to comprehend the essentially spiritual nature of love. And I find it odd that she who danced to the Gitagovinda, who advocates a non-conventional morality based on love, who wrote *My Story* and the most sensual and erotic love poetry in contemporary India, insists, "I hate sex."

"Yes," I admit. "I am always surprised when a sexual feeling creeps up on me."

"It doesn't creep up at all on me, and I feel that is probably a loss," she counters. "I was always like a river in spate …"

"A river in …?"

"In spate, you know, during the monsoons. It means without control – unbridled, rushing forth."

"In spate" is the kind of person I expected Kamala to be from her writing. And perhaps a small part of that Kamala still lives in this "switched-off" Kamala, if only in the regret for what is gone. I have to open myself to the thought that orthodoxy and rebellion coexist within her, as do other seeming contradictions just beginning to surface. Clearly, the "love queen" veneer is simply a shiny initial layer of her many selves. What is not clear, and what I can not yet imagine, is how complex, mercurial, many masked, and multi-layered Kamala really is. And how the connections and collisions of our different worlds will change both our lives.

I walk to the beach and face the sea that Kamala often and variously uses as an image in her poems. The water is tepid, neither cool nor warm, clear enough to see my feet, green rather than blue, the horizon mounting halfway into the sky. Michael, the dark-skinned lifeguard, joins me, assessing the force of the high, rolling waves, then leads me in. He tells me to plant my feet apart and bend my knees to withstand the surf, then talks me through the ten-foot wall of crashing water. "Stand, wait, dive," pulling me through the wave when I'm sucked under, "swim, swim!" pushing me toward the next when I lack force, yelling "dive, dive," as we plunge through the final crest into the calm waters beyond the breakers where he leaves me, continents away from father, lover, brothers, children, in the vast, unfurling Arabian Sea.

> Go, swim in the sea,
> Go swim in the great blue sea,
> Where the first tide you meet is your body,
> That familiar pest,
> But, if you learn to cross it,
> You are safe, yes, beyond it you are safe,
> For even sinking would make no difference then …

Eight AM, not yet bubbling hot, a comfortable time to take the elevator five floors up to Kamala's flat one last time. We hug, arms around each other, holding close for comfort and encouragement. We have hugged like this before, but Kamala is reserved in front of local people, which I attribute to the gossip nipping at her heels. Because of her support for women's causes, her friendships with younger women, and "The Sandal Trees," her short story about love between women, she has been disparagingly called a lesbian. She doesn't need a foreign writer mauling her in front of others. "I don't touch you in public," I say.

"Why?"

"You don't need it."

"You are right."

Kamala has caught her granddaughter's flu and is just recovering. Nayanthara had fever again today, and Kamala hovers near her, swept away in the overwhelming family tide, as I often am, immersed. She can't imagine travel now, although she admits that sometimes "this life stales on me and I feel like travelling." I talk about her forthcoming visit to Canada and the United States and remind her that, once on the plane, she will shed layers of care.

"Be another person," she says.

We both know we are strong, able, and interested in the world outside the family life that nourishes and troubles us. We like each other, two grown women, immune to most external approbation but vulnerable to what the other thinks. Both capable of caring for others, of loyalty and love, beginning to care for each other. Kamala is sputtering in the domestic wave now, and I am not. I do my best to remind her of a potential she knows but cannot feel.

Wrapped in a black sari with gold-embroidered red pallu, she slumps against the wall near the elevator, beautiful, graceful, vulnerable, soft.

I'll get her slowly walking in the fresh country air. I'll get her a Dictaphone to tell her stories to. I don't know what she'll make of me or my life. I rarely know what she'll say or where she'll be coming from next. I must trust her. Trust her honesty and my desire to match it.

She is framed now by the black metal bars of the elevator. I smile and throw a kiss. She turns on her heel and, before the elevator leaves her floor, she is gone.


I hand-carry my tapes of our meetings through customs. I don't want them erased. I am at the research and collecting stage where I'm terrified of losing my "material." The thought is like a sinking torpedo, subcutaneous buzz, a rising gorge. The security guard calls me over and rifles through the cassettes.

"How long have you been in India?"

"Three weeks."

"Music?"

"No. Recordings."

He is fingering them, opening the first one.

"Kamala Das," I say.

"Ah, Kamala Das." And I am through.

# TWO

# Montreal, the Laurentian Mountains, New York, 1995

My skin dries like the bark of a birch
my hair smells of spruce

# 6

## Maple Leaves as Red as Drying Blood

Finally the funding is in place, and next week Kamala is coming to Canada. I call Cochin to finalize arrangements, and someone answers in Malayalam.

"Kamala Das," I say as the woman on the other end of the line repeats whatever she is saying. I am repeating Kamala's name again when I hear, "Hello, hello."

"Kamala." I raise my voice, inflect it with what I hope sounds like pleasure but sounds like a yell.

"Merrily, where are you?" Her standard opening – it gives her time to focus.

"I'm in Montreal." Then I'm flummoxed. I'm not in Montreal, I'm in the Laurentian Mountains forty miles north of Montreal, but the connection is echoing *Kamala, Kamala*, so that I have to hear that whole thing again.

"How are you?" I ask.

"Fine. I'm excited." Her voice is light and clear as a bell. Mine is still asking, *How are you.* I don't know how to talk to minimize the confusion.

"Merrily, the travel agent has taken my passport to Delhi to get me a Canadian visa. I hope it will come in time."

"The Indo-US Subcommission will help you," I assure her.

"It's a Canadian visa," she tells me.

She emphasizes *Canadian.* I am so preoccupied with what I want to ask that I wonder why she is bringing this up until I realize later that she can't get into Canada without a Canadian visa. One of her first faxes asked for official invitation letters to facilitate visas for Canada and the United States, and we sent them. But this summer the Canadian government barred entry to Algerian feminist filmmakers because they feared they might stay. Kamala Das is from a country in the South. She knows the job of immigration in the North is to stop her, a woman with a heart condition and diabetes, from sneaking into six months of below-zero ice and snow, without the cook, driver, and admirers she's used to, because Canada is the best country in the world – for men.

The line is echoing *help you.*

"The letter from the university will get you a Canadian visa," I promise: *a visa, a visa.*

I should ask whether she would prefer to be carried up two flights of stairs to our city apartment or stay in a hotel nearby, but I should have warned her about this before and I can't bear to hear it twice.

*static*

I feel bad about her long, upcoming flight, the cold Montreal weather, that I'm not flying to meet her in New York, that she may miss the din behind her, that I haven't been able to bridge all this.

*sound waves across the Atlantic Ocean, the European continent, the Arabian Sea*

"Merrily," her tone familiar, playful, r's rolling, syllables somersaulting, where does that voice come from, what source, detachment, love of life – "Merrily, you sound nervous."

I laugh to assure her I am okay.

Hah, hah *hah, hah,*

Hah, hah, ha, ha *ha, ha, a, a.*

It sounds harsh and a little nuts. Irresponsible. If I were her, I wouldn't come. I can't *hah, ha, a, a* say anything else.

Behind the echo I hear the singsong Malayalam of Kamala's visitors. I can't believe I've undertaken the responsibility of bringing this great writer, this woman who listens for the underground sound of the Saraswati River, this beloved feminist heroine, to Montreal and the isolated Laurentian forest beyond.

"Ahh," light as a sun shower, "I too am nervous," she says. "Merrily, let's not have a nervous breakdown together."


I take a break from writing and lie on the Tibetan rug I use for exercising, wondering if coming from Delhi to the Laurentians is as much a shock as the other way around. I breathe in deeply and press my back against the rug, exhale and straighten out, thinking that coming to the country from the city requires a sense of resignation. Without the distractions and energy of other people, I feel myself slowing down and turning inward. I don't know if Kamala can do it. Or if she does something like this in other circumstances all the time.

She calls from Delhi. She's sleeping at the home of her eldest son, Monu, then flying straight through – Delhi, Frankfurt, New York, Montreal – sixteen hours in all.

"Merrily, I will have two hours in New York. Will they forget me?"

"It's considered a legal amount of time for a connection. The stewardess will meet you with a wheelchair and take you through customs."

"Good, then. Merrily, I hear it is cold there. Shall I keep my overcoat out? Is a cardigan and a shawl enough?"

Is it? What experience does Kamala have of cooler climates? It's the middle of September, supposed to be sunny tomorrow but what temperature? "Maybe not. I will bring you a coat."

"Mmmm," she concurs, "so I don't tremble in the cold."

Monu takes the phone. "Amma is looking forward to seeing you," he says, underscoring my responsibility for Amma, his mother.

I ready the country house so it shines. This house has fewer steps than our city house, and I decide it's the best place for Kamala to recover and for us to meet again.

I set the table with the most succulent fruits, breads, cheeses, and salads, in the West. And I put out the tape recorder. It would be wonderful if Kamala kept a journal, as I do, but so far she's described us only in occasional columns. To preserve her impressions, I'll try to record her regularly, as a journal-on-tape.

*Merrily, let's not have a nervous breakdown together.*

*So I don't tremble in the cold.*

Kamala makes me smile. The way she cuts to the quick. The things she says. The way she says them. If I can only get the logistics under control, this visit will be fun.

"When Merrily Weisbord told me that she would try to get me over to Canada," Kamala says, when she settles in and begins her taped journal, "I was amused. For one thing, I didn't have the health to travel that far alone. Then, of course, such promises have been made by visiting writers several times. I didn't think Merrily was 100 per cent sincere. Then I read something Merrily had written. I thought her a very bold woman. Sometimes I wondered if she was really bold, or was waving her boldness as a child might wave a flag at a parade? But when she came, we got on well. It seemed possible then that she might take me to Canada to write a book.

"The trip was very arduous, very difficult for me alone. I had started out early in the morning from Cochin, and when I reached Delhi, I was exhausted. My son said, 'Are you sure, Amma, you can travel all that way alone? Right now I could phone and cancel.'

"I said, 'No, that's not the way.' I knew what it meant to Merrily and I didn't want to disappoint her. And I thought what I might lose is some kind of peace I might get in Merrily's company. I knew that we belonged to the same tribe, although we came from different cultures, different backgrounds, so I said, 'It's all right.'

"I took a warm bath and rested, changed. They brought me at midnight to the airport, put me on the flight. Then there was the getting out at Frankfurt. This really bothered me because I am helpless at airports and railway stations. They are so frightening. I always think that I have crossed over to the other country, the land of the dead, alone with only strangers. The white faces are strangers' faces, you don't recognize anyone, and you are not recognized at all.

"It was a relief when I boarded the flight from New York because I knew at the end of it, although I was tired and somewhat dizzy and weak, I knew there would be Merrily and her wide smile. I dozed off a little, and I woke up when they announced that we were landing in Montreal."

Kamala is wheeled out looking smaller and thinner than I remember, and incredibly beautiful. She is sixty-two and her face is unlined and calm despite days in transit. She checks the international watch Monu has given her: 3:30 AM Delhi time.

We settle her in the front seat beside Arnie, whom she has just met, and on the drive north she observes the industries, shopping centres, empty fields, the General Motors factory.

"What are those houses?" she asks when she sees the grid of clapboard cottages near the plant.

"Homes for the workers," I say.

"They must be so happy there, they can make friends. How do they get to them?"

"They have cars."

"So much richer than Indian workers, houses and cars."

She dozes as we pass acres of fields and takes stock again when we turn onto our country road. "There aren't any people here," she comments. "Only the occasional car, with a light even though it's not dark. How many people in Canada?"

"Twenty-nine million," Arnie answers.

"Where are they?"

"This is the second biggest country in the world," Arnie tells her.

"Our friend Ellen was here, but she didn't like it," I add.

"Did she find it eerie?"

Does Kamala? I wonder.

"Even the airport looked deserted. There weren't many people around," she writes in the first English-language column she sends home.

It was as if Canada needed more people. I was coming from an overpopulated country and this was a rare sight. Merrily and her friend Arnie came with me in the car. I was very tired, I didn't even know what to say but I was safe. After hours of being insecure, untended, once I sat with them I knew that I was secure. I saw lines of tenements meant for the labour classes, slate grey huts like barracks. Everything was deserted. Roads were wide, vistas empty, not a soul walked along the sides of the road. No one. I have to adjust myself to this space, the vast areas, not finding any human being. That takes time.

Then I came to Merrily's place which is a wood and glass house built deep in a forest amidst the boulders. Dark boulders which look like elephants to me. Tall trees, maple trees, birch, all these trees. My eyes were thirsting for the sight of trees because in India most trees have been felled by contractors abetted by the government. The trees nod ever so gently. The leaves of a few trees tremble. They have shushed the birds to silence. They seem to know how keenly I desire it. Silence is the only lake I can dive into. I shall lurch in it like a sporting dolphin.

"I'm going to my dad's for few minutes," I tell Kamala once she's well settled.

"Take Arnie with you," she cautions. "The dark, loafers, muggers."

I smile as I leave the house. Dad lives with his wife, Phyllis, five minutes away on a road I have walked since I was a child. In the 1930s my Zeda (grandfather) lost his eye making railway ties on a defective forge, and with the $3,000 accident compensation he bought this sixty-acre valley. When I was a child, Zeda, Dad, and my uncle built summer cottages here and rented them to "comrades," who shared their love of square-dancing and volleyball and their communist ideals – a heritage that adds to my interest in Kerala, where Marxists regularly lead a democratically elected government. I spent every summer of my childhood in the Laurentians. The land was blessed with lakes, ponds, mountains, forests. And we children were cherished by adults who believed they could make a better, more just world, and that we children were its future. Naked until I was six, bare chested until puberty, I swam, danced, played, and ran safe and free.

"Kamala is a real ballsy woman," Arnie laughs. "She has no idea where she is, but she trusts us."

Dad walks me home and bounces though the door in a yellow nylon jacket and jeans. Kamala is relaxing in a caftan, without shoes. She apologizes for not helping more in the house.

"Do you have any Jewish blood in you?" Dad teases. "Maybe you have Jewish guilt." Then he says, "Do you kiss where you come from?"

"Yes, it's okay."

He kisses Kamala on both cheeks. "That's what the French do, so we say we're French."

"Such a charming man," she says when he is gone. "He has a twinkle in his eye."

"Merrily's father who is eighty-four came and kissed me on my right cheek," a friend will translate from Kamala's Malayalam column:

That was the way he welcomed me: "We the French people kiss both cheeks," and he kissed me again. Merrily burst out laughing seeing my confused face. Old people have the right to kiss people as much as they want. Pretending they have the right, they also exploit it.

It is now 4:30 AM. Merrily will get up only after 9. Yesterday morning I searched the kitchen and found the jar containing Tata tea. There was milk in the refrigerator. While I was relaxing and drinking tea, Merrily's fiancée, Arnie, came up the stairs. He offered me golden-hued bread and butter.

Merrily got married twice. Both marriages were failures. She told me therefore she never desires to marry again. She has been living with Arnie for over twenty years and they have not thought of marriage. They love each other. Arnie is a film producer.

In the bathroom here, there is only a bathtub. Being used to pouring water over my body, the bath was not satisfactory. To sit in water used to wash oneself is pitiable. I do not use oil when I go on a foreign tour. For a good bath, I have to get back home. In my son's house I can bathe using a bucket and a mug.

When I woke tonight at four, my Dictaphone was handy. I turned it on and could hear Nayanthara's song, "Crow, crow, where is your house ..." When I heard her voice, I suddenly thought of the happiness I would experience when I reached home. To embrace Nayanthara. I had travelled a lot and my world had shrunk and found itself in four-year-old Nayanthara. She is my abode of hope. My future.

It is silent here. It is a very quiet place. The silence is calling shrilly.

"The last time I experienced silence of this kind was on holiday many years ago at the Panchgani hill station near Bombay," Kamala tells me. "In those days there was something trapped within me. I could not speak much, I could only write. My husband said, 'You were such a bright person, so merry and full of laughter.' He wondered why I had withdrawn into silence. But I could not feel at ease with my husband. I didn't know how to explain, even define what I wanted. I knew only that there was something. I don't know why I remember all these things now. Maybe because the trees are similar, the air is clean, pure like it was at Panchgani."

She writes, "After breakfast I go to Merrily's library and sit at her desk. Margaret Atwood is the Maharani of Canadian literature. I sit and read her novels avidly. The hunger to read books burns in me again and again here. I bring the book close to my face and read causing pain to my eyes. The old hunger is thus satiated."

When I appear with the tape recorder, Kamala moves to the dining table or settles into the upholstered armchair.

"In India about sixty years ago, our ancestors used to set out for a pilgrimage to the holy city of Benares," she says into the mike. "They would go by bullock carts and walk a distance, taking half a year to reach there. Then, after praying at the shrine for fourteen days, some would try to return. And nearly always, exhausted with walking and travel, they would die. But those who died at the shrine were considered very fortunate. Sometimes the others would return and say, 'We left behind so and so, but they were cremated on the banks of the river so they are lucky.' Because when you cross sixty, you are expected to go on a pilgrimage and die at the shrine of Shiva. I am old enough to go on a pilgrimage. I am old enough even to die, but I won't. Maybe I will try to write three or four more books. Maybe I'll eat yogurt with blueberries. I have never seen a blueberry in India. These things really tempt me to live."

She leans back in her navy satin dressing-gown, eyes half-closed, hair in a top knot, gold bangles shining, snake ring flashing, Jaeger diamond earrings casting a bluish light.

"I have come at the best of times, autumn, when the maple leaves are turning brown, copper. I have come at the right time of my life too. If I had come when I was young, I wouldn't have found the peace I can now accept within myself and soak up as if I were a blotted paper. I lie on my bed because I am sleepy all the time, and I soak up the beauty and the silence of this place. It's as if night was a warm animal like a large cat moving against the house, rubbing itself on the house, on the glass panes."

It's fascinating to hear Kamala's stream of consciousness, and also to see her grope, weave, rephrase, structure as she struggles to write out loud. The only problem is that I'm recording her, and although it's her monologue, I'm there listening. Kamala should be free to talk or write about us, privately, as she does in the Malayalam columns she hand-writes in close-packed script and mails weekly to Kerala. I don't know how the columns differ from our recordings, but they must. It's a question of context, voice, the reader she's addressing.

In Malayalam, I know it isn't me.

I ask Kamala if my presence inhibits her discourse and how it differs from writing alone.

"Certainly, holding a microphone and having someone else in the room might inhibit," she says, "but I think I am getting used to this. Merrily, I haven't thought of you as a friend to be kept at a distance. I accepted you when you came to me, and I have trust in you. I am not so sure of others who come only to pass judgment on me."

"Does this recording process affect your writing?"

"I think it can upset the mental balance if you go on talking when you don't want to talk. Then it is not unlikely you will feel a bit unsettled within the mind because it is not as easy as writing. You bring out words and sometimes there is regret that you used a certain word, phrase, some emotions you feel later should have been left concealed. But then I feel as if I have moved into a confessional and there is a presence near me, invisible, asking me to confide, asking me to trust. It's all right as an exercise. I think it's all right because most of my writing is confessional."

That evening, in her Malayalam column, she writes:

Although I am recognized as a poet abroad, in my own country I am a slave with a begging bowl. Still I am living. I laugh when I get the opportunity, and celebrate life. I do not have any feelings of guilt. I don't have to perform sayanpradakshina [a ritual offering to the gods] in the temple or go to the ashram in Potta to sing the praises of Jesus. I have dipped myself on many occasions in the sacred waters. I have swum in the holy water of love. I have played Thiruvathirakkali [a dance performed during the Thiruvathira festival] and revelled in it. There are no stains or blackness in my body or mind. I have lived and accomplished my undertaking.

# 7

## I Shall Carry You with Me

Arnie returns to the city to face the crises endemic to a fledgling film company, and I am not alone as I often am. The country house is warm with the presence of Kamala. I feel her in the room above, curled up under the duvet, venetian blinds drawn to protect her eyes. No longer fearful.

In our normal lives, Kamala and I are often both essentially alone, children gone, mates more or less departed. Now we have the comfort and respect of our companionship. We have each other.

"And at two-thirty, I don't know if it was Indian time or Canadian time," Kamala writes, "I could not sleep any longer so I put on the lights, groped around, opened the door. Upstairs there wasn't anyone sleeping. I went and ate a green apple. I sat in Merrily's kitchen for a long, long time. It's as if I have found another sister. I feel close to this girl who is my new friend."

When the sun reaches the skylight, I walk upstairs to greet Kamala and prepare our morning tea. Flush with night-time thoughts, I switch on the tape recorder as usual, then hesitate. I tell Kamala that although we talked and worked together like this in India, I feel more uncomfortable doing so here because she is my guest.

She generously assures me I shouldn't. "I came for it, Merrily, I am offering myself. In the time I stay here, you can ask me any question and I will answer. Any awkward question."

"And we can discuss later if the book is published in Kerala," I suggest, concerned lest her conservative compatriots attack her again.

"But if it isn't, the Kerala people may be furious. It's just that it will make things a bit awkward for me. I also have a family, a sister, brother-in-law, all of them puritanical, not trusting me enough. I keep quiet about my work."

I know too well what she means about upsetting family, having censored myself much more than she. I ask if she thinks all memoir writers have the same problem.

"A writer moves away from family, old relationships, very far with the speed of a falling star," she says. "Otherwise the writer is destroyed, and only the member of the family remains: the mother, sister, daughter, wife. The writer at some point must ask, Do I want to be a well-loved member of the family? Or do I want to be a good writer? You can't be both at the same time. The days when you are with the children and are being a very good mother, you cease to be the writer. You feel repelled by the pen and the paper, which are definitely going to come between you and your loved ones."

I make assenting sounds as Kamala describes the conflicting pulls of motherhood and writing. Not everybody understands this conflict, and her blunt rendition of our predicament brings me closer to her. When I was a single parent with small children, I too felt torn between family obligations and writing, and I tried to talk about it to my dad because he was helping me raise my kids.

"I am overwhelmed by all that is asked of me," I confessed to him, and quoted writer Tillie Olson who said, "All women who manage to write are 'survivors.'"

"We are lucky if people ask things of us," my dad admonished me. "It means we are needed and responsible."

I reminded him that before I got pregnant at nineteen, I had written for radio, newspapers, literary journals, and I seemed set on a writing path. But as soon as I was a mother, I was expected to clean, nurture, and earn money. I had to struggle to give myself the mental, physical, and temporal space needed to lose myself in writing.

Dad said he saw his male clients struggling in business too. He was sorry, but he didn't really see a difference between men and women writers. And although over the years he continued to help me practically, even anticipating my needs, like many non-writers he couldn't understand my need to write or the circumstances obstructing it – until I showed him a letter from a friend: "The children fill every inch of cubic air, squeezing me out, requiring constant tending, rendering my stomach knotted, body a board, brain in seizure. I am frantic to get back to the book. My poor people hang in mid sentence. I know how to finish it, I want to finish it."

"I had no idea," said Dad, handing back the letter. "I'm eighty years old and I'm just beginning to understand."

"The pen and paper are a real impediment if you are seeking relationships that will last," Kamala amplifies. "The writer might fall in love with someone, she might have a love affair, but if she becomes a total writer within that phase, the relationship is subtly destroyed."

I think I understand, but I ask her to clarify why this happens.

"Because the writer can give all of herself only to that task of writing. She will have to write against her loved one, put him under the microscope, dissect him, analyze his thoughts, his words. After a while he is no longer the man you held in your arms at night. You have cut him into little slivers, everything is burst open, he is seeds and pulp and juice all spread out in little bits on your writer's table. After that, you can't go to his arms the same way."

Yes, I nod empathically. In my case, I stopped keeping a journal when I realized that the journal and Arnie were irreconcilable. Like Kamala at Panchgani, I was not speaking much, only writing thoughts and feelings in my journal. I had given up trying to work through problems with Arnie because the journal and I faced them more easily together. I watched him and us for it, and this helped me cope. But Arnie was out of the loop. And often by the time I had figured things out, written them down, and told him about it, the past and the present were out of sync. I was living in the time warp of me and my journal.

"If you are very wise, you try to conceal from the loved one that you know everything about him," Kamala warns. She says that even if she sometimes detests herself for it, she can't stop scrutinizing people, even her children, and herself too, "every move I make, every thought that comes." She uses images like "butchering my loved ones, slaughter them by analyzing them and their motives," to describe her instinct for seeing people as "material," not just as themselves.

I understand Kamala's need to write "so avariciously," and her shame about her nature hurting others, since I am similarly compelled. She may want to hug her loved ones as one human being to another, or she may throw herself into bliss – and then something in her says, "Don't waste this. Put it down on paper. Don't trust memory, it will go away." Like the scorpion that drowned because it stung the frog carrying it across the water, she can only say, "It's my nature."

"You can't help yourself," I acknowledge.

"I am not talking down from the heavens. I am talking from my own hell looking up to you. I feel really cursed with this kind of power to take the juice out of everything like a fruit crusher or something. There is a sugar-cane juice machine at every road corner in India. You put in hard stalks of cane and out comes frothy juice. I am trying to get some juice out of all the sugar cane that I take clumsily, without any mercy."

"Don't you think that we can still love somebody even if we do this?"

"That's true. I am a great one for loving. But who would believe me when I say I 'love'? If I were to write twenty stories about a man I love, would he, after reading those stories, think that I loved him? I would like to hold him, reassure him of my feelings but it is impossible. He would say, 'Well, I was only a victim, you used me.'"

"That's a problem."

"That is a problem, but there is a solution too. What happens is you write a beautiful poem regarding that separation. In some secret corner of your thoughts, you welcome the pain too. You feel grateful to the man for abandoning you. But then, who can abandon a writer? A writer is powerful in some way, isn't she? Powerful destroyer. If I were not a writer, I would stay far away from writers. I wouldn't get into their orbits."

"It's a dangerous thing to do," I repeat, waiting for the rest.

"It's very dangerous because they are working on you all the time."

"That's why I think what we're doing is brave. In my case I have a fascination with what's interesting, so I don't care if what's revealed is bad or good."

"But Merrily, what is interesting?"

"I think it's interesting that we are writers from different cultures talking honestly to each other."

"Totally different cultures. That makes a difference. And me coming from an orthodox Hindu household. We'll have to be honest because there is no compromise, otherwise the book will be a fake. We would be called fakes and that would be a calamity. Let's be honest even if we are going to be hurt in the process. If we are honest, they will accept us, as one of the injured tribe. Only the dishonest will hurt us … It's getting a bit too hot for me now, Merrily."

"I will turn the tape recorder off."

"Finish your breakfast. You have not eaten a thing."

Kamala writes in her English column:

Mid morning, I went with Merrily to meet her aunts Sue and Katie. They lived in separate houses. They are people with old world charm, an old world courtesy. I could relax in their drawing rooms.

Auntie Katie, the matriarch of the family, stays in a small house made of wood, a house I dreamt of while I was a child and addicted to Hans Anderson's tales. She had covered every bit of furniture with crocheted rugs and doilies and looked like a porcelain figurine all pink and blue and gleaming. She embraced me and kissed both my cheeks. She told us that her small house had only sweet memories. She told me of the poverty they once experienced, about her younger brother Nathan who built houses on the estate, and also about his painless death.

Aunt Sue and Uncle Joe were busy packing to drive to Florida. Sue had shampooed her hair and tied it with a towel. She was bent forward a little and the chiffon of her cheeks brushed against my skin.

I feel as if all the fences have been pulled down and life is an expanse like an ocean. I have no time sense here. I sleep when I feel sleepy, I eat when I feel like eating and Merrily doesn't disapprove. It's almost as if I am leading the life of a baby who is allowed demand feeding. I write a little but every minute of my stay here I am conscious of the fact that I am a writer. I thought I might miss India, I might miss my people. But there is some kind of languor stealing over me here.

We leave Auntie Katie's and return to the long pine refectory table at home. I serve the fruit, cheese, bread, and avocados Kamala likes, and we eat leisurely. When she is ready, I turn on the recorder and ask the question that has been nagging at me ever since she queried me about Arnie in Cochin.

"In Cochin, you asked what of Arnie belongs to me," I remind her. "What did you mean?"

"I had no doubts of my husband belonging to me," she says without hesitation. "Accepted by society too. In India, legitimacy counts a lot. Marriage is a promise on stamped paper. Yours is a promise on blank paper without much validity. When one partner dies, what is the other partner left with? She is not even called his widow. The widow at least gets the widow's pension, she's accepted by his friends."

I tell Kamala that because of her prompting, I researched Quebec's Napoleonic Code and learned that no matter how long Arnie and I lived together, he would have no legal responsibility to me because we are not married.

"I'm sorry I disturbed you," she says, looking not at all sorry. "I shouldn't be interfering, I know that. But maybe I took a liking to you and I wanted you to be safe."

"I think from your perspective living together unmarried seems silly and romantic."

"Eighteen years is a very good relationship. You might as well legitimize it. Everybody loves him in your family, they'll celebrate it. What did Arnie say, then?"

I wonder how to summarize what happened between Arnie and me when I returned from Cochin. I would not have traded the trek, meeting Kamala, or the journals I wrote for anything. The weird thing was that I returned disinterested in sex. I had enjoyed being alone, working at my own rhythm, having my own hotel room, and physical sharing didn't attract me. Two months of celibacy, plus Kamala's propaganda about "invasive" sex, had made me happily self-contained. It became more normal to sleep beside Arnie as time went on, but I still had no desire to be entered physically.

I remind Kamala of the day her friend Gita visited and they talked to me about being happy alone and intact. "You used the word 'intact.' And after months on my own rhythm, I saw I could live like that."

"I am so sorry Merrily. What a scene you have created here."

"So I didn't want sex, but I wanted to get married."

"If you had got married, you would have slipped into sex."

"I slipped into sex anyway, because part of sex for me is holding and sleeping close together. Slowly I got used to Arnie again, and slowly I wanted to hold him and be close to him."

"What did Arnie say about marriage?"

These discussions are much harder to summarize. Kamala had questioned what Arnie and I meant to each other and what obligations and responsibilities we accepted toward each other. Her prodding made me face difficult practical and emotional issues that I had dismissed, then suppressed. If Arnie and I were married, for example, I would be his legal heir. But as his common-law partner,

I would inherit nothing unless it were specified in a will. Kamala's expectations of commitment normalized needs that I had judged weak and materialistic. Her viewpoint concretized my feeling that Arnie and I should take care of each other, and I urged Arnie to make a will. When he understood, he did.

But the marriage question was thornier. I tell Kamala that Arnie said, "This is very surprising, because this is not the understanding we have had for eighteen years," and asked for time to think. As days passed, I said, 'You're behaving like an adolescent,' and he said, 'Maybe I am.'"

"So it is settled that you will not marry, is it?" she asks.

"No," I say, still unsure what's best for us.

"How I would love it to see you both married. I could marry you according to Hindu rites right here. We must get a little thing, a little locket which you must place around your neck, or an exchange of rings – at least two flower garlands to exchange. I could be the priestess getting you married. But then, Merrily, you are married. There is no going back."

This is a scary thought. But as a friend pointed out, I already have the responsibilities, adaptations, and compromises of marriage, without the position or protection of the married state.

"Why are you wanting it?" I ask.

"Probably because I want you to be safe. And then there are the financial reasons. When a husband divorces, he settles an alimony on the wife. When a lover leaves, he doesn't have to. You should be more secure."

"Are there reasons besides finances? Married people are no safer from breakup. My relationship with Arnie is twice as long as either of my marriages."

"But how do you introduce him? 'Here's my friend Arnie'?"

"That's a problem. We call each other husband and wife. We say 'companion.' Sometimes 'compadre.' My friend calls her boyfriend of ten years 'my pelvic attraction.' There's no word that gives enough weight to the relationship."

"When you stop enjoying sex after sixty or so, then what does he become? Helper in the kitchen? Really, what does he become then? Because there is a time in a woman's life when she feels that her body should be hers. Even the legitimate entry becomes removed after a while."

"In this culture this may or may not be so."

"Really? Do you think your father is sleeping with his wife?"

"I know they're sleeping together."

"How can they, at this age? How can a man be potent at this age?"

"Sometimes he is, and sometimes he's not. And if he's not, they don't worry, they wait until he is."

"She doesn't mind sex?"

"I think she likes it."

"She likes sex? She told you?"

"I think it would be interesting for you to talk to her."

"No. I behave like a Nalapat woman now. Their frigidity came to me after sixty and has settled on my soul like snow. I don't have many unfulfilled desires, or any desires at all. I wanted to come and see you."

"But you more than anybody in the world …"

"I have dissected the subject, gloried in it, that's true. Now I don't think any man or any woman in the world can cause me a sexual flutter. All I want is to put my feet up, relax, chat, have plenty of people come laugh with me. I am like a beach where the sun is about to set. But the beach wants children playing on it. It wants to retain warmth for the people who come the last few minutes before dusk."

On the phone that night I tell my friend Linda about my efforts to negotiate a relationship with Arnie that feels more secure. I say I could never have allowed myself to want marriage enough to ask for it, or to brave rejection and female stereotyping, until I met Kamala. I tell her that Arnie has always earned more money than I and if he is against marriage on existential principle, I will request a notarized domestic agreement for security in case we separate.

Linda says she understands the need for a will, but with all our independent feminism we have painted ourselves in a corner, and can I really ask Arnie to provide support if we stop living together? She reminds me that our generation, and that of our daughters too, believes in the equality of the sexes, and that part of that equality is pulling our own weight, sharing expenses, and supporting ourselves.

"Shouldn't we give up on the idea of anyone looking after us like our daddies did?" she asks. "Won't Arnie see this as a lack of faith that he will do the honourable thing?"

I tell Linda that Arnie would probably want to do the honourable thing, but it might slip his mind. I would have to remind and nag and feel demeaned, and he would be bothered and irritated and forget why he wanted to be honourable in the first place.

"It took me awhile to arrive at this position," I say, agreeing that at first Kamala's marriage propaganda seemed uptight and conventional, and her longing for "responsibility and belonging" seemed old-fashioned and needy. But Kamala was so alarmed that I had to re-evaluate my situation. And when I did, I realized that my arrangement *was* insecure and that, to be honest, the insecurity made me feel insecure. I asked myself why money should be considered such an importnat arbiter of equality. If both of us worked hard, and if we were equally committed to each other, shouldn't we share *emotionally, physically, and financially*? "First I had to believe that the concept of responsibility was right and justifiable," I tell Linda. "Then I had to have the guts to ask for a legal commitment."

As retrograde as it may seem to Linda, my new perspective feels liberatingly conclusive, and I am ready to move on to Montreal for Kamala's scheduled meetings and major public appearances. She brings her readers in Kerala up to date:

Leaving the paradise that was Merrily's country home, Merrily and I drove to Montreal at noon, a hot sun beating on our faces. I climbed the steep staircase of their elegant house very slowly and reached the doorway without much pain. There are 26 steps to the Parishad in Kochi, and I have climbed them many times. That thought gave me courage.

The apartment reminded me of 117 Park Street in Calcutta where I lived as a child. The bedroom on the west belonged to Anna, Merrily's youngest daughter, and had been made ready for me. At night when I opened my door, Anna appeared like an apparition, her golden hair gliding with her. Her eyes sparkle with innocence. She has the glow of an oil lamp remembered from the past, one my grandmother placed on her window each evening. After a spell of rest, I listened to Alasdair's music. Alasdair, Anna's boyfriend, stays in a room beyond the large kitchen. He played the bouzouki and mandolin as one possessed.

The next day, an expert in organic farming called Jerzy came as an overnight guest.

In the evening my friend Jerzy reads Kamala's poetry, and because she's a love poet, he presents her with a short story he assumes she will enjoy, "an organic farmer's erotica" about two naked hippies copulating in the soil.

"Watch out for the farmer," Kamala warns me as soon as I get up next morning. "He gave me a pornographic story. Do not to have him in the house without Arnie. Do not hug him or he will lust after you. Just say 'Mr Jerzy, today I have the flu and I don't want to pass on the virus.' That will avoid a situation."

But Kamala is more upset than I realize. "I am afraid sometimes people's concern for their friends seems very abnormal here," she says after Jerzy leaves. "Here I don't know what kind of a question can be asked, what kind of a statement I can make. A woman of my age is supposed to ask, 'Are you all right?' She goes around showing concern. If she doesn't, she's not on her best behaviour, she's indifferent. This morning when I came to the kitchen and saw that farmer friend of yours, to be social I offered him a cup of tea. When I was making the tea, I asked him about his family because it seemed a friendly thing to do."

She writes home to her readers, "Then, he said I was like his mother, inquisitive. I felt shocked. The remark made with a wry smile made me realize that I came from breeding different than his. Another month in a Canadian city and I would begin to feel like an ill-mannered, clumsy villager."

"But he loved his mother very much," I assure Kamala. "You misread his response."

"He used the word 'inquisitive.' I wasn't at all. Who is interested in some farmer living somewhere? Organic manure and all that. Blue potatoes, the size of potatoes, he is very excited about potatoes. Then, turnips. Merrily, how long can you sit and talk about these things? I really salute you."

"Had he used the word 'curious,' would you have felt better?"

"'Curious' would be nice. It is just that I could not make something for a man without talking because I am not paid to do it. If I was paid to do it, of course I wouldn't talk, he would be my master. You see, only a servant keeps quiet and cooks and serves. If it's a friend, you talk. So these are codes of behaviour which I will have to learn. I wonder sometimes how you picked me as a friend. Such a different culture."

The following morning, balanced between the banister and Alasdair's arm, Kamala descends the stairs for her appearances at Concordia University, where I am this year's writer-in-residence. We drive past ex-Prime Minister Trudeau's art nouveau mansion and circle up Mount Royal to enjoy the Lookout's splendid view of Montreal and the St Lawrence River.

"I want to be totally frank," Kamala says as we descend the mountain on our way to the university. "In American serials, they are always kissing on the mouth, then ripping the clothes off and leaping into bed. Is kissing such a great thing that it must always end in bed?"

I let Alasdair go first. I think he can't believe this is happening. "No," he says after a while. "Sometimes it is something all by itself."

"Or it can be a prelude to lovemaking," I add. "But it can go on a long time before lovemaking."

"In serials, it is like animals. And the young people are being influenced."

"The TV serials aren't true," Alasdair comments.

"But is kissing so erotic?"

"Yes," Alasdair and I chorus in unison.

"Don't they kiss in India?" I wonder.

"Not on the mouth."

"What happens before lovemaking?"

"Tickling. The man kisses the foot, nibbles it, then he moves up slowly. Women take longer than men, they have to be warmed up."

I am contemplating having my foot nibbled and remembering a dinner where a male writer asked Kamala if he could kiss her goodnight. Although in India no man is allowed to hug or kiss Kamala, she graciously pointed to her cheek and said, "You can kiss me here." I guess I'd feel the same way if a strange Indian writer asked if he could nibble my toe. I'd point to my thumb and say, "You can nibble right here."

Merrily took me to her classroom where the students ranged from age 20 to 60. I have found Canadians to be less racist than others of the white community, and I told them many times of the writer's need to free himself from any nationality in order to belong to all who read his books. A poem, however perfect, is incomplete until the reader fills its frame with his own experiences, philosophy. If a poem is likened to a house, it is for the reader to inhabit it.

"Once I fell ill and doctors suspected leukemia," Kamala tells the students. "To verify, they aspirated my marrow. That was very painful. They showed me the marrow, which I never dreamt of seeing, something hidden within yourself, without which you are not yourself. Poetry is like that. If you are prepared to go deep into yourself and aspirate the marrow of your essence, you become a poet. You have a new vision which is a poet's vision. Everything is poetry."

Kamala addresses the Writer's Union of Canada, Concordia University's Department of Education, the South Asian Women's Association. After two days, her Montreal appearances take their toll, exhausting her.

I put the microphone between us, and her shoulders slump. Her body crumples into the couch. I stop.

In the city I could not write anything but letters. The rooms seemed full of floating voices. They spoke a language I could not comprehend. They were not hostile to me, but my presence stirred them up. It was as if in the early hours of the morning the dead ones were coming alive to communicate with me. They seemed to want a listener for their tales of despair.

I too am finding this whole thing harder than I thought. Perhaps it is because as sole assistant to a world-famous writer, I am organizing engagements in Montreal, New York, Houston – feeding, entertaining, worrying about stairs, a wheelchair, health, trying to provide enough of whatever Kamala needs so that she is not homesick and longing to leave.

I cannot imagine Merrily without the phone receiver in her hand. She sets down dates and fixes schedules for her friends. She is continually interrupted by long-distance calls. She leaves her tea untasted. After an hour I throw it away. I have not seen Merrily sit down to complete a meal. Often she stands up eating, nibbling at some dainty thing while she converses with people on the phone. Once I saw her gulp down some apple juice.

It's disconcerting to find that the me Kamala sees is the busy me, arranging her tour. It is clear from reading her columns that the observer affects the thing observed. I am busy in the way I am because she is here. She thinks this hectic pace is my life, although it is merely my life during the visit of Kamala Das.

And, I admonish myself, what I am observing, affecting, and writing about is merely Kamala's life during her visit here, with me.

# 8

## Child Bride

Merrily has to attend a meeting so her younger brother, Hyman, agreed to take me back to their house in the countryside. Hyman looks like a handsome Italian with a round face and black hair. His eight-year-old daughter Emma phoned while we were speeding along. Hyman used the little phone in the car. The sky was grey and near the western horizon it had a tinge of gold. Canada seemed vast, stupendous, unbelievably grand. I would have loved that drive to go on forever, the untamed wind crying out in our ears. Canada has by its beauty and its largeness removed all terrors from my mind. I no longer fear robbers, violent gangsters, or even death.

Then exactly at 6:30, I sat at the groaning dining table of Merrily's parents to join Uncle Joe, Aunt Sue, Aunt Katie, Nat's widow June, and Merrily's father, Syd, while Phyllis, the hostess, fussed around serving delicious food like kugel (baked with potatoes, flour and eggs) and challah (braided egg loaves). It was New Year's Day and the ceremony began with honey poured onto the plate. Apples slices were dipped into the honey and eaten to make the new year sweet. There was a sweet preparation of carrots and shredded fruit, meat for those who liked it, a salad. White wine was served and toasts drunk.

I told them of my marriage and of my life as a child bride.

The following day, I walk the country road with Dad, thrilled to be outdoors, noticing blood bursts of autumn leaves along the way.

"How do you like Kamala?" I ask.

"Very much," Dad answers immediately. "She's fascinating. Last night she kept everyone enthralled." Then he asks, "Do you know why she talks so much? Is she trying to be an entertaining guest?"

"Probably," I agree, and we continue along in companionable silence.

Then, surprisingly, Dad says, "I was shocked."

"At what?"

"Well, you know, that she was punished because she failed her math exam."

"You mean married off at fifteen."

"Yes."

She told Dad that her father had shouted at her, calling her "a dunce," his face purple with rage. "You have disgraced our illustrious family. I will not educate you further. Now it will have to be marriage. What else can I do with a girl like you?"

"But the law forbade girls under eighteen to marry," she told Dad. "Girls of my class didn't marry so young. And it seemed brutal and crude, and I didn't like it one bit."

My father stops walking. He looks uncharacteristically confused and angry, and I don't know what to say. I know Dad would always help me any way he could. And if he is protective of me now when I am grown, how much more protective he must have felt when I was fifteen.

Faced with my dad's distress, I feel the magnitude of Kamala's father's betrayal.

I loved you father, I loved you all my life ...

Dad and I retrace our steps and turn onto the gravel road leading to the pond. When I was a young mother, I sat on a log at the side of the pool like my mother before me, watching my kids play and swim. Kamala too had a pond at Nalapat. She floated there, her grandmother guarding her, the sun warming her, the coldness of water under her.

I want to reassure Dad that despite her father, Kamala's childhood was also blessed. I tell him about Nalapat, Kamala's ancestral home and lands in rural Punnayurkulam where she spent her summer holidays with her mother, grandmother, maternal grand-uncle, great-grandmother, mother, aunts, and their children, all related through a common ancestress. I tell him the women owned the land, because here we women also proudly own our land. And I tell him Kamala cuddled with her grandmother, swam with coconut floats, presented theatricals with her brother, and read in her grand-uncle's library – as I did in Dad's, my anticipation mounting each time he reached into the shelves to hand me the keys to another, exciting, unknown world.

Mostly I tell Dad about Kamala's "plump, fair-skinned" Ammamma (grandmother) who held her, hugged her, treasured her, slept close to her at night and for the noonday nap.

"Such kind eyes she had and shiny, black, straight hair," Kamala remembers. "She took two baths a day, and her throat, whenever I nestled close to her, smelled of sandalwood."

Ammamma "opened the portals of mythology" for young Kamala, taught her to pick medicinal herbs, light the sacred oil lamps, apply vermilion, sandalwood paste, and oils. Ammamma bought modest long skirts to cover her granddaughter's legs, gave her oil baths, and washed, untangled, oiled, and braided her long, curly hair.

There is a house now far away where once
I received love …

I tell Dad everything I remember hearing about Ammamma and describe how she took Kamala at eleven to the privacy of the *tekkini* (the women's quarters) for the traditional Nayar pre-puberty ritual of wearing the *onnara* (an undergarment). How, as the music of the breeze filtered through the mango trees, Kamala learned how to fasten yards of mill around her waist, then draw the fabric between her legs and into delicate folds behind, securing it at the back. How once, protected by her grandmother, Kamala felt proud of herself, of her slim, strong body, her little-girl breasts, and the *onnara*-augmented swell of her hips.

I want Dad to know that while I had support from my family, especially from him, Kamala had her extended family, particularly her maternal grand-uncle, a prominent Malayali literary figure who admired and encouraged her. Most especially, she had her grandmother.

"My grandmother was my safest, most loving refuge," Kamala tells anyone willing to look beyond her public persona. "She was my first love, and has always been my love."

I sit near Dad on a wooden deck chair, watching softly hued leaves flow downstream over the dam to our summer cottage. At Nalapat, Kamala's extended family lived together in a *nalukettu*, the traditional home of the Nayars, with tiny rooms surrounding an inner courtyard "beautifully framed by round pillars with granite bases where the women of the house sat taking the snarls out of their long, glossy hair, exposed to the afternoon sun." I think of the freedom I took for granted as I roamed our family land, and wonder how much greater Kamala's sense of entitlement must have been at Nalapat in the 1930s, when her family was one of her village's five rich landowners, with over two hundred families to serve them.

I think Nalapat is Kamala's emotional centre as this place is for me. I store images of the land I love – the path to the Back Lake, the granite rocks and tree roots I leap over, the stream chorusing hallelujah over pebbles and rocks, the fields of ferns, and arches of cedar. The Back Lake is imprinted on my memory cells – the glacier boulders left since the Ice Age for us to lie on, the ring of evergreen and white birch, the clear, cool water calm as silence, or rippling in the wind and sparkling with pure light. In hard times these images are my refuge. This is where I go.

Kamala too has stored images of childhood and immortalized them in books – the pillars of the patio, the dark interiors forever fragrant with incense, the hedges with flowering creepers, the lichened idols in the snake shrine, the granaries, the enormous *palmyra* tree near the stone-walled well, the old *bakul* tree she swung from as a child, the magnolia-like *neermahalam* whose fragrant flowers scent the house, the frangipani, mango, *amla, parijatham, jac,* slender *bhel* trees, the *vaka* whose bark is ground to powder to use as soap, and especially the bathing pond in which she floated, face turned toward the sun-blanched sky and where, in the silent hours of the afternoon, baby waterfowl emerge from bushes of yellow *arali* and henna to prance around and cry "*kwar kwar kwar.*"

The pond and its association with childhood joy is a primal connection between Kamala and me, and Kamala's overwhelming feeling at Nalapat could just as well be mine.

in all those unfenced hours, she had felt
no fear, not even joy, but
an anonymous peace ...

It is a treat to have Kamala in the country house, and even as I write I think I should return and see if she needs anything. We are three weeks into the visit, and she has found a place for me: I am younger sister, she is elder sister, and yesterday I was allowed to rub oil into the dangerously cracking skin of her very slender feet.

Taking care of her makes me understand how Kamala could devote herself to her ailing husband and miss that total commitment when he died. Caring for someone takes you away from ego, out of yourself, its dictates relaxingly clear.

For me this dedication is tiring, and a new kind of pleasure.

Merrily is looking after me as best as she can. Yesterday she rubbed vitamin E cream into my drying feet and massaged them.

From four to six I sat in the library and wrote one poem and two articles. I should travel to other countries at least twice a year. Then I will get rest. My near-dead poetry will bloom again. With travel I will rejuvenate myself.

Kamala has written more of her "Backpage Banter" columns, enough for a fortnight and, glory of glories, a poem.

"My husband never read my poetry," she says. "He thought it was silly, like making a little bit of lace to stitch onto your collar. And it didn't earn enough money. Now he's wrenching it out of me." She reads aloud, her eyes sparkling, voice tripping,

> I have torn to shreds the tarot cards of my fate,
> I walk the highway alone.
> He was a sunshade, he was my home,
> now I walk naked as a babe.

This new poem, even though it's sad, makes her joyful. Her early poetry blossomed in the cultural ferment of Bombay, Calcutta, and Delhi, but she says that in "powerfully inhibited" Trivandrum and Cochin, she feels like "an Egyptian mummy all wrapped up in lint." Here she sits in a path of sunlight, hair loose, writing without interruption. Admiration grows in me for her courage, but more so for how the words flow from her heart through the prism of her mind to the page. She follows the exhortation of the great French writer Marguerite Duras, to "write at one's own pace and in accordance with what one is experiencing at the time, one ought to eject what one writes."

And she heeds her own spirited cry to

> Write without
> A pause, don't search for pretty words which
> Dilute the truth, but write in haste, of
> Everything perceived, and known, and loved ...

This time when we return to the table, I jump-start our ongoing comparative sexuality discussion by telling Kamala I probably slept with fifteen men – "a bit on the high side," one of my friends said, but not unusual for someone of my generation. I excavate names and I count: two marriages, ten relationships, three liaisons, and an eighteen-year non-married cohabitation that makes Kamala cringe.

I tell her I married at nineteen because I was pregnant, remained married for two years, then wheeled my baby home to my parents' house, divorced, then married and divorced again.

She stares ahead and tries to ask a polite question.

I ask how my life with men seems to her, and she says "immature." She thinks a mature person would have had more patience and not given up so fast. She didn't leave her husband because she didn't want to lose the respect her children might have had for her.

"I didn't want them to think of me as a shirker. The children wanted a father. That was part of their wealth." She thinks that without my dad's support, I would not have had the guts to leave my marriages, and she didn't have that support. She lived in Bombay, her parents lived in Kerala. Her father had asked Das to take her off his hands, and her mother was distant. Anyway, since women were expected to make their marriages work, she couldn't expect parental sympathy for her plight.

"The only thing I envy you is your friendship with your father, because my father was never very friendly with me. Your father maintains this dialogue, and with a father like that, you could get your escape, get your release. His words must be like feather strokes, they don't hurt at all."

"Never have they hurt," I agree.

"When we were bruised, my grandmother would dip a feather in some medicated oil and paint our bruises with it. And it didn't hurt at all. Such gentleness."

This prompts me to ask if my affairs, marriages, divorces, seem as cruel to her as her early married years do to me.

She looks at me briefly, makes a decision, and says, "Except for the pain, of course."

Then all semblance of shared experiences – joint and extended families, ponds, in-house libraries – disintegrates as she describes how our paths so violently diverged.

She is fifteen, a schoolgirl. She runs so fast, she can hear the wind rushing past her ears.

She fails in mathematics and is given in marriage to a husband of thirty-five. He holds a secure, if lowly, government position in the Reserve Bank of India.

… You cannot believe, darling
Can you, that I lived in such a house and
Was proud, and loved …

Young Kamala knows male/female love only from prayer books and literary books. She expects her husband will take her in his arms and stroke her face, her hair, her hands, whispering words of endearment. She imagines conversation, companionship, warmth. She believes that with one sweep of her husband's benign arms, he will remove all her loneliness.

Sex plays no part in these imaginings. She knows nothing about sex. She knows there's a hole where you urinate. But not about any other orifice.

Her husband knows love only from the fast, feudal mounting of serving girls. For ten days he rams at her, unable to open her up. He is much too big for her.

"I'm sorry, I'm not normal," she apologizes.

And he agrees.

"I have no opening," she tells the village serving maid.

The girl advises her to try sex on the fifth day of her menses, and that day her husband thrusts and thrusts at her "like a bison."

"It was horrible. A horrible punishment for a child. It hit at my cervix and I bled. I developed lesions."

The lacerations are so painful that she is unable to move or to pee.

"So much bleeding there was and pain."

She says that when her husband's resting penis lay on his belly, it reached his navel, "not like a normal person at all, like a horse."

And he is proud of it.

"Das is a very lucky man," his uncle instructs the child bride, "and the woman who marries him is lucky too."

"It is your fault you bleed," her husband berates her. "You are lucky. Look at this, you've got this."

Kamala turns away in fright.

Shortly after her first son is born, Kamala leaves her husband's small apartment in Bombay and returns to her grandmother in Nalapat. She is happy there, and Das is happy with his boyfriend, but her mother-in-law complains that her son is all alone and Kamala has to go back.

"Such pain there was then," she remembers.

By age nineteen, she is the mother of two young boys.

"My cervix was so broken down, they had to operate. I had to have the mouth of the cervix cut and I bled and I bled. My God, what a way to bleed."

"The surgery is caused by the husband's penis," diagnoses the lady doctor. "It will hurt this girl all her life."

Kamala tries a second time to leave and return to her ancestral home with her children. Her great-grandmother, also at nineteen, had left her philandering Raja husband and returned in a palanquin with her child to Nalapat.

"The homecoming of a proud and dignified woman," Kamala remembers. "Not a single eyebrow was raised, not a single face darkened." Kamala considers it her birthright as a Nayar woman to return home and live in peace. But by the 1950s, the matrilineal *taravad* had become nuclear and patriarchal, and Kamala's duty was to her husband, not her extended family.

"Go back," orders her grandmother. "Obey Das. Nalapat women are good wives."

"He is your husband," pronounces the doctor who staunched her bleeding.

"Father will allow you to live in the village and sell produce from the lands, but he will not allow you to marry again," says her mother.

Kamala is faced with the choice of living alone in a village or living with her husband in Calcutta, the city she considered "the axis of the cultural world." There she and her group of "young hopefuls" felt the influence of the great Bengali novelists Bankim Chandra Chattopadhyay, "Sarat babu" (Sarat Chandra Chattopadhyay), and Rabindranath Tagore, and "the Bengali touch like old lace enriched the silk of our writings."

She returns to Calcutta and keeps to the kitchen, hoping her husband will forget her.

"He would leave at seven in the morning, come home at eleven when I was asleep, and call me up for my duty." She obeys, waiting for it to be over so she can drag herself to the table and write.

"Every night this digging went on and on, and I almost thought he was burying a body every night. No tenderness there was. No preliminaries, nothing. Probably he couldn't love me. At the moment of sexual intercourse with him, I wished he would gather me in his arms after the act. Had he caressed my face or touched my belly, I would not have felt the intense rejection I felt after each union. Then again he would want. After about fifteen minutes the man gets up again. Bury. Shovel. I felt rotten, like a corpse was within. When I felt his semen in me, I just wanted to wash it out.

"Such humiliation I felt.

"Then I'd go, sit in the bathroom, try to wash it out. I have a feeling that my heart trouble originated from this period of love because there was no love on my side. I loved the children, of that there is no doubt. I would have done anything for them. And I didn't want him to fall ill because he was the pillar of the family then, and I would have been left destitute."

Kamala tries one last time to escape the cramped apartment where the cook and ayah whisper continuously in her presence, eyeing her with disdain, "spying and reporting to my husband thinking I was mad because I sat up at night and wrote stories."

She is found and returned by her husband's friend, who says her elementary education prepares her only for the brothel and assaults her, his rough hands groping within her blouse and his body crushing her limbs.

Finally, at age twenty-two, Kamala concludes, "This is my destiny."

… Dress in saris, be girl
Be wife, they said. Be embroiderer, be cook,
Be a quarreller with servants. Fit in. Oh,
Belong, cried the categorizers. Don't sit
On walls or peep in through our lace-draped windows.

"I was part of this society, like an exposed nerve that hurt. Talking to my readers, I found my private voice and my peace."

… for I know I have a life
To be lived, and each nameless
Corpuscle in me, has its life to
Be lived …

When she is thirty-seven, Kamala hemorrhages and a surgeon removes her womb.

"It was very fashionable for people in the Reserve Bank to get rid of their wives' uteruses. The Reserve Bank paid for it. Of course I was just a little too young to be walking around without it. I needed hormones to cruise through my blood. So the doctor prescribed estrogen tablets. Taking them gave me the biggest heart attack of my life, and I landed in the intensive cardiac unit."

After her operation and heart attack, Kamala has even less inclination for sex, but her reputation dogs her. Bureaucrats send love letters, men call, editors assign articles on sex.

"I am fated to dazzle the idiots," she writes. "The brilliant ones keep away. They do not approve of the way I tear myself into shreds to feed my readers. My readers have tasted all of me. They have dug their fingers into the hollow where my womb was … They are my cannibal cousins, the real excuse for my staying on."

In the mid-1970s, the success of *My Story* makes Kamala a commodity, and her relationship to her husband changes. He takes over her business affairs and handles her contracts and public appearances. She buys a new car, presents it to him for his birthday, and gives him all her earnings.

"One way to earn some men's love is to give them a lot of money, and there was no doubt I was really loved. What I wanted from my husband was a man who would sit around on the porch, meet people, send some my way, send up food for me, and guard me while I sat upstairs writing. What he wanted was somebody with a reputation. When I was famous, he respected me, hugged me, and massaged my feet. Life became quite blessed after that."

In 1983, Kamala's husband retires from international consulting, and Kamala maintains him from then on. When writer Geoffrey Moorhouse visits the rambling Das bungalow in Trivandrum in these later years, he finds Kamala "utterly self-possessed, confident of her ability to amuse, and strong in the knowledge that the power now resided in her. But she did not exult in that shift of emphasis and, had I not read her revelations of the marriage, I would have assumed that they had always been uncommonly and tenderly devoted to each other."

At the end, Kamala's husband is "a weak man, very pale, very frail, a white blur on the porch of my house." His face lights up when Kamala opens the gate, he asks about her adventures, giggles at her sharp observations, and preserves her press clippings. He makes Kamala feel that "no one will ever take as active an interest in my life, or be as proud of me as he."

When she craves new jewellery, she requests it from him. He asks her for a bank draft and buys her gold bangles with interlinking hearts.

I turn off the tape recorder. The new gold bangles Kamala gave me jangle when I make them move. I think of the bangles now to distract me from images of young Kamala – dissociating while her body is used, dragging herself from the "sex fiesta" in her husband's bed, clearing the kitchen table of plates and chopping utensils, setting out paper, pencils, writing hundreds of stories and poems, stopping only at the clank of the milkman's wagon when she buys milk, heats it, and serves her husband, her children, and does her chores until nightfall, when once again she writes.

> If I had not learned to write how would
> I have written away my loneliness
> or grief? Garnering them within my heart
> would have grown heavy as a vault, one that
> only death might open, a release then
> I would not be able to feel or sense …

Kamala's bangles make me happy and constrained, a dichotomy I had projected onto Indian brides. But I am not projecting anymore.

How presumptuous of me to ask if my affairs, marriages, divorces, seemed as cruel to her as her early years did to me.

"Except, of course, for the pain."

In that light, lilting voice of hers.

Of course.

# 9

# Riding a Tiger

I am eating, Kamala nibbling. She has written:

I have been up as usual since 5 AM. I made myself two cups of tea and a sandwich with peanut butter. I ate an apple.

The chair beside the divan is my favourite seat. There is a reading lamp behind it. If one is too tired to read, one can look to the right and see the trees which seem to surprise us each day with changed colours. It is a riot of colours outside. The lakes glimmer silver. I am smitten by the land. It is wreathed in smiles today.

"So, your Arnie didn't turn up last night," Kamala says, pouring tea.

"He stayed in town to view film rushes. Are you getting any deeper insight into my life than before?"

"Of course. Coming to think that we are all of one type, the difference only being the opportunities presenting themselves."

"Were your opportunities constrained by being a woman?"

"My reach was very wide. If you were to liken the marital bed to a cross and I was lying there, suddenly I would leave and fly in all directions. I became not just one but thousands of birds flying together, a multitude taking over the sky. Even while the man used me on the marital bed, I was flying. I only gave the dead body on the cross. The moment he fell asleep, I was resurrected. And I was always on the mount with a sermon ready for my audience." She laughs at her bravura.

"Did that save you?"

"It saved me that there was an audience to listen. Younger poets like Balan Chullikkad grew up listening to my sermons. And my writing flowered, because when the body lies like a dead heap, the mind sits up like a

Lean greyhound,
Awakening
and leaping up …

"Yesterday I was thinking of Merrily walking down dark paths and then Merrily becoming the path. Sometimes in my youth when I took walks, I would get that exalted feeling. Strong, you know, rising in all directions, flying through the trees, the streets. I became the street so much so that I felt

… the street-lamps
Shall glimmer, the cabaret girls cavort, the
Wedding drums resound, the eunuchs swirl coloured
Skirts and sing sad songs of love, the wounded moan …

"I became the street, the hot thirsty roads, the heat. Then I became not only road or heat but the whole summer. Sometimes, floating in the sea, I suddenly felt I did not know where the sea stopped and I began. I had turned myself into the sea. That way I became this and that, and in return I had such powers, such strength. So my husband could not destroy me.

"Merrily, you carry weights and your arms become muscular. It's like my mind carried weights. There was no one to erase the pain, so I knew I couldn't give up. Every night I thought, 'My precious mind will have to be saved. Once he touches that, I have lost.' And my mind is healthy still. It revises and renews its vision."

"I think you've even opened your mind to a western woman's experience."

"It seemed very strange at the beginning, but now I think if you are liberal minded and if you are civilized, you accept these things. The person who wrote *My Story* would not balk at it."

I tell Kamala that when I was sixteen, my twenty-four-year-old boyfriend wanted to make love and I made two lists: pro and con.

"That was your first sex act?"

"Yes. The 'cons' were: my parents wouldn't like it and I could get pregnant. The 'pros' were: I'm curious and unconventional, so why bide by convention?" I admit to her that the imaginings of a young girl were very different from actual sex, and that it was a while before I found sex pleasurable.

"In my case, the stress is always on happiness, not pleasure." Kamala differentiates, reminding me of Professor Bhatnagar at Concordia who explained that sex in North America has become part of material goods. "North Americans forget it is both a physical and spiritual exercise. They think sex is a route to pleasure. And pleasure is a route to happiness. That there is a one-to-one relationship between pleasure and happiness, and sex is the way to get it."

I think about what Kamala said about being happy when she was in love, and I review my past relationships. On consideration, happiness was not a major distinguishing characteristic. Kamala's model of "being near him, touching him, him holding me, and conversations that went on and on like music endlessly" is more tender.

"I am amazed at the sex lives of unmarried girls in this country, because in my country virginity is still the grand thing you save up for the right man," she says, jolting me back to the present. "I wouldn't want a man to sleep with my daughter unless there was the legitimacy of marriage, so she wouldn't be discarded later."

"Here a non-virgin can marry as easily as any other, if she wants to marry," I inform her.

"It would worry me, Merrily. I think the body is entitled to certain safety measures, and if there is something which commands the body, that power should be more dutiful and loyal toward the body, should consider the body precious."

For me, sexual liberation meant hospitalization, fungal infection, and cystitis. For one of my friends, it meant four abortions, one septic and life threatening, and two cryosurgeries. Other women I know suffered pain, disgust, a botched abortion that almost killed, doctor's words that scarred the soul, infections obstructing fertility. And while Kamala talks, my favourite student lies spread-eagled in a white room while a male doctor shoves a clamp up her vagina and freezes her cervix to minus 70 degrees. Luckily she does not have a sexually transmitted disease, cancer, or AIDS. She has a pre-cancerous lesion, the risk of which is increased in teenagers by prolonged use of birth control pills. The lesion is excised and must be monitored forever.

Kamala makes me recognize the price there is to pay.

"But can a girl in Canada just plan a temporary alliance?" she persists. "Do you choose a partner because of his sexual prowess? Suppose the country goes to war, could you sacrifice sexual activity? Could you live without it?"

Now I balk. Kamala has so misunderstood my sexuality that she wonders if I'm pathological or compulsive. I find it ludicrous until I remember that after *My Story* she was attacked in shocking, vulgar terms and called a nymphomaniac merely for her writing.

"Just because I have had some sexual experience doesn't mean I'm a nymphomaniac," I correct decisively.

"You are not a sex addict?"

"No, I am a fairly normal Canadian woman, and you know I am not trying to change your feelings."

"You can't change me anyway. And I won't be able to change you. We are both set in our ways, but we are free to experiment with thoughts. Even while differing from you in my views, I have a great deal of respect for you, for what you have stood up as. You are standing up straight and looking them in the eye, 'Yes, I am Merrily Weisbord. I had some affairs. I discarded somebody. And I am living with this man. It is not a legitimate relationship, it is not marriage, yet I hold onto it.'"

I guess from Kamala's perspective this is a brave way to live. But in Quebec, over half a million couples, or 30 per cent of all couple-families, live together without marriage. Of these, half have children at home.

"Whatever our pasts, we are here now and we know who we are," I say. "It is interesting that although we are from incredibly different cultures, both of us have survived with some strength."

"Yes, a young poet quoted me saying, 'I shall wail in his nerves, as homeless cats wail/ From the rubble of a storm.' 'Kamala's like that,' he said, 'wailing in the reader's nerves from the rubble of a storm she herself has created.' He's a smart critic. I am like that."

I don't get it. Supposedly, Kamala blazed a whole new path for women. And many conservative Malayalis and Indians hurled obscenities at her for rejecting their moral norms.

When she was thirty-one, she published *Summer in Calcutta*, after which Oxford University Press declared: "The mentors of sham manners and peddlers of decadent morality wound up their shops and ran out by the backdoor."

At thirty-seven, she wrote *My Story*, her confessional memoir, which hit like a bolt of lightning, illuminating the instinctive nature of woman's desire and the longing for communion in love. Not yet forty, she published *The Old Playhouse and Other Poems*, once again defying taboos with poems about marital discord, sexual ecstasy, loneliness and longing. Critics hailed her for burying nineteenth-century diction, sentiment, and romanticized love, as no Indian woman had done before.

"Kamala set many women thinking and some feeling bold enough to change the course of their lives," testified the Indian scientist Shubha Narayanan, whom I met by chance on a bus to Oxford University.

Yet sometimes she sounds like a morality ad for the 1950s.

"Balan Chullikkad told me you always fought hypocrisy," I try, searching for missing links.

"So that one could face oneself. My mother and my father were supposed to be an ideal couple, but every night they quarrelled. Their generation never looked into the real mirror which showed little people making furtive gestures, covering up their little meanesses, pretending to be what they were not. It ate away at them, disintegrating their core. I wanted people to be what they are."

"Is that why Balan gives you so much credit?"

"Balan's generation grew up listening to me and adopting my totally different code of morality. 'Don't think you can ride the cart of tradition into a future that is going to suit you,' I told them. I didn't want them carrying the myths and prejudices of generations."

"What were they carrying?"

"Superstition, belief in religious rites, and belief in the myth of religious difference. I also said it is immoral to go on living as an ideal couple, quarrelling, disgusted with each other, using a woman for sex when you hate her and she hates you, just because it has been legitimized by society. One is married to one's man if there is love. The feeling you belong to each other is enough. I removed the hypocrisy of ideal marriages, and that is what they celebrate now."

This makes me laugh. "It's interesting that in Canada when you see the actual result of what you advocated, it freaks you out."

"The fulfillment of my dreams I see here, and I'm worried."

"If you talked in India like you do here, they would love you. All you talk about here is marriage."

"I won't show that face to India. This is the true face of the one who is trying to study. I am grateful to you, Merrily, for letting me see all of this, the difference in our lifestyles, everything. Even if we quarrel, we quarrel in such a friendly way. And we are analyzing ourselves. And something good will come out of it, I am positive. I can almost see it arriving like a cyclone, but the only thing is that it's a merry cyclone. The cyclone won't affect us, only others."

Today, Kamala and I are equally nervous. Tomorrow is her big public lecture, and I hope I have filled the hall.

"It is difficult to perform to empty seats," she warns, putting me on notice.

Arnie returns from Montreal with a headache, says hello to Kamala, and goes to bed. Kamala and I search through her poetry looking for a poem to end her lecture.

"The lesbians hiss their love at me," she suggests from "Composition." She adds, "They looked like men and wanted to pinch my breasts," describing poets she met at a Commonwealth Writer's Conference in London.

"That's a very politically incorrect thing to say here," I advise. "People here will think you are closed minded. Let's find another poem."

"Yes, we'd better stick to love. A little bit of adultery on the side," she laughs, "a side dish. With that you're okay." And she wanders away to switch on *The Bold and the Beautiful*. "Lovely, here they all are. I was missing them."

We lie on the couch vegetating, "like rag dolls," she says, "limp, at rest, so nice."

At 8:30 PM. she drags herself to her quarters and sequesters herself, and I go downstairs to write the introduction to her talk.

"Kamala swam naked in the ponds of Malabar, and I in Laurentian lakes. Her joint family home was called Nalapat House, mine was called The Acres …"

Next morning Arnie wakes me, snuggles, kisses my nose, says, "I have to go," takes a shower, no breakfast, carries Kamala's heavy bags to my car, and leaves on a business trip to Paris. He'll be gone eleven days. I arrest the sinking feeling. Kamala is here and there's lots to do.

Kamala writes to her sister,

My main appearance is to be at the Concordia University. I pray God that I prove myself to be adequate. My theme is the Writer as an Emotional Revolutionary. I shall wear a green silk sari and the black coat which I shall remove while speaking. I am going bravely on keeping the Nalapat flag flying but my heart palpates with anxiety.

Remind Amma of the eldest daughter now globe-trotting on feeble legs.

with love

Amioppu

Not a seat is empty. People crane around in their seats, taking in the mix of young, old, women, men, Indian, black, Japanese, Middle Eastern, Arabic, Dad, Phyllis, students, brother, writers, kids, professors, the overflow on the steps and standing at the back of the hall. The theatre buzzes as the audience identifies Kamala Das on stage in sea-green Kanjeevaran silk. On her lap she holds a handbag containing her passport, without which she fears she can't return home. She appears perfectly composed.

The co-organizer, Riva Heft, thanks our sponsors. The dean thanks Kamala and introduces Concordia's current writer-in-residence – me. I clomp in high heels to the microphone and introduce Kamala.

"You never know what Kamala Das is going to say," I hedge.

Kamala removes her glasses and walks gracefully to the lectern, black hair cascading over an iridescent gold palu.

"Dear friends, let me express my gratitude to all those who made it possible for me to come to Canada," she begins. "These past weeks I have been staying in Merrily's home in a true forest with birch, oak, poplars, maples, and I have smelt their leaves. When Merrily collected the pine and the spruce, I thought I must write about the forest. I had stopped writing poetry. There was a block. And here poetry has come back to me."

She fixes the audience with the intimate regard of the visually challenged, and in a dreamlike voice, without notes, addresses each individual facing her.

"I grew as a child with the British ruling my country, and therefore it wasn't possible for me to think of English as *not* my mother tongue. English was the language of my awareness."

Sentences trip off her tongue like the confidences of a friend or the telling of a bed-time story. The audience laughs at the payoffs and stays with Kamala through readings, digressions, and confessions so seemingly frank that only because we've gone further do I know she's holding back.

And then she stops, extends her hand to me dramatically, and I remember her saying, "I make my recitals seem like pure theatre." On cue, I bring her *The Best of Kamala Das,* a poetry collection that includes the ten "Anamalai Poems," first published by India's national literary council, the Central Sahitya Akademi. To provide context, Kamala describes the 1984 elections when she ran as an independent candidate on the platform of "A House for Every Woman."

"I was drunk with the attention, the absolute silence of those listening to me, loving the heady experience. But after losing the election, the deposit money, the support of my family, and my voice, I became utterly lonely and physically disabled. To save me from dying, my sister took me to Anamalai, a high peak in Tamil Nadu, and gave me a tape recorder. 'If you feel very sad, speak into this at night. You will be less lonely,' she said.

"I spoke out of loneliness and despair, and she collected all that into the 'Anamalai Poems.'" She rifles through the pages and then reads:

> ... If only the
> human eye could look beyond the
> chilling flesh, the funeral pyre's
> rapid repast and then beyond
> the mourner's vanquished stance, where would
> death be then, that meaningless word
> when life is all that there is, that
> raging continuity that
> often the wise ones recognize as God?

She hands the book back to me, rearranges her palu, draws the loosened hair from her face. Her diamonds sparkle.

"I didn't even think of God in the days when I was producing children, looking after them, falling in love. Because all these things were good enough for me. It was only in the wake of the election campaign that I began to think there was some all-pervasive power. I was born a Hindu, and I used to go to temples because the relatives went and it was considered decent to go and worship. And then I realized that if there really was a God, he would not allow himself to be housed in temples, chapels, shrines, mosques, to be a prisoner. No building can contain God, he's all-pervasive like ether. And God probably has no name despite all the names we give him. No name, no face, no postal address, you can't address a letter to him. You can reach him only by becoming fully aware of him, or her, or it. It's creative energy only."

She stops abruptly, searching for me. "Have I taken up too much time, Merrily?"

Has she? An hour has flown by. She's made people comfortable, uncomfortable, empathetic, incredulous, made them laugh, made poetry live, cast a spell of contradictions that she dares *not* to package, and she's used me as a straight man.

Satisfied, high, sensing she's captivated the audience, she's winding down.

"The whole world is full of my friends, an ocean of friendly faces," she says, including the audience. "Merrily called me only eight months ago. She came to Cochin and I got to know her, but not so well. After coming here, I have made friends with her family, and what a family, almost like the Nalapat family. The only thing is, they don't all live together. There are houses for each of them – Merrily, Uncle Joe and Aunt Sue, Merrily's Auntie Katie …"

And then, just as I am swelling with embarrassment and pride, and just as the audience is chuckling at Kamala's enthusiastic embrace of all things Weisbörd, she says, "And I saw a documentary on dowry deaths, bride burning. Let me tell you, it doesn't happen. Horrible film made by an Indian educated at Oxford, nothing Indian about him. If women die, saris getting caught on the electric cooking range or gas stoves, men die too. You hear of several deaths taking place in hotels where the chef died. I don't think mothers-in-law try to kill the young girls. India does not kill brides.

"Are there any questions?" she asks. "I love questions."

There is a surge, quick as an involuntary gasp, toward the microphones on the floor. A determined line forms.

"I am puzzled and perplexed," a young woman kicks off. "No brides burned? I wish you were not lying. I suspect you find the truth too hard to face."

"I am disappointed about bride burning," an older woman follows angrily. "I came far to hear you. Parking is difficult and I don't like to pay for parking. You have had an upper-class, privileged life. Not all Indian women can choose to marry. Most are sold."

Kamala purses her lips, waits a beat. "I'm very sorry about the parking. Perhaps I could pay."

The hall rumbles uneasily. Many feel betrayed.

"I see violent movies coming from the US," Kamala reacts. "People killing without hate like spilling tomato sauce over your cutlets. Should I think every-day in the US someone gets shot down? I used to think the US was a wicked place with everybody either having sex or killing people. I thought Canada was almost as bad, and I come and find a marvellous family. Don't go by the films you see."

Anger simmers as more-forgiving fans line up to praise Kamala's writing, courage, and activism. She holds her head high, cheeks dimpling, lips puckering, her smile tilted to me.

Next she will be live on Canadian public radio, saying whatever she wants. I have recommended she stay away from lesbians, the pernicious nature of four-letter words, and dowry deaths. When I tell her a respected professor just reported that two Punjabi families in his immediate circle lost daughters to kitchen fires, she says, "South India is a totally different country." She doesn't want westerners to think that Indian men, her sons, for example, burn their wives. Or that mothers-in-law, her, for example, egg them on.

"I'm against negative stereotypes," she tells an irate Indian student who calls later to berate her. "I speak of Kerala. I haven't been to all these North Indian places. This comes from my own little orbit. Until sixty years ago a Nayar woman could be polyandrous if she could afford it. I don't want to tell all those gloomy foreign tales. We expect a permissive free sex society in the West, but conservative people also live here, just as gentle husbands live in India. They don't all set fire to their wives. In Kerala, women are cherished."

She protests to me, "I am a real Indian." "Perhaps that is the problem. Here people are used to half-westernized Indians. I am a real Indian."

We retreat to the country and burrow back into our peaceful routine. If I were Kamala, I'd be gnawing on the public confrontation, but veteran Kamala has moved on. Conscious that our time together is running out, I raise the ethical question of how and what to write about living people, and quote Elias Canetti: "The story of my life is not really about me./But who will believe that?"

"Yes, there is the ethical question. How much can you publish?" Kamala responds. "But there is no ethical question involved about writing. Write it down. And you have to be faithful. I don't know why I romanticize the whole thing, but I think it is a great responsibility being a writer because you are a chronicler and what you write should be very truthful."

"What are your thoughts about the ethical question of publishing the diary you wrote when your husband was alive?"

"The diary is lying there unpublished, yes, because of how perverse he was in many ways. If my son were to read that, *he will hate me.*" Her voice drops to a whisper.

"He will not believe those things of his father, and he'll say, 'What a wretched mother I have.' I don't want to risk that because I value my son's friendship and affection, and if I lose that too, I have nothing, no." Her words break.

"What a thing. What a dilemma," I commiserate.

"I have no moorings without them."

"I know. I understand."

We sound like a hopeless chorus.

"Kamala, are you sorry you can't publish your diary?"

"I'm sorry, because it would be a powerful book. But I don't want to lose everybody. I hold onto this relationship that I still have with my sons, I clutch it. So that role should not be taken away from me."

"I know, it's just —"

"Don't take a chance, don't hurt your children."

"Or Arnie. I could lose Arnie."

"Don't hurt him. Yet. You might begin to want to hurt, and that will be the final revenge. But your position should be made more secure before you take the attacking position. It is like battle. Before you become the aggressor, see that you are the strongest and nobody can slide you off the chess board. Nobody. You should become that strong. It is for us women to be strong, Merrily."

Kamala finishes reading "Blood Notes," my abandoned memoir, and calls me over.

"I shouldn't say this. You are in love with Arnie, but how would you like to marry a nice man about fifty-four, a planter living in Munnar, greying at the temples? His wife just died and he told my sister he wanted a cultured woman he could show off. He comes from an ancient family, a Muslim. He told my sister that colour and class do not matter. He wants a cultured woman, and you surely fit the bill."

"But I couldn't wear my T-shirt. I wouldn't have my land."

"This chap was educated as a Britisher."

"In my life now, I'm not obligated to entertain or do small talk."

"Forget that."

"I would have to do that, wouldn't I?

"I should not even talk about marriage to you. How can you understand it?"

Yet Kamala has given me permission to think of marriage in a positive light – to have done with de Beauvoir and Sartre. I'm becoming attached to concepts like belonging to, being protected by. "Now I do want to get married to Arnie," I say. "We've been together so long, I don't think we would revert to traditional roles. You've influenced me after all."

"If I didn't love you, I could say, 'Oh, let it be. I can write a book which is miserable and sell your grief.' But I think you love this man. So instead of looking for somebody else, let's see that you marry this one."

"Still, it is amazing to think there is somebody like this Munnar planter who is actively looking for a wife."

"Who is civilized, who is brilliant, who is good-looking, moves in high circles. But how could you leave all this?" She gestures to the lake, the trees. "And he will not want to leave India." Then she solves it. "Three months here and three months there."

We wrap ourselves in shawls and stand on the porch facing the photographer's Haselbad for a portrait to commemorate Kamala's first visit to Canada. She assumes a regal stance and looks so directly into the lens that the photographer jerks the camera from his eye. I stand to the side, bemused. I am hoping for more intimate photos than the distinctly separate ones we took on our first meeting in Cochin.

I position myself beside Kamala in front of a tree with yellow leaves and the grey granite boulder that reminds her of an elephant's back. "Kamala," I say distractedly, "you're not even looking at me. Don't you think we could put our arms around each other?"

"Merrily," she answers, ramrod straight and addressing the lens, "what if I am the prime minister of India and you are the prime minister of Canada?"

She allows five minutes for the photo session and moves unsmilingly off the porch.

A heavy rain falls and I have to rest. My throat is sore and I am tired, drained. Now Kamala will see Merrily-the-machine slow to a healing pace, recharging for our trip to New York and Kamala's talk at Columbia University.

Rain pounds the roof and through the venetian slats I see the familiar slick, dark trunks of maple, minus their burnished, pointillist haze. In a month Kamala has watched gaudy trees strip to naked stalks. She has become part of my family, and of a season's change.

I have seen the maples turn yellow and later burgundy red. I have smelled the forests and clear waters of the lakes in Quebec. I have watched the wild geese flying away yodeling. The hourglass will soon be empty of sand. But one of the best things that happened to me is Merrily. The book has not progressed at all. But the friendship has.

Gathered together at Columbia is an intimate group including poet Meena Alexander, writer Amitav Ghosh, our friend Ellen Coon, and Kamala's host, Ted Riccardi, chairman of Columbia's Middle East and Asian Languages and Culture Department. We sit in a semi-circle listening to Kamala's perfectly pitched tremolo as she reads us famous poems such as "Composition," "Blood," and "An Introduction," interspersed with commentary.

"I am a writer, that's true," she tells us. "By the time I was six, I started filling a notebook with verses. Yet even today, learned professors in India say, 'This is not English, she has forgotten the word *the*. We should have each note rising out of *the* sea, out of *the* wind.' But it doesn't agree with my ears.

> The language I speak
> … voices my joys, my longings, my
> Hopes, and it is as useful to me as cawing
> Is to crows or roaring to the lions, it
> Is human speech, the speech of the mind that is
> Here and not here, a mind that sees and hears and
> Is aware …

She continues: "'You write the way you like it,' I told Professor Ezekiel. 'My gait is different. I danced all that, professor. I want rhythm in my writing. When I write a poem, I am speaking, moving, my mind is dancing. Notes come and go, the rhythms like Sanskrit stanzas I know. With this language, which may seem distorted to you, I will bring out my emotions. I will lay them out as wares in a sweetmeat shop. If you don't like it, don't come as a buyer for my sweets. You go where English is "spake"! Go there, what is it to me?'"

And after my talk, my friend Andrew Arkin invited me to the Lotus Club. Invited all my friends too. Riccardi of the Columbia University, Ellen Coon, Meena Alexander, David, Merrily, and the alluring Rebecca. Andrew had invited three wealthy widows whose capped teeth were gorgeous. In America the rich people can never look old. At the Lotus Club I drank mimosa. Toasts were made and everyone laughed for the sheer pleasure of being alive. I posed for photographs standing beside the picture of Mark Twain.

In the taxi after dinner, tired, knowing we are going to part, Kamala lets her head rest on my shoulder like a child. We hug on the curb outside Ellen's apartment, and I watch her walk away wrapped in her black shawl, a small, dignified figure swaying slightly on heavy legs, looking back, so I run to her and we hug again.

"Oh, Merrily, Merrily."

"Till we meet again," I promise, surprised by the love I feel for her – love, not respect or admiration but love, and fear for her fragility, her naked spirit, and the suffocating effect of communal expectations. And now I am leaving her after a month of caring for her better than I have cared for anyone else, with more warmth, generosity, intelligence, and pleasure, because she has let me, has put herself in my hands. Now she is leaning on Pushpa's arm (does Pushpa know to warn her of a step?), not turning back as I watch her enter the building and pass the first-floor window. For three weeks I was devoted to her and learned the happiness of caring for someone you love.

I miss you, my elder sister.

I call Kamala at the home of her son's friend in New Jersey. She is happily ensconced in a comfortable chair, absolutely alone, TV on, kitchen stocked with food, fruit bowl overflowing.

I tell her that Arnie and I have signed a notarized domestic agreement and she doesn't have to worry about me being destitute anymore.

She says she's happy.

She says, "Merrily, one thing I want to tell you, the bathroom of the Lotus Club has scented toilet paper coloured like heliotrope. I have never seen such luxury."

She says, "Merrily, without you as an escort, I feel like a peeled banana."

I lie on the turquoise bedspread in my daughter Anna's Hampshire College dorm, looking at photographs of Kamala and my daughters, Kamala and Auntie Sue and Uncle Joe, Kamala and Dad smiling.

I have decided to remove the bangles Kamala gave me. They no longer chime like Kamala getting up, or tinkle like a Kamala-stream flowing from room to room. Now the bangles sound like money and scratch when Arnie comes close. I don't need them to prove how much Kamala likes me or to show her gratitude. It's ten days since we parted, and I think of her, her words, our friendship, every day. I talk about her. She is part of my discourse, part of my life.

I will have to lather my hand and ask for Arnie and Anna's help. The bangles have my hammy hand to traverse. Not Kamala's long, supple palm, but one that chops wood and carries bags, attached to a muscled arm that dismayed Kamala when first displayed. Arnie can fold in thumb and pinky while Anna manœuvres the bangles over the ridges. Or I could cut them off. I will miss their glow, like sun on the Arabian Sea, moonlight on the Malabar Coast. But they are choking me.

We stand in Anna's bathroom, at a sink facing a mirror. Anna squeezes my hand and Arnie yanks until it hurts too much.

"You'll have to do it yourself," Anna says, folding my palm in two.

I soap and pull them off. And the ghosts of Kamala's bangles flap uncertainly around my arm.

# THREE

# Delhi, Cochin, Kovalam, 1997

*I give a wrapping to their dreams*

# 10

## Orbits of Friendship

I call Cochin every month to catch up with Kamala and to hear the bright, sweet music of her voice. When I put down the phone, I feel lighter and stronger, and I think she does too. There is a complicated connection between us now, born of an empathy that Kamala suggests comes from being of the same writer's tribe, and for me derives from an attachment to a treasured friend whose enigma itches like a word on the tip of the tongue.

My own experience takes me into Kamala's life, then leaves me in unknown waters. And many of the Kamala scholars I read careen from label to label, mystified by her repeated insistence that sex is distasteful while at the same time maintaining sensuality as her constant theme. Sensuality is a theme vital to Kamala and to me, the emotional DNA of who we are and how we developed. Knowing Kamala's cruel sexual history, I understand her distaste for genital sex and her staunch celibacy. Yet she is a great love poet. Only she can unravel the apparent conundrum of how, despite her marital history, she retained a passionate, yet unsentimental celebration of sensuality. And this is not something we can discuss on the phone.

I await the opportunity to be with Kamala, and a year and a half after her Canadian visit, my life is calm and undemanding enough for me to return to India.

Monu, Kamala's eldest son, meets me in Delhi where I stop over en route to Cochin. He welcomes me to India and advises me that Kamala must travel to Madras for emergency cataract surgery soon after I arrive. We will have some time together before the operation and several weeks after she returns. Meanwhile, Monu is on filial duty.

I look out the car window, disappointed by the change in plans, then quickly buoyed by the pleasure and excitement of people and places I've never seen before. I try to conjure up Kamala with talk, but Monu, chief of bureau of the *Times of India*, prefers contemporary Indian *real politick*. He informs me that like-minded Indian military, journalists, politicians, and young rocket scientists are fed up with western countries telling India what to do about Kashmir, the Tibetan question, its nuclear program.

Then, he tells this story:

"A low caste young man hides in the bushes and watches the king's master archer teach five young princes. The young man learns the movements and practises on his own until he can outshoot all five princes. He then presents himself to the master archer saying, 'I have outshot them all. What shall I do?'

"'Cut off your thumb,' the master responds.

"This is what Indians feel the West is saying to them," Monu says. "It makes me uneasy seeing their political interference drive India away from the West." He says that until there is total disarmament, India has a right to control its own bomb, delivery systems, and satellites and not be under America's wing. "India must create its own destiny," he insists.

His intensity reminds me of Kamala's fierce Indian pride: her rejection of foreign loans, denial of dowry deaths, and dismissal of expatriate Indians who pronounce on Indian literature without knowing any Indian language except English. In Kamala's "Indianess," I sense the seeds of Monu's strategic nationalism. But when I remember Kamala's candidacy poster for the 1984 state elections, I see the difference between mother and son, and miss her all the more.

THE SOLE CANDIDATE WHO
BELIEVES IN THE RELIGION
OF LOVE

KAMALA DAS MADHAVIKUTTY

VOTE FOR HER

Tamil and Malayalam film music fill the car, and its headlights carve space in the Delhi night. We drive thirty-five kilometres from the city centre, through spewing traffic, to Monu's house in the new city of Gurgaon. Guarded by a ferocious dog, his gated building looks more like a barracks than a housing development, and inside it's a plaster-filled renovation site. I remind myself, when next I visit Delhi, not to forget Monu's amazing proclivity for domestic dissociation, and I call Kamala to arrange my arrival. I can hardly wait to see her.

"You can come any time, Merrily, you are my sister."

I hardly sleep, wake frayed, and leave at 6:45 AM for Cochin.

I place bags of gifts around Kamala's chair, and she unwraps them with such pleasure and gusto I wish I'd brought more. Then she launches into an attack on the city's beautification campaign that has displaced the homeless people, and even though she's moved to a new apartment, I know I'm back. We talk through dinner and I feel like I've never left. I follow the maidservant to Kamala's spacious guest apartment, marvelling at the sense of homecoming I feel so far way from home.

Next morning I return to Kamala's sitting-room and find her in a flowing burgundy dress, talking politics with the Brahmin attorney who defended her during the Emergency, and discussing logistics with the co-founder of a free legal service for women, many evicted on a husband's whim.

As soon as they leave, Kamala retreats to her AC bedroom with round-faced Mrs Rajasekharan, "a good girl, clean, but her mother-in-law's always picking fault with her," and forty-seven-year-old Aparna, whose husband hasn't made love to her for fifteen years. The women sit beside the bed and lean forward to talk. Kamala rests on her back, squirms, stretches her arms, finally settles on her side, her housedress draped over the womanly arc of her hip. She wears no makeup and says she learned from me to have a fresh, open face. She also says that like me she has stopped dyeing her hair, but of this I am not sure.

"I have no money of my own," Aparna confides. "Sometimes I feel like a beggar. I tell my husband, 'I need money,' and he snaps, 'How much do you need?' and I shrug, 'Whatever you like.'" She says she thinks of suicide and at the same time dreams of travel, or of an intellectual, non-physical love affair. She says her daughter is about to have a baby, which makes her realize how soon she'll be a grandmother and how much of life she's missed. "It makes me sick."

Kamala listens as if she's heard this before, and I listen amazed by Aparna's public confidences. I'm used to people "putting a good face on things" and confiding only in trusted confidants. I feel I should acknowledge Aparna's trust in some way, but Kamala is already up and moving toward new visitors in the sitting room. She is greeted by Surendran, a journalist who has been doggedly waiting all afternoon.

"He is stationary," Kamala whispers dryly.

But, possibly, visions of Mata Amritanandamayi Devi, the popular Hindu swami dubbed "the hugging god woman," have alleviated his ennui.

"She receives with a big smile and embrace," Surendran volunteers when her name comes up. "People say there will be a peculiar pleasure, an ecstasy that is sexual. She gives lots of kisses on the neck and rubs your body. For a male it's a rare chance to embrace a fatty woman. She has big breasts. She embraces very closely. That is the chance Amma is giving to everybody."

He smiles broadly, realizes what he's said, and frowns censoriously.

"Mothering," Kamala says, reinterpreting the God-woman's embrace. "The body has some resilience," she admonishes Surendran. "It has something of the spirit and of the mind."

I long to talk to Kamala alone, but more visitors arrive and her drawing-room duties take over the day. I make my excuses and leave to prepare for the trip I will take while she is away, hoping we will have plentiful time together when her operation is done.

Next morning I awake in time to see Kamala in white khadi wafting out of her apartment on her sister Sulu's arm. Family ranks have closed around her, and everything – the wheelchair, car, sister beside her, youngest son at the car door, first-class plane reservation, Monu in Madras, post-op hotel suite – has been planned with protective, private perfection.

"Hi, beautiful," I holler, so incongruously it makes Sulu laugh.

Then as completely as she was here, Kamala is gone.

To distract myself from missing Kamala, I board the Parasuram Express heading south to the seaside tourist attractions of Kerala. The train picks up speed at an alarmingly slow rate and arrives late in the state capital of Trivandrum. I hire a cab, and eight hours after leaving Cochin I'm in the breeze, ease, and relative privacy of Lighthouse Beach, Kovalam.

To keep busy, I decide to see and do everything – tourist beaches, rock swimming pool, ayurvedic spa, rebuilt traditional Kerala houses, Kashmiri shops, the pool at the Ashok hotel.

To experience *ayurveda*, I meet Deepa, my masseuse, in a palm-thatched cabana with pale-blue cement walls the colour of her sari. Deepa mimes undressing and points to a chair between a large wooden oil-bath and a massage table. I strip and sit. Deepa vigorously slathers my head, arms, hands with medicated oil and leaves me sitting naked in it. When she motions to the mat on the floor, I lie down gratefully on my back. She hitches up her sari, stands astride me, grips the thick rope hanging from the struts above, and hoists herself up. She touches her toe to the centre of my body and her finger to the centre of her own. Then, with expertly controlled force, her long, narrow foot and supple, splayed toes come to life. Toe, heel, full foot, up, down, around, and into the crevices of my body. Sweeping across me like an exercise at the barre, her muscular leg gathers speed, kneading diagonally from right foot, across stomach, skirting nipple, along my arm to my left hand, the oil granular as pumice, her prehensile caress like the coarse tongue of a primeval beast.

I open my eyes and look up to see a long, brown leg, the frill of a white petticoat, a blue sari, and Deepa's calm Malayali face.

Yet I am not really here. Through the hotel's open shutters, beyond the coconut trees, I see the sea. It's quiet except for the waves and crows, and despite the activities, I ache for home. I returned to India to be with Kamala, and without her I cannot "work," or learn what to write on my return. Alone with the prospect of "the book," I realize how woefully inadequate I am to write about the world I'm in.

I return to Trivandrum and am considering the cultural complexity of the Kamala-and-me project when Surendran, last seen stationary in Kamala's sitting-room, joins me for lunch. He has retrieved Madhava Das's personal archives, stolen from the Das Trivandrum home, and says he's keeping them so that Kamala doesn't "just give them to the first person who asks."

Expecting rare Kamala memorabilia, I follow him to a room full of newspapers and magazines, and he urges me to read his scrapbook of "nasty, abusive" English and Malayalam letters. At first I think the letters are awkward attempts at love poetry, and realize later that even exposing kissing fantasies to a South Indian matron of Kamala's generation is improper, obscene. Then, the letters begin to sound like dirty phone calls with lists of specific sexual demands. Surendran watches me like a voyeur, and it makes me uncomfortable. I reject the letters in disgust, but he insists on quoting even more abusive Malayalam letters attacking Kamala for speaking improperly, for her prurient, lustful, vulgar, sex-obsessed, moral aberrations, and "calling Amma to sexual intercourse." So frightening is this personal assault on Kamala that I am relieved when he closes the scrapbook and I am done with this small dose of what Monu laconically called the post-memoir "difficult times."

As soon as Kamala is back in Cochin, I rush to the train station for my long-awaited return, then stand there totally lost. I know the time the train leaves for Ernakulam, I know my platform number, but I have no idea where to go. "Ernakulam? Where, where?" I call, my meaningless cry escalating raucously, my head whipping around for help. Finally, I give up and drop my bags. When I look up, I see a wiry old man in a dhoti and orange top. He circles, points at the clock, says things in Malayalam, strides away, returns. Fed up, he hoists my suitcase onto the coil on his head and takes off. I scoot after him, about to yell, but he stops, asks "Ernakulam?" and when I nod, goes directly to the First Class AC ticket booth. Holding my pull-case close, he indicates the fare, pays, hands me the ticket, pockets the tip, and, fulfilling his unsung hero's role as an Indian porter, sees me safely installed in my proper compartment.

He says good-bye and leaves us, three men and a woman with a severe fright/flight response, avoiding touching. The top bunks are taken by two semi-clad men with mustaches. I am calmed by the swami on the bottom bunk, nodding and waving to his followers through the window. Draped in white, slender with long wavy hair, he sits prim and graceful as a girl.

The train chugs out of Trivandrum, and another semi-clad man appears in the door of the compartment. He spreads a starched white sheet over the swami's berth and fades from first class back to third. I lean forward on the edge of my bunk to hear the swami talk.

He tells me he's been helping people be the best they can, and assures me there is good and light in everybody – "even you." "Guru means light. Swami means God," he says, referring to himself. He susses my interests and directs the talk to writing. He looks deep into my eyes. In a divine, abstract way, fleshed out by flashes of a slim, brown torso glimpsed under arms raised in exhortation, he seems to care. "I am a psychologist of the spirit," he says.

I contemplate giving up my lonely existential search and letting the swami solve it all.

"Open your hand," Swami commands and I instantly open and proffer my palm. Into it he drops a small gold Christian cross.

"Sound has a great power," he calls toward the bunk where I've retreated. "GUN, for example." He points to the middle of the top of his head where sound resonates. "GUN," he chants, drawing out the NNNNNNNNNNNNNNNNN.

Then it's my turn.

"GUNNNNnnnnnnnnnn," I echo.

"GUNNNNNNNNNnnnnnnnnnnnn," he develops further.

"GUNNNNnnnnnnnnnnnn," I try again. It feels good.

"Is your head vibrating?"

"Yes," I assure him.

He nods, pleased. "Anyone can do GUN. But only your guru can give you a mantra."

Swami rests soundly on his crisp sheets, plumb as a perfectly straight tree. I wrap myself in my newly bought hand-loomed bedsheet, glad to finally be returning to Kamala.


Kamala receives me lying in bed at her sister's house, her hair loose and flowing, as close-cropped doctor Sulu pulls up her older sister's satin sleeve, plumps up a vein, and injects a shot of insulin. Kamala is recovering from post-op high blood sugar under her sister's supervision, but when Sulu leaves, Kamala says she feels "caged," wants her freedom, wants to go home.

We talk as if we have never been separated, and it feels like our work is beginning again, although it's increasingly difficult to think of it as work. It is a growing friendship, and this meeting feels like a deepening of sorts. Less predatory – a deepening of acceptance, appreciation. We discuss our work process, and Kamala says her eyes will hold her back. Before this recent operation, the cataract in the centre of her pupil let in light only from the side, and her vision was vague. She scanned text with her head tilted sideways and pushed herself to write four weekly columns so she would be "a good worker and have my dignity." She says she would like to work with me, "But what shall we write about?"

Once more I list the material I've collected, including our conversations, my journals, her poems. She offers me her English and Malayalam columns, and repeats again that her paid columns deplete her energy and visual capacity. She insists she has nothing left over. For now, she suggests that I ask questions and record.

While she rests, I float on the living-room swing, avoiding the ramifications of what she has said about my writing on my own. I am losing myself in an oblivion of heat when Kamala and Sulu return to the room. From inside my haze I hear Sulu extol her in-laws' inclusive behaviour.

"You must have earned it," I murmur. "You seem to do the right thing."

"But what is the right thing?" Sulu counters philosophically. "When I lived at the tea plantation in Munnar, the managers and their wives were always kissing hello and dancing with each other. That was right for the plantation, but not for my conservative home."

"I guess I mean a more profound right," I suggest, "like not hurting anyone, doing what's morally right, even if it's not conventional. Kamala doesn't hurt people, but she's not conventional."

"I'm sure I hurt my family by publishing *My Story*," Kamala interrupts sharply. "My father thought I was so cheap."

This snaps me out of my haze.

"Irshad came to see me," Kamala says when Sulu has gone.

Irshad Gulam Ahmed is the younger of two partially sighted Muslim brothers. Kamala housed and educated him at her home in Calcutta from the time he was seventeen until he was twenty-two. She read to him, encouraged his poetry, and included him in her monthly salon. Irshad became a professor of literature and the author of the critical study *Kamala Das: The Poetic Pilgrimage*.

She says he came to ask permission to publish disturbing information about Madhava Das. "He said people vilified me for how I treated my husband, and he wanted to set the record straight. He said I was a saint and he knew my husband was not."

Kamala says Irshad wanted to tell the world what he knew, but she begged him not to. Her youngest son admired his father's honesty, and Das *was* honest, she assures me again. She says although she has hinted at her husband's sexuality in her writing, "I always kept my husband's reputation."

I nod at this, not knowing what to say because I don't know what the disclosure she describes means to her. Irshad's information seems to be new, but not as surprising or devastating as I might have expected. She obviously wanted to tell me about it, but I feel it was a prelude to or part of something left unsaid. I am unsure how to respond until I know what's really being broached.

I am saved by Balamani Amma, who wanders out of her room shadowed by a maidservant. Her ethereal figure stops in front of the television, where she watches the pregnant young wife of a rich old man huddling in a locked hut. A tribunal of overfed Brahmin men waits impatiently for the woman to name her lover so they can punish her. Outside the tribunal, young girls giggle as they practise faking fits to make them themselves unmarriageable. Balamani Amma responds to their giggles with sweet, soft laughter.

"Aren't you lucky, Merrily," Kamala says. "You won't have to be married off to an old man."

Finally the TV husband dies, and his widows keen and howl as they renounce their status and their ornaments. Balamani Amma emits sympathetic sounds and shuffles off on Sulu's gleaming rosewood floors.

Later I will meet Irshad, and he will speak bitterly about the unfairness of Kamala's disreputable reputation. He will tell me she was so puritan that when Das was in Sri Lanka and she wanted to see *War and Peace*, she bought three tickets so no man could sit in the adjoining seats. He will describe Das chasing away a BBC journalist and sending Kamala to lie down. "And she went quietly." And he will report that in 1986 Kamala stopped writing poetry because Das discouraged it, saying, "Poetry brings only mental satisfaction. Prose brings ready cash." Irshad repaired Kamala's typewriter and bought her paper, and for twenty days Kamala wrote a poem a day, many of them collected in *The Best of Kamala Das*.

He urges me to project Kamala's "true image." He tells me that the image of the Das marriage in the public mind was "'Her husband was so kind. He tolerated her. He was a saint, she was a stain.' The opposite is true. He was hopeless."

That night I wonder anew how Kamala survived her marriage, and I remember a scene she once described. She was nineteen, and Das, home late from work as usual, sat drinking beer and nagging her about her reputation. "The neighbour said you're seen out walking with boys," he complained. "She said I can't control my wife."

Kamala reminded him that *he* didn't like to walk or play, and only the gawky boys next door would escort her anywhere. But he persisted. "Why are you playing chess with boys? Why do you go with them?" Now he was shouting.

So Kamala raised an unopened beer bottle and said she couldn't stand it any more. "I don't care if you are my senior. I will smash your head with this bottle, your brains will spill out, and you will die. I am not a great quarreller, but I can act."

She said she was scared and knew she wouldn't do such a thing, "but I could always threaten."

She was influenced by one of her grandmother's stories about a bruised, beaten snake that had sought guidance from a sage. The sage counselled the snake to change his nature, believe in non-violence, and then he would go to heaven where things would be lovely for him. So the snake followed his advice, and six months later returned to the holy man with terrible sores, crushed here and there, its beauty gone. "You look so different," the holy man said. "Yes, I followed your advice and people have been stepping on me, throwing stones at me, and I never bite them," answered the snake. "Yes," said the sage, "but I never asked you not to hiss."

Kamala said she had to frighten her husband because he was a big man and she was a little girl. "I didn't want to be pushed down like other women, to become so colourless. I had to."

The story helps me imagine nineteen-year-old Kamala, still full of the pride, almost a familial ego of an aristocratic Nayar South Indian family. I think of the creative life she had enjoyed at Nalapat and the confidence instilled in her by her grand-uncle Nalapat Narayana Menon, a brilliant writer and renowned literary patron who translated Victor Hugo into Malayalam and wrote a six-hundred-page encyclopedia on sex. He gave Kamala a taste for salons and wit, and free reign of his eclectic library, from ancient palm-leaf manuscripts to Oscar Wilde. Kamala galloped through Maeterlinck, Turgenev, Flaubert, Tolstoy, Hugo, Dickens, Mansfield, Chekhov, Whitman, Wilde, Fitzgerald, Colette, Woolf, and Isadora Duncan.

"Ask the books that I read why I changed," she says. "Ask the authors dead and alive who communicated with me and gave me the courage to be myself."

But Kamala's grand-uncle told her it was not enough to read; she also had to think. "It was he who first made me conscious of the importance of nurturing my individuality."

I sat on the swing suspended from the ilanji tree, moved up and down slowly and taught myself to think. While I thought, I saw the trees on the edge of our pond, the bushes of yellow arali and henna, the coconut palms in the burning ground in the southern compound, the fields on the north and the neemathalam tree in the snake shrine. I heard the mantras chanted by the water flowing through the canal from the pond to the field and the messages the south-west wind wafted through the branches of the kanhira, ilanji and mango trees. I almost felt I could hear the sound of the waves on the distant stretch of the Arabian Sea.

By age fourteen, a year before her marriage, Kamala had read the British, European, Malayalam, and Sanskrit classics, and she had published her first poem in *P.E.N. India*.

"In front of my grand-uncle, I never had to despise myself or feel inferior. With profound kindness, this philosopher encouraged me to develop a sense of superiority that might have been illusory but that nourished my spirit."

I lie awake thinking of this spirit as an inheritance that helped Kamala survive and transcend her marriage. She says that being a Nayar was helpful to her as a young woman because without it she couldn't have shown such courage "in the face of the patriarchy."

But even this courage couldn't extricate her from a marriage I can't yet fathom, a marriage she presents mostly through the prisms of poetry, mythology, duty, and pride.

Unless she tells me, I will never know what she was trying to broach with the Irshad revelation, or what she means when her face darkens and she says, but doesn't explain, "how perverse he was."

I fall asleep thinking that only Das knew how discreet the "confessional" Kamala Das could be. How much she didn't tell.

# 13

## Life Is but a Dream

Out my Ambady Apartment window, above the rooftops, morning birds soar and chatter in coconut fronds a block away from the cars, bikes, auto rickshaws, and motorcycles on MG Road, where the Parthas Department Store sells silk and khadi, Arun develops one-hour photos, the Ayurvedic clinic offers its five-thousand-year-old healing system, and I can walk to the post office, government handicraft store, pharmacy, tailor, and foreign exchange, and the restaurants of the Avenue Regent Hotel.

Kamala has returned to her own apartment, and I can walk two floors down and see her too. A new sign is posted on the door.

KAMALA DAS IS RECOVERING
POST SURGERY
STRICTLY NO VISITORS

I follow a gaggle of schoolgirls past the "No Visitors" sign into the sitting-room where phones ring, maids scurry, and an ex-maidservant steps forward, touches Kamala's feet, displays her child, and begins to cry.

"Why are you crying?" Kamala asks.

"Because I am so happy," the maidservant sobs.

Kamala goes to the bedroom, gets a hundred rupee note, and stuffs it in the baby's pocket. An old friend who knew Kamala as a young bride joins the throng.

I long to talk to Kamala alone but it's impossible with the Canterbury Tale-like circus surrounding her. She is now listening to a western businesswoman describe her newest business venture, a marble egg she's producing in India to sell to a Scandinavian sexologist as a sex aid to tighten women's vaginas.

"Next step is to put a chicken in," Kamala retorts, "scratching, scratching."

The next day we begin carving out our work routine, and I raise the question of working together on the book.

"Don't forget," I say, "I always keep a journal. What you do in your mind, which you sometimes say and I record, I do in my journal. We'll have lots of material. I could mould it together in some form, but you would have to work with me after that."

"Merrily, let it be your book," Kamala hardly waits to say. "I've helped you with it, that's all. Say 'I am grateful to Kamala Das for helping me, assisting me.' It's yours."

"What if I take the material and put it in a shape, and then you and I will meet together," I demur, resisting taking full responsibility.

"That's fine. Because I don't think I'll have the strength to sit down and write now. Not for one year at least."

I leave Kamala and return to my airless apartment. Defying malaria, I slather myself with citronella and open the windows. At 2 AM the mosquitoes begin to bite. I close the windows, take a shower, spray on cancer-implicated mosquito repellent, and take stock. I could move to an AC hotel, or get a mosquito net, or go to Delhi and escape the heat, escape Cochin – most of all, escape my unease at what is happening now with Kamala, me, the book. My impulse is to go. I can no longer hope we will co-write, and for the first time I think the book may not happen. Perhaps Kamala doesn't like me taping or scribbling while we are eating. Or, I have been lumped into the general unpleasantness – operation, Sulu's house, hangers-on, takers, lack of old friends. Or, maybe Kamala has decided that Merrily too just wants something from her.

I lie writing on my stomach, positioned so the fan cools my back. The air is ancient and the room smells of mosquito repellent. It *is* the full moon. There is that too.

Early next morning the maidservant delivers an 1888 Victorian coin from Kamala for my niece Emma. The phone rings, and P.G. Joseph invites me to an English Department conference at Union College. Kamala calls and we exchange pleasantries.

"Have I overstayed my welcome?" I finally venture.

"That is such a western concept," she protests. "We get fonder of people. Last night I felt something was incomplete, some compassion was needed. 'Does she have a headache?' I thought. You left so quickly, Merrily."

"I heard you say you don't receive after 7:30 PM, and it was 8 PM."

"I meant men. You're not a man, Merrily."

"I know. I checked this morning."

This, thank goodness, makes her laugh.

"Then I thought, how can I expect someone from a foreign country to love as I do? Merrily, you honour me by coming here. Yesterday when you ran away, I thought it was because my hair stinks. Since the operation, I have not been able to wash. Somehow I made the girl wash my hair so I could embrace you."

The frozen knot inside me thaws. "Do I bore you?" I blurt.

"Oh, Merrily, don't think such negative thoughts of me. If there is some friendship in this world, it is ours. It makes me happy to know I can ring you and hear your voice. What is it? Did you have a bad dream?"

I tell her last night was the full moon. Even though "all that" is over, my juices still run the wrong way.

"Do you fight with Arnie then?"

"Sometimes. Usually I know what it is. Sometimes I am sad, or full of energy, sometimes I write."

"Shower and come," she says.

I am greeted by Kamala, her maids, the widowed neighbour, the neighbour's daughter, sister Sulu, brother-in-law Unni, daughter-in-law Devi, and the grandchildren. Kamala hugs me, holds my hand, puts her head on my shoulder, tells everyone what a good friend I am, gives me a sprig of *tulsi* (basil) to hang over my bed and a *rudraksha* bead (a dried fruit used to make a chain for saying prayers) to keep mosquitoes, disease, and chill away. I am flying, glowing, cells filled with leavened air.

When the family leaves, Dr B. Hariharan enters, grinning like the teenager he recently was. When we met at the Canadian Studies conference in Trivandrum, Hari told me that Kamala awed him with her fantastic bilingual talent. Face to face with the legendary Kamala Das, he restrains a compulsion to reach out and touch her, "to believe I am really standing in front of this person." Instead he tells her that he bought *My Story* with money won by betting his father he could eat an entire plate of chili-dosed food.

Strangely, this makes Kamala infinitely sad. Hari's story has reminded her of another young man whose letter she quotes by heart.

Dear Madhavikutty

I bought *My Story* and was reading it when my father came in the room and saw me. He grabbed it out of my hand saying Kamala Das was a hussy, an evil immoral woman, and he was going to immediately burn the book. Several weeks later, I went into my parent's room. My mother was asleep and my father was on his side holding the book and gazing at your picture. My father saw me seeing him. That night he swallowed something and the next morning he was dead.

"I felt terrible," Kamala says, and looks it. "I wrote to the young man and told him I was so ashamed for writing such a book that I felt guilty and responsible. I asked what I could do for him."

"It is not your fault," the young man wrote back. "My father was secretive and full of hypocrisy. I am not sorry for him, only for my mother who does not know why he died."

"You live in such a censorious culture," I explode. "They pick at you like vultures."

"Yes, I see them as if they have sores all over their bodies, pus coming out, stinking," she says with unusual venom. "They are horrible."

Outside in the energy-conserving blackout, Hari reports to me that Kamala told him in Malayalam that she doesn't know what more to say about the proposed book. Her belief is that good writing can't be programmed: it should "emerge like a rash of prickly heat," only when there is so much to say that it has to come out. Her literary creation takes place in the mind whenever she's awake, and perhaps even in sleep. "When you ripen for a poem and a poem ripens for its debut, it gets born. There is no easy way to get it out, no miracle remedy for its delayed gestation." Hari thinks Kamala's low spirits are because she feels she can't produce what is expected of her. He urges me to reassure her that everything about the book is okay.

I am grateful for his counsel. I sense there is much more that Kamala could say, but I don't want to pressure her or be a burden. Anyway, it wouldn't work. She knows her writing must build up to overflow, and I know that confidences too need time to be expressed. I return to her apartment to reassure her, but Sarasu, the maidservant, peeks through the chained door to say Amma is sleeping. I go back to my apartment, take the tape recorder out of my backpack, and retire it to the safe.

Today I am to pick up a ruby ring that I have carefully selected, designed, and had fitted.

When Kamala hears this, she tells me about her doctor friend, a jolly man who one day decided he wanted a ruby ring. From a choice display, he chose a large, exquisitely cut, light pink ruby, to be set in gold. "Careful," friends warned, "rubies can be dangerous to your health." But believing only in science, the doctor fetched his treasure, put it on immediately, and hurried home to show his wife. No sooner did he enter the door and extend his ruby-ringed finger than he had a stroke and died.

"He died?" I say weakly.

"He had a stroke in the right side of his brain and died," Kamala confirms. "Precious stones have medicinal qualities. Rubies have something to do with heart and blood. I believe they should be worn only by Geminis."

As a non-Gemini, I am very relieved when Rajesh P.B., astrology columnist for the *Times of India*, manifests in reply to Kamala's summons. He records my birth date, consults charts, calculates, and says I am able to wear a ruby.

I should also wear one pearl. The pearl represents the moon and the moon is the planet for the mind. Wearing the pearl will release my tension. Wearing these two stones will give more strength to my eyes, and the ruby will give strength to my heart as well.

I should wear the ruby on my ring finger.

I should put it on one hour after sunrise on Sunday morning.

I should wait until Monday to put on the pearl, an hour after sunrise.

I grin across the counter at Mr Sathyanda, who is seated like a fat frog on a lily pad, buttocks comfortably spread on 117 years of good family reputation. The ring is more elegant and better crafted than I had imagined. I lust to see it on my hand but force myself to heed the astrologer. I buy the pearl, take my purchases home, and wait.

The Sunday after the purchase, one hour after sunrise, I don my ruby ring. It looks more gorgeous than any of my other jewellery, and it fits. I can barely wait to rush upstairs and show it to Kamala. I go to the bathroom to fix my hair, look in the mirror, and see my eye is obliterated by a swathe of blood. It's unbelievable. My eye is swimming in blood.

I rip off the ruby and run to Kamala's. Sarasu is bathing Kamala's feet in hot water. Mr Menon has come, asking Kamala to intercede with his wife, who has left him, but I am in no mood to listen to his story. I show Kamala my eye and through the blood see her concern. She sends me with her driver to an ophthalmologist. Still in his *mundu*, Dr Varma leads me to a clean, equipped examining room, and I count the seconds until he suits up. Exactly 170 seconds later, he returns in a surgical smock, takes my history and blood pressure, shines a light in my eye, and diagnoses a burst blood vessel that will be absorbed in ten days. "Don't worry," he says.

I reassess the bloody mess, happy it won't impede my return home in three days, and lock the ruby ring in the safe with my tape recorder.

"And I suppose Arnie will accept you in any crumpled form," Kamala consoles.

# 12

# The Husband Who Neither Loved Nor Used Her but Was a Ruthless Watcher

Kamala and I sit together on the settee at the end of our penultimate day. "If at all you write about this woman," she says, touching her chest, "let my husband come out as a good man. I don't know if anyone else would forgive him, so I think I have to. He used to like talking about me being immoral, then he's the grand one, forgiving all."

"In *My Story*, you wrote about how he treated you," I remind her.

"Yes, but pushing me to the boss, that was ugly. Some of my friends might have known, I haven't talked about it to people. I wrote a little about it, and some of my readers might have guessed. But if I don't talk about it to you, people will think I threw myself at his boss. *Summer in Calcutta* was dedicated to this man."

Having heard this teeter-tottering before, I quickly recognize Kamala's high-wire attempt to balance loyalty to her family with justice for herself. She suggests I say her husband is a "good" man – but if I do, people won't know he engineered her affair. It reminds me of other covert references to her husband's perversity, with the difference now being that I am leaving tomorrow and time is running out for setting the record straight. I think Kamala may realize that hiding her experience misrepresents and obscures her history and that of many women of her generation. The problem is critical, because once I'm home, I'll start drafting the book. Kamala knows that without her testimony no one will know why she wrote the way she did.

"What is the point of hiding?" she finally says. "Why did I get frustrated? Why did I write such sad poems? Why did I become a celibate so young? If I don't tell the truth about my husband, *My Story* is only half a book.

"There was so much of sadness in me," she begins, finally opening a path into her hidden life. "My husband was always talking about young men, and about the old men lying over me. Only a man's naked form could excite him. He would ask about the man he fancied, 'Tell me, what did he say to you? Did he touch your breasts?' – asking me to narrate the incidents, even to describe his genitals. "Tell me how he did that." He wanted to visualize the man in bed with me. Only then would he get excited. And I'd have to fantasize, because I was not one to receive any man in my body."

She says her husband never really slept with her but always with an imaginary male lover. To get through it, she would close her eyes, secretly thinking of Krishna. "Because when I thought of Krishna, I felt clean." She tells me she felt she was both the crab inside its shell and the shell outside, and "sometimes I would lose my identity."

I wait, because this behaviour is so outside my experience that I haven't fully understood what she's describing, much less how it might affect her.

"My husband was always pushing me to his superiors so he would get a promotion," she says, looking to see my reaction.

I knew her husband expected her to flirt with his Brahmin boss and entertain him. Now she tells me that when her husband found a fan letter to her from a high-ranking minister, he sent her to the minister to get him a better job. "You must go," he said. "Don't you want to help me?"

Kamala says she obeyed her husband because she believed she owed him this duty, because he was educated and she was not, because she didn't think she was beautiful, and because without him the family wouldn't survive.

I went to him for half an hour
As pure woman, pure misery
Fragile glass, breaking
Crumbling ...

"No, my husband didn't tell me to come. I'm the cunning one," she told the minister. "It will help me. I'll be able to shop."

Soon Kamala's husband had a good job with a prestigious title, and Kamala felt "dirty, and humiliated." She warned Das that she would not live with him if he were dishonest, and she assures me yet again that although he authorized large loans and could have skimmed a commission, "he was scrupulously honest."

But that was not the end of it. During an international banking meeting in Bombay, coveting an opportunity to work in international finance, he sent her to a superior one last time. He told her a senior banking official admired her poetry and wanted to meet her.

"I know myself I was a woman of great physical and mental charms," Kamala says with a mixture of pride and regret. "Prime of my life, trained to charm his superiors, offer the right kind of drink. A good, hospitable woman, very, very hospitable." Once again, she charmed a prospective employer, and her husband became an international financial consultant.

"But I didn't like it. I was playing a role, like I was cut into pieces, and I felt sordid."

She hated the lecherous hugs and slobbering kisses, and could not reconcile herself to this "metamorphosis into a carnal object." Her pride rebelled. She felt shame at being coerced and used by her husband.

"It was so sad to be just a plaything, that's all. The whole thing seemed dirty to me. I was happiest taking my children to the comic store, buying them ice creams, walking with them."

Yet she kept up the charade for her readers, masking her grief.

I am a freak. It's only
To save my face, I flaunt at
Times, a grand, flamboyant lust.

The end came when Das returned from a work trip to Burma and showed Kamala photos of himself with a much younger "special" man on his lap. They were holding each other so affectionately that she asked Das if he loved the young man.

"Yes," he answered, describing details she didn't want to know.

Only then did she feel justified in relieving herself of further sexual duty.

"Because he had others, I was afraid of disease, and his constant talk of those he slept with was like graffiti on lavatory walls. So at about forty-five, I thought, I will give him the freedom to sleep with whomever he wants, and I will give myself the freedom to sleep alone, take a wash, be clean, and have a good sleep. I told him, 'I want the freedom of my private parts. You can do what you want. I will even finance it.'" She asked her husband for permission to be celibate. "And he permitted me."

Throughout this astonishing recitation, astonishing because it comes out of nowhere and because Kamala is as agitated as if it is happening now, she keeps repeating, "No one knows how I suffered being the wife of a homosexual," and then says, "I loved him so much, so much I loved him. I always obeyed him."

And she almost always did obey him. But now, older, she is becoming more blunt about the damage her husband's proclivities caused her, and more bitter about the society that gave the stranger who married her the licence to rape her. "The rape that went on and on because he had the licence to do it. One night coming home drunk and using me five times. In the morning I was broken and lacerated." She cried silently then, "Somebody crushed me. My whole body hurts."

Forced sex is like an auto crash, Kamala says: fear, pain, blood, and confrontation accompany both. She says girls forced to have sex begin to look at men with fear in the same way as people are afraid to get into a vehicle after an accident. "That is why their eyes seem dilated and their palms grow cold like lotus stems. Gradually they come to know that sex is a war and that lust is a kind of terrorism."

I feel so terrible about the torment Kamala endured that I go overboard in acknowledging the feat of her survival.

"I didn't survive, I went mad," she corrects me tersely. "A nervous breakdown." She recalls the doctor giving her sedatives, warning that if pills didn't work, she would be taken to his clinic. The dosage was three pills a day, and when she stopped medicating herself, she would smash things, screaming she couldn't stand it any longer and wanted to get out. Finally, "miserable as a trapped animal," she went to the terrace to jump, and a neighbour saved her. Then, for eleven months, she took the full dosage of pills and slept and slept.

"Afterwards a new person emerged," she says, "a person who had more control of everything."

This new person accepted that "marriage to Dasettan was not good, but my destiny." And since we are all just instruments of destiny, it was useless to struggle against it. She accepted her fate, tried to get some fun somewhere else, and became complicit in a marital cover-up. Speaking in her husband's favour, she says he never sullied her reputation or spoke harshly to her. In later years he acted as her manager and protected her so that she could write. She gave him money and celebrity by association, and he gave her the status of wife and the happiness of being a respectable mother, which she loved.

"In the end," she says, "he gave me that." And she gave readers "Jaisurya," one of the most beautiful birth poems ever written.

> It was again the time of rain and on
> Every weeping tree, the lush moss spread like
> Eczema, and from beneath the swashy
> Earth the fat worms surfaced to explode
> Under rain. It rained on the day my son
> Was born ...
> When rain stopped and the light was gay on our
> Casuarina leaves, it was early
> Afternoon. And, then, wailing into light
> He came, so fair, a streak of light thrust
> Into the faded light. They raised him
> To me then, proud Jaisurya, my son,

Separated from darkness that was mine
And in me ...
Out of the mire of a moonless night was
He born, Jaisurya, my son, as out of
The wrong is born the right and out of night
The sun-drenched golden day.

Still, I wonder how Kamala managed the emotional contortions required to play a man for her husband and a courtesan for his superiors. It's hard to know, because even the writings that allude to these situations are so couched, they conceal her feelings.

After bathing me in warm water and dressing me in men's clothes,
my husband bade me sit on his lap, fondling me and calling me his
darling boy.

It confuses me, and Kamala sees the question on my face. "People think I should be outraged, but I surprised myself by keeping my balance," she tells me. "The two of me did not become agitated. One suffered, and one watched and wrote. I managed because I loved my children and I somehow loved him."

I look at Kamala and wonder how she could love her husband, or say so often that she did. Then I remember her telling me how she made herself be generous to a critic who'd demeaned her, in order to overcome her hatred of him, so that life would be renewed. "It's not enough romanticizing things, romanticizing even hurts and slights. You've got to continue to live, accept your enemies as attackers, but still serve them a cup of tea." She told me that making friendly gestures to our enemies stirs something within us that removes the hate and makes us begin to like them. "Hate is a thorn in the flesh," she said. "I would rather prefer to love them, if love is not very difficult to achieve. I try."

I think she tries her best to unequivocally forgive and love her husband. But her husband's prolonged assault on her body and womanhood cut too deeply into her nerves and memory cells to forget. Although she is infinitely more adept at emotional channelling than I, she remains cursed by "this wound which has never healed."

I can't help comparing Kamala's social constraints to the permissiveness that allowed me to divorce twice with much less provocation than hers. In early 1960s Montreal, when I left my first husband, it was an oddity to be a twenty-year-old "single parent divorcee," but by the late 1970s when my second husband left me, divorce was easy and rampant. Children were thought better off removed from the clash of male and female destinies (a generation from the late '70s divorce explosion is now reeling from this supposition), and in my children's downtown city school, divorced parents were the norm. I too countenanced a failed relationship longer than was healthy, hoping to make a marriage work. But when I confronted my husband, I found support in the writings of like-minded women, in the expectations of the women's movement, and from my parents.

Kamala had no such support and says she had no option but to remain married to Madhava Das. She knew she was being exploited, but if she "failed" as a wife, society would judge her broken marriage to be as "distasteful and horrifying as an attack of leprosy." People would say she didn't deserve any better, because "she's not an educated girl, she's nothing." She would be shamed and ostracized, and no man would marry a divorcee with small children.

"Write, write, it's the truth," Kamala says defiantly when I ask whether these disclosures should be published. She says the hypocrisy of her marriage was "part of the face of respectability that my society bore in those days." And I've learned that her experience mirrors that of many women of her generation, just as mine mirrors that of North American women who came of age with bohemians, existentialists, Playboy bunnies, Twiggy, free love, with the pressure to be "liberated," not "uptight," and to enjoy premarital sex whether we liked it or not.

"I'll write a first draft of this," I offer. "But I'm worried that if I send it to you in India, you'll have a different reaction to what you'd have in Canada."

"I'll give you both reactions. I'm only worried about my children." She thinks for a moment, then grabs the other horn of the dilemma. "Why should they claim me only as their own? I'm a writer. I'm not family property."

Still, no matter what she says, Kamala's unresolved ambivalence about her allegiances and conflicting loyalties remain. To Das? Her children? History? Herself?

That night I look for the poems Kamala said were written years ago when she was being "utilized and misutilized" as a sex object. "Writing a good poem is like thrusting a needle into your breast bone to aspirate the invisible marrow within – a painful procedure," she has said. And, in a metaphor that one critic called "surreal," she confessed, "I have often wished to take myself apart and stick all the bits, the heart, the intestines, the liver, the reproductive organs, the skin, the hair and all the rest on a large canvas to form a collage which could be donated to my readers."

But these particular poems, she warns me, "smudge out" the facts.

I find the relevant poems in *The Old Playhouse* by referencing the word *toy,* a word Kamala uses as a metaphor for a woman sent as a plaything to a man. To protect her sanity, the woman creates a self detached from herself, one who behaves like a mechanical toy.

But the schizoid schism tears her apart.

I am sinner,
I am saint. I am the beloved and the
Betrayed.

Kamala begins the poem with her husband's betrayal, and concludes with her father's betrayal – for me, the saddest betrayal of all.

I do not bother
To tell: I've misplaced a father
Somewhere, and I look
For him now everywhere.

I put the poems on the sideboard and turn off the light, with more wonderment than ever that Kamala's themes of love and sensuality survived her personal experience of what she called "the phallocentric superiority, phallocentric sadism" that eroticized women and fetishized parts of their bodies, "converting women into consumable luxury goods." My thoughts turn to Nalapat, to the nurturing she had from the household of women, her grand-uncle, and the physicality of being held, groomed, and dressed ceremoniously by her grandmother, dancing to the Gitagovinda, acting the role of Queen Noor, and performing the undulating movements of Manipuri dance. She told scholar J. Devika, a Nayar woman decades younger than she, that "women didn't cover their breasts at Nalapat, there were beautiful bosoms. All sagged, with pinkish tips. I remember my great-grand-mother's breasts, and the scent of sandalwood paste they bore. We never thought of them as vulgar."

Devika extols Kamala for recovering "the erotic potential of the female body" and for not degrading it into mind-centred romantic love or depersonalized pornography, "an event of significance in the history of love in Malayalee society."

"How do you do this? What kind of shaping of the mind makes you like this?" she asks Kamala, sounding like me.

Maybe, as Devika suggests, books, or contact with the warmth of the servants, opened Kamala's mind to erotic potential beyond romantic pap or porn. Maybe it was her experience, one foreign to me although she has tried to communicate it, of holding a man and feeling Krishna in her arms; thinking of Krishna, his eyes, his radiant mouth; believing that the eternal soul transcends the bodies of Krishna and Radha, the original lovers, and travels from body to body, loving, mating, uniting; feeling exalted by the sacred act of love, that she is the goddess, her lover the god.

"It is not pleasure, it is happiness. You are giving immortality to your feel-ings," she tells me.

In marriage, Kamala's body belonged to her husband to use as he wished, but her mind leapt free. She thought of Krishna, flew above her body like a bird, merged with the sky, the streets, the natural world. She wrote so that her life wouldn't choke her, and created a persona to free her and mask her grief. Mis-understood as a consumer of erotic pleasure, feeling crucified over and over on the "cross of male lust," she searched for the love she read about but never had: the worship of the body in love like Radha and Krishna in the *Gitagovinda*, the impossible love of *The End of the Affair*, Isadora Duncan's exuberant free love, Lawrence Hope's passionate romance. Above all, she longed for the gentle lover who would not objectify her, or mistake her sensuality for lust, but would unite with *her*.

To cap the visit, Kamala sends me to a neighbour who owns a video-cassette player so that I can view *Rugmini*, a Malayali movie based on her short story "A Doll for the Child Prostitute." The neighbour lives next door in a three-bedroom flat with her ninety-two-year-old father, eighty-three-year-old mother, fifteen-year-old daughter, eight-year-old son, sister, sister's son, and a maid. When I arrive, Grandma prepares tea, the son inserts Kamala's tape in the player, and a haze of sticky cooking gas invades my lungs. Everyone sits stoically facing the TV and coughs. Finally, to counter the smell of gas, the daughter grabs an aerosol can and squirts it liberally, enveloping us all in a protective chemical mist.

Grandma and I start watching the film, and the others watch me. I look over at Grandma and see her entranced. We watch twelve-year-old Rugmini's mother sell her to a brothel after her stepfather attempts to rape her. Grandma looks grim. Kamala has told me that a week ago the old lady came to her, begging to stay in her home. Her daughter had brought her and her husband to Cochin for ayurvedic treatment, commandeered their pension, dismantled their ancestral home, and sold their land. When Grandma asked to return home, her daughter said, "You have nowhere to go."

Grandma and I enter the harsh world of Bombay prostitutes, brothel keepers, abortionists, and johns, through Rugmini's innocent eyes. As research, Kamala had taken a cab to a brothel, and while the driver pretended to fix the engine, she observed:

Two young girls probably in their early teens played hopscotch on the sidewalk. Just then, a thin man, totally bald, appearing to be a clerk appeared and climbed the staircase shielding his face with a newspaper. A minute later, an elderly woman came up to the window and shouted out "Rugmini." One of the young girls stopped hopping from square to square. She said to her playmate: "Sita, I shall be back in a few minutes. Please don't move the piece."

The girl called Sita went on playing a solo game nonchalantly. She was emaciated and had a yellow tinge to her skin. She had applied collyrium to her sunken eyes. The time was about three in the afternoon.

After a while Rugmini came down the steps and resumed her game. Her hair seemed dishevelled. Her cheeks were flushed.

Even in incomprehensible Malayalam, I find the film moving. Girls vie for rooms, the madam's prodigal son returns, the most beautiful prostitute falls in love with an idealistic student, an abortionist negligently murders a client, and Rugmini's vulnerability finally touches the heart of the elderly police inspector, her client. Rugmini looks like a young Kamala. For a brief moment, Kamala saves her.

Kamala says she showed the film to UNICEF delegates in Delhi, to NGO delegates in Cochin, and at film festivals, hoping it would shame politicians into enacting laws against the sexual exploitation of children, a cause she passionately supports. "But although there were no scenes of sex or violence, the film's setting made it suspect in the eyes of Kerala's prudish middle class." Bowing to vociferous public indignation, India's public broadcaster, Doordarshan, apologized for its broadcast.

As soon as the film is over, Grandma disappears into the kitchen. The son switches tapes, and everyone watches fascinated as rival Malayali gangs fight like Hollywood gangsters. I leave as quickly as possible, cradling images of Kamala's film.

At 8:45 PM the apartment bell rings loudly, insistently, three times. I am too exhausted to answer.

An apologetic watchman knocks on the door. He announces that Balan Chullikkad, the charismatic poet scheduled to visit earlier today, has appeared.

"Too tired. I'm asleep," I groan, dozing off as the watchman's steps recede.

The alarm wakes me early next morning. I dress, lock my suitcase, and the phone rings.

"Congratulations," Kamala announces. "The watchman told me you sent Balan away."

I cry in the elevator, accompanied by the maidservants, bags in the car, driver waiting. I want to go home, am ready, eye still red, face and shoulders pocked with mosquito bites, but Kamala and I live far apart and I never know when, or if, I will see her again. This visit, perhaps the most intimate of all, she's pulled me closer as a confidant. She's been more direct, demanding, and reflective than when she was recently widowed – restless, as if she's finding her footing, assessing the next way "to live so that it would be an incentive to live."

Yet even as I move on, and sense her moving on, I could never imagine the adventure ahead – how far Kamala's life-force would take her, and how much more deeply I would be drawn both as observer and participant into her unpredictable life.

The burst blood vessel in my eye is reabsorbing into washes of yellow and streaks of red. I fasten the protective rudraksha bead from Kamala around my throat and board the plane.

# FOUR

## Cochin, Calicut, Malabar, 2000

his perfect teeth became my necklace of prayer beads

# 13

# Bliss in the Scent of His Perspiration

I don't know about it when it happens, and can't imagine why, but suddenly aristocratic, upper-caste Hindu Kamala Das, lover of Krishna, descendant of rajas, decides to embrace Islam. Without any hint or warning to me, she bursts back into the glare of CNN, Asianet, media across Asia, in the biggest scandal of her scandalous career. On 16 December 1999, amidst a storm of controversy, in a one-minute home ceremony, she converts.

I have no idea what's going on, neither do my informants, and I'm embarrassed Kamala hasn't told me anything herself. I try to call her, but her phone is disconnected. I reach her son Monu in Delhi, and he says a state restraining order prevents Kamala from speaking to journalists or groups, that she is receiving death threats, she travels with a bodyguard, and there's a price on her head. He gives me her new number but warns me that the phone is probably bugged.

I contact anybody who can tell me more, and Hari, my scholar friend in Kerala, forwards clippings.

"Islam is the religion of love," I read Kamala saying. "Hindus have abused and hurt me. They have often tried to scandalize me. I want to love and be loved."

She tells an interviewer she is taking Krishna from the Guruvayur temple, naming him Mohammed, and making him a prophet. "If you go to Guruvayur, you will not see Krishna there. He is with me."

"But you're so fond of Krishna. How could you abandon him?" asks the astonished journalist, aware, as is everyone in Kerala, that Guruvayur is a Krishna temple and also the temple of Kamala's ancestresses.

"I haven't abandoned him. He's still with me, he's in my house."

"How can he be in a Muslim house?"

"I've just had to rename him Mohammed," she says, confounding conventional religious logic, or asserting one more ecumenical. "My grandmother told me as a child I was married to Krishna. I have seen Krishna, played with him and eaten with him. I love Krishna, and that love will never die. The essence of Krishna is within me, it's only that the name has changed."

I follow up on the Internet and read that Kamala's life is being threatened, that the leader of the Vishwa Hindu Parishad (a Hindu extremist group) has taken her to court for abusing Hinduism in her remarks about Guruvayur, and that she converted because Muslims promised her a seat in government or an Assembly candidature, or so that Ishmail Merchant would film one of her books.

"I was travelling from Malabar to Kochi," Kamala responds in the *Times of India*. "I looked at the rising sun. Surprisingly, it had the colour of a setting sun. It travelled with me and at 7:00 AM it turned white. For years I have been looking for signs telling me when to convert. Finally, I got the message."

"Kamala has found a new and improved way to shock the fabric of her society," says a friend.

"May Lord save Islam," concludes a local intellectual.

A month after her conversion, Kamala's enlightening letter arrives.

Dearest Merrily,

Life has changed for me since Nov. 14 when a young man named Sadiq Ali walked in to meet me. He is 38 and has a beautiful smile. Afterwards he began to woo me on the phone from Abu Dhabi and Dubai, reciting Urdu couplets and telling me of what he would do to me after our marriage. I took my nurse Mini and went to his place in my car. I stayed with him for three days. There was a sunlit river, some trees, and a lot of laughter. He asked me to become a Muslim which I did on my return home. The Press and other media rushed in. The Hindu fanatics, Shiv Sena and the Rashtriya Swayamsevak Sangh (RSS) pasted posters all over the place, "Madhavikutty is insane. Put her to death." I refused the eight policemen sent to protect me. There are young men, all Muslims, now occupying the guest flat and keeping vigil twenty-four hours a day. I have received court orders restraining me from going out or addressing more than six people at a time. Among the Muslims I have become a cult figure all dressed in black purdah and learning Arabic.

My Hindu relatives and friends keep a distance from me. They wish to turn me into a social outcast. My sister visited me twice but wept all the time. I cannot visit my old mother. Otherwise life is exciting ...

> Affectionately,
> Kamala Das
> (Suraiya)

I get an Indian visa and boosters for inoculations, anguish anew over malaria pills versus mechanical protection, buy long skirts and long-sleeved blouses, and break the plane journey to India with a stopover at my friend Angie's home in Oxford. Four days later, I find myself scribbling under a mosquito net in the Madras flat of Gita Krishnankutty, Kamala's Malayalam-to-English translator, wondering what awaits me this time in Cochin.

Jet-lagged and tired, I open myself to a laughing, entrancing Kamala in burqua and black. We've been talking for hours, between and over the heads of the new cast of Muslim visitors. Lulled by her lilting Malayalam, I follow the bewitching movements of her slender brown arms, elegant fingers curling and extending, palms opening, arms rising, hands circling, punching the air, reaching out. Her hands perform a hand dance, hand mime, hand directions, hand tones, resting just a beat before the next arabesque.

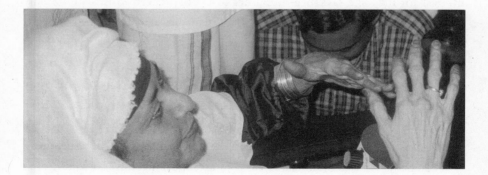

I meet businessmen and scholars who come and go, but as the hours pass, I notice a constant stream of slim young men in western shirts and trousers who glide through the sitting room, answer the phone, and settle familiarly at Kamala's feet. I begin to recognize four of them, but soon realize I'm not expected to get to know them. When I try to draw them out, Kamala answers with a collective designation. These slim young men are "the commandos," mysterious members of her new entourage.

I notice too that Kamala's posture and body language are looser and more relaxed than on my last visit. She says Muslims are friendlier than Hindus, and with them she feels a complicity and trust. There's more laughter in the house and she looks radiant – dark eyes bright, full lips puckering, gold on neck, diamonds in nose – her face dramatically framed by a regal, high-capped, black *chador* (Muslim woman's headdress).

Whatever her new reality, Kamala's warmth to me is unchanged. She shows me a shiny silver cell phone resting like an idol on a pedestal, and says it is a gift from thirty-eight-year-old Sadiq Ali, Islamic scholar, national Muslim League MP from Malabar, and her absent lover. All day she wears the phone on a gold belt slung rebelliously around the waist of her black dress, keeping the line open and, as he requested, "dedicated to our love." As her bangles flash and her visitors delight, Kamala listens for the phone strapped to her body. She longs for Sadiq Ali to call. And when the visitors leave, she tells me that after their first meeting, he called for days, at midnight, every night.

"After my husband died, I found myself insecure and totally untethered. I lost my zest for life," she says, beginning her love story. "Even in this supposedly modern age, Hindu widows are regarded an inauspicious sight. They're not the right omen at the beginning of any journey. They're lacklustre, like a mud lark. They can't fly. They drag their wings in the mud."

She had spent decades being celibate, extolling its virtues, "carrying my body around like a corpse," accepting loneliness as the permanent climate of her life. "In a sense I was lying in wait for death. Everything seemed to be dead, or deadened, even poetry. I shrank pitifully, feeling diminished for no fault of my own."

Then Sadiq Ali asked Kamala's cousin to arrange a meeting. He said he had admired Kamala for years and wanted to meet her. Kamala gave him a two-hour appointment, and Sadiq Ali drove five hours from his small town to Cochin.

"He sat at my feet laughing the attractive, reckless laugh of a monarch. He was a preacher who delighted large audiences with ballads and narratives lasting five hours. He held his listeners in a spell with his four-octave range and a pure voice that resembled a newborn's cry."

Sadiq Ali charmed Kamala with his eloquence, scholarship, rough wavy hair, white teeth, and "smile of wondrous innocence." He asked if she would permit herself to be photographed with him, and they posed on the cane sofa, nibbling on plum cake, laughing together. "I no longer recollect the topics of our first conversation, but laughter entered our home as spontaneously as sunshine that morning, filling each crevice of emptiness."

"Feed me," Sadiq Ali requested playfully, when Kamala allowed the two hours to stretch into lunch.

"But I cannot touch your lips," Kamala responded. Her grandmother had warned that Muslims ate the corpses of sacred cows, which made their breath stink, and that touching them led to exile. "A staunch vegetarian like me would never touch the mouth of a *mlecha* [flesh eater]," she said.

"Then I will feed you," Sadiq Ali offered, breaking food into small pieces.

By the time he left Kamala's home, his flirtatious play had stirred long-buried feelings and desires. "For many years I had not witnessed the blush spread on the cheek of a young man finding himself embarked on a new love."

And it had been many decades since she had felt desire, that slow ache in the abdomen, blood surging as on a fast-moving swing.

Minutes after returning home, Sadiq Ali called Kamala to say he had been thinking of her throughout the journey. Breathlessness made his voice even more attractive. "You follow me like a melody," he said.

Then, every night for eight nights, whether from Abu Dhabi or Dubai, he called Kamala to sing Urdu poetry and speak passionately of love.

"Such sweet talk. It was a new experience for me because I had imagined love affairs but I never had what I imagined before. This boy made me feel like a woman for the first time, his voice resonating like a temple bell. You could hear it ringing after he was gone."

Sadiq Ali had two wives, but as a Muslim he was allowed four. He invited Kamala to stay in his rural villa, and she accepted because after a month of intense courtship, she had fallen "irrevocably" in love with him. The lovers dined leisurely and talked, served by Kamala's maid, Mini, and by Sadiq Ali's second wife, who respected Kamala as a scholar. Kamala reciprocated by sending Sadiq Ali and his family to their village feast with her driver and her car. She watched them disappear, then lay down to rest.

"I was almost asleep when Sadiq Ali climbed in beside me, holding me, breathing softly, whispering endearments, kissing my face, breasts. It hurt when he kissed my toes, they're delicate from diabetes, so he moved up my leg, licking me where I had never been licked before.

"'What are you doing?' I asked.

"'Just kissing you.'

"And when he entered me, it was the first time I had ever experienced what it was like to feel a man from the inside. Not with my hands, or face, but with my insides."

Afterwards, Sadiq Ali suckled like a baby and Kamala didn't know what to do. She held him tightly as she could. "I feel like I have made love to a virgin," he said.

He pulled her down to the river in her nightie and she bathed.

When he dried her, she said, "I was thinking of your fingers looking for treasure."

"My fingers were pilgrims on a pilgrimage," he murmured.

Kamala tells me she had never before imagined that a man could be such a pleasurable playmate.

The next day, she had other thoughts. "I feel sullied," she told Sadiq Ali, feeling dishonoured by the illicit nature of the relationship.

"But we will get married," he promised, "twelve days from now. You will live in my Delhi home and be my Delhi wife. If I marry you, the others fade."

She dressed in a clean silk sari, preparing to leave, and he sat on the windowsill sobbing until she consented to remain one more day. That day he named her Suraiya, "the morning star," and said she would have to become a Muslim before they could marry. When she finally left, he cried like a child, "You can't go. I won't be able to enter this room again."

Filled with love, not wanting to waste precious time, Kamala stopped halfway home to announce her imminent conversion to the press. Newsmen and television reporters were on her doorstep when she arrived. She avowed her long-time interest in Islam and described the vision that convinced her to convert.

The reaction was immediate and extreme. Within the week, Hindu extremists had put up posters offering 50 lakhs for her murder. Obscene postcards taunted, "You like it circumcised don't you?" And fanatics threatened to burn down the cinema in her ancestral village if it showed a documentary on her life. As writer Paul Zacharia explained, for the Sangh Parivar (a family of Hindu organizations built around volunteer associations called the RSS, which promote Hindu nationalism), "the cruellest blow of the conversion was that Kamala belonged to the Nalapat tarawad, the crème de la crème of Kerala's Nayar Hindu elite," and her conversion desecrated this honour.

When the tabloids named Sadiq Ali as Kamala's lover, the threats intensified. Callers shouted that her high-caste Hindu birth was a stroke of good fortune, and she had betrayed them. An anonymous man threatened to kill her in twenty-four hours. Another warned that when the milkman arrives, "there will be a surprise. Along with the bag of milk will be Sadiq Ali's intestines."

Sadiq Ali went into hiding. The wedding room reserved at the South Park Hotel in Trivandrum was cancelled. Kamala was left alone with the press, and the mess.

"Certainly her action has electrified Kerala's somewhat moribund social scene," wrote Leela Menon in the *New Indian Express*. "The state, many feel, is evolving into a land of widows, with women outliving men and depression stalking the land. In such a scenario, Kamala may even appear to provide an alternative."

"When I was a Hindu widow, no one would pay any attention to me," Kamala says, handing me her conversion scrapbook to photocopy. "Now, one of the greatest Muslim scholars proclaimed on stage before thousands that Suraiya is the star that will lead Muslims into the twenty-first century." She says that pilgrims stream to her home, young people seek her endorsement, she was the only female speaker addressing three thousand men in Bombay, she will be Haji's guest at the Sheraton in Qatar, and a twenty-five-year-old suitor may show up in Calicut.

"The Muslims are pampering me. Everyone who comes loves me."

She says she is learning a religion filled with song. She would like to dance.

I am moved by her infectious hope. Her dance card is full and her world ripe with piquant possibility. She has thrown away caution, duty, and propriety, providing a grand alternative to austere widowhood. She has renewed herself in the face of sickness and aging and leapt, full of life, to the edge. For other widows, such as journalist Leela Menon, her electrifying decision "injects not only optimism, but euphoria."

Yet Kamala aches for Sadiq Ali in her bed again. After decades of callous sex and defensive celibacy, a master lover, "my only love like I read about in books," playfully, tenderly, poetically aroused a lifetime of dormant erotic desire. Sadiq Ali lives in Kamala's nerve endings, and every moment they shared plays like a film loop in her head. She longs to repeat the night they had together, a night that came only once in her lifetime, and that when she was sixty-seven.

"Would you have moved to Delhi to live with Sadiq Ali?" I ask.

"I would have done anything."

"Did you consider the reaction of your family?

"I didn't think of anything, losing the family or friends. I thought he would be my family. He would be everything to me."

Next morning we breakfast with Kabir, a reserved, thirty-three-year-old writer on comparative religion and Islam, one of Kamala's new regulars. Kamala beguiles, entertains, and toys with him. She quotes a poem about a love paler than the morning moon, a fading love that the desperate poet renounces, knowing she will be poorer for losing it, "because love is so wonderful."

Kabir tilts his head, acknowledging the Sadiq Ali subtext. His reaction is so controlled that Kamala can't help teasing him. She says he has a man's body but a child's face, even with his beard. "A puritan with a child's face," she laughs, "isn't it so, Merrily?" – trying to draw me in. Then, because Sadiq Ali is always near the surface if not bubbling over, she complains that he just told the press his relationship to her was a sacred one, like mother to child, and that she is going to marry Ishmail Merchant, whom she has never met.

Kabir is more concerned about Kamala's upcoming speech in Calicut than about Sadiq Ali. Drawing on his knowledge of Islamic texts, he suggests that for the upcoming anniversary of a Muslim woman's magazine, Kamala could quote the phrase "Heaven is at the feet of the mother."

"The last prophet said this," he tells her. "The mothers will like it."

As soon as he leaves, three middle-aged editors arrive from the *Malayalam Daily Chandrika*, the Muslim League's popular mouthpiece, to arrange Kamala's trip to Calicut. Chief editor C.K. Hanifa sits across from me, a well-dressed man with steel-grey hair, electric energy, and interested, intelligent eyes. Much to Kamala's surprise, I find him charming, and since he and I have no common language, she translates and I learn: the Muslim League is a small political party in coalition with the ruling Congress-led United Democratic Front; the commandos, sent by a friend of Kamala's as an alternative to police protection, are members of another group called the NDF (National Democratic Front), a fundamentalist Muslim network that emerged to defend Muslims after the recent rise of Hindu fundamentalism; the more moderate Muslim League works within the secular constitution of India, and the NDF divides society on communal (communities defined by their religion) lines. Eventually the exchange bores Kamala, and she tells a story instead.

I almost sleep during the following long, animated travel arrangements. I live down the hall in an apartment normally used for public audiences and guests, but until I came, the commandos were sleeping, eating, and camping there. My bed has no top sheet, so I contort to keep myself covered with my mundu and my shawl. More distressing, I can't get the mosquito protection under control. When I make the AC cold enough to render mosquitoes inactive, it's too cold for comfort. And although I've gerrymandered a single-bed mosquito net over the venetian blinds and mirror with wires and hooks, it barely covers the twin bed. I spend nights debating whether to wiggle to stay covered or stay still to keep the net in place.

I manage to stay awake through the three hours Kamala entertains the gentlemen from *Chandrika*. When they leave, I see that she too is totally done in. Now, a younger, scruffier group of Muslim men from the NDF storms in, insisting it is Suraiya's duty to speak in their "program" before the Muslim League event. Kamala responds politely in Malayalam, smiles, and demurs. To accommodate these men, she would have to leave tomorrow, drive nine hours in the opposite direction from Calicut, sleep over, drive nine hours home and another five hours to Calicut. The young men persist doggedly. They declaim, repeat, and unrelentingly press their case.

When they finally leave, I look with complete empathy at Kamala's exhausted face. I have been here less than two days, and I don't know how she does it.

"As a good Muslim woman I am forbidden to write poems having to do with love, or sex," she says, returning to her eternal theme. "So, to test them I wrote a poem about how Allah should punish me because I loved someone more than I loved him."

This is the best news I've had since I arrived. I expected love to inspire Kamala's poetry but thought she would be censored. I'm excited to hear she is still writing.

"Your poems will reveal more than all those newspaper clippings," I say, knowing poetry is the truest mirror of her self. "I would very much like to hear the poem."

"Later," she says, and waves the topic away.

This unexpected withdrawal unsettles me. Why would she mention and then dismiss a poem she knows I want to hear? Perhaps my interest set off alarms for unknown dangers.

"What would happen if you left Islam?" I venture.

"They would kill me," she says matter of factly. "I am an icon for them."

It's 8 PM and we still haven't eaten when a new team of NDF men – "boys," Kamala calls them – takes over the mission of pressuring her to drive eighteen extra hours to their meeting. Calmly, then with increasing unease, excusing herself much longer than a person with a survival instinct would ever do, she explains that she's a heart patient, under doctors orders, too frail. She collapsed after her Bombay speech, surely they saw the newspaper photos of her on the ground. Unmoved, the disgruntled crew persists in arguing, beseeching, complaining, until they finally back out of the room, still pleading.

The maids are setting the table when a burly, older commando strides into the sitting-room, his three "brothers" waiting in the hall outside. He pushes a stool close to Kamala's chair, plunks himself down, spreads his legs, proffers a program, and stabs at Suraiya's name. Kamala shrinks back in her armchair. He harangues angrily. Kamala fiddles with her headdress to keep it straight. The man jabs at her, repeating that Suraiya must come, his group will lose face if she attends the Muslim League program in Calicut and not theirs, talking louder and faster when she tries to protest.

This exchange is translated for me later. Now all I hear is his threatening voice and her few, meek responses. All I see is her growing agitation, hands flying at her headdress, words tumbling out in abject apology, him leaning closer, intimidating, tormenting. She seems so helpless, he so overbearing, it's outrageous. Who is he to treat Kamala this way? Why does she stand for it? No matter how distressed she seems, he won't leave her alone.

I get up from the settee and place myself in the small space between him and her. I help Kamala to her feet and support her arm.

"Let's go, Kamala," I say. "Come lie down in your room."

I turn her toward her room merely fifteen paces away, and he stands to head us off. I pull at the wooden sitting room screen, attempting to make a barrier to halt his approach. She is facing him, making feeble protests, him more vehement, aggressive, staring her down. I turn her forcefully around, ushering her to her room.

"She can't," I say in English, almost crying. "She's sick, she can't."

He doesn't move and our eyes lock. In his I see a look I decipher immediately although I have never seen it before – blinding hate and rage.

I turn away quickly and find Kamala leaning crumpled against the wall of her room. "I feel I'm being bullied," she whispers. "So much pressure. I want to die."

"Who are they?"

"Terrorists." Her words are a sigh. "They kill."

She decides to go only to Calicut. She calls the police to report her travel plans, we finally sit to eat, and the phone rings. I answer and pass the Malayalam speaker to the new maid, Mini. Mini holds the phone to her ear, nodding yes, yes, face crunched with anxiety, moaning assent, crouched near the phone table for what seems like a very long time. She straightens up, shaking, crying, and Kamala tries to question her. It sounded like a Hindu voice, Mini says, someone who threatened before, but she's not sure. Neither Mini nor I remember the caller's telltale choice of appellation: Kamala or Suraiya. What Mini does remember, very clearly, is the caller's warning: "She must *not* speak at either program. She must *not* go to Calicut, or she will never reach there alive."

"You've just had a death threat, " I say, amazed.

"Yes, " Kamala agrees. "You should have been here when there were real death threats. This is a cup of tea."

She calls the police again, and they dispatch a guard to the house. She assures me the guards are "gunned," but I'm scared. First I provoke the head NDF commando into a murderous rage, and now someone else, from some other murky depths, threatens to off my hostess. All too soon I will have to go down the hall to my apartment, to a bedroom with easily broached windows, alone.

"Before, a big poster offered fifty lakhs (US$100,000) to kill me," Kamala says to reassure me. "Then the price went up to one crore (US$200,000), and Monu sent his congratulations. They threatened to cut out my and Sadiq Ali's intestines, wrap them around each other, and float our corpses down the river."

"Come to Canada," I suggest.

"Temporary relief," she demurs. "This will never end until I am dead."

The phone rings and she snatches it before Mini reaches it. She listens, making quick, animal-like sounds – "chee, chee, chee" – like a forest bird with people close to its nest. Mini sits on the floor, cradling her head. Within the Malayalam words, I hear Kamala say, "death threats," but mostly she makes those strange sounds while Sadiq Ali's wife berates her for stories published in a recent scandal sheet and for the resulting ridicule her children endured at school.

"I am actually sick of his wife shouting at me, crude girl," Kamala says afterward. "The first wife has eczema, some disease, he can't touch her. The second wife is thin as a stick. He's irresponsible. Sometimes he leaves them without money. I sent 25,000 rupees for his boy's treatment. I'm willing to take responsibility for the whole wretched family. But she shouldn't harangue me on the phone."

My face is interviewer-proof unflappable, but inside is a high-decibel "*Whaaat!*" Reflexively, I feel sorry for the wife and disapprove of the husband-stealer. On the other hand, it's wives, not wife, and the husband is allowed two more. I can't imagine what the wives are feeling. They seem upset, yet they accept Kamala's money.

The phone rings with Monu's return call about the trip to Calicut. "These threats are normal for you. Just go."

Finally, the night cops arrive, dark-skinned, resplendent in starched mustard uniforms, beautifully hatted, belted, gunned. I have never ever been so happy to see policemen. One, I swear, is as handsome as Krishna.

"We will definitely protect you," he says, twinkling wildly.

The phone rings with final arrangements for Kamala's trip to Calicut.

"Maybe I won't go," I tell her, exhausted beyond belief.

"You're scared, Merrily?"

"Yes."

"I'll put you at Sulu's."

"But you're going?"

"I get these death threats three times a week. Only this time Mini picked up. Usually, it's me. I say, 'Yes, yes, we'll see.' I'll go with the policemen, that's all. I've always been brave."

She begins rummaging in the cupboard, pulling out camp cots, while I lug mattresses into the corridor for the policemen. I help make the beds and all of us, Kamala, cook, maid, policemen, are chatting in the makeshift, low-watt hallway dorm when I hear Kamala say, "After the nuclear blast, we can stand tall. When I get up to make a speech now, I say, 'I'm not a Gandhian. I believe in violence when necessary.'" I lean against the wall. I'm so tired and her comment seems so incongruous, I start to laugh. In the afternoon, when she despaired of losing the kind of love she'd had with Sadiq Ali, I reminded her she's only been interested in men for three months.

"Yes," she admitted. "I'm interested in death too."

Well, I'm not.

Yet I want to see Kamala in action, feted, being the star she enjoys so much. I wave good night, noting uncharitably that her black purdah now seems less glamorous than my first impression, and open the door to the heat wave in my room. I fumble with the mobile phone Kamala left me and connect to Canada Direct. First I reach my youngest daughter, Anna, then Arnie. Anna takes the long-distance pulse, assessing the gravity of the situation, not sure what I should do. Arnie says, "Come home."

I hold the dead receiver in my sweaty hands. The AC is broken and the windows must stay shut in case the mosquito net doesn't hold. Should I go to Calicut. Or not?

# 14

## Beyond the Outskirts of the City

I sleep fitfully, and in the morning find Kamala lounging in her chair, comfy and at ease. I rest too, relaxing my legs under my big skirt and smiling at the memory of "switched-off" Kamala, so certain no one could ever rekindle her desire. And as I'm thinking of the change in her, she says, "I'm all fingerprinted with him," her cry constant as the call of a mourning dove. "I feel like I've been in rehearsal for this all my life. He was in a taxi going home and there were bunches of Hindu fanatics on every corner. He got scared."

I ask again about the poem she dared to write, and to please me, or to share her suffering, or perhaps because transforming sadness into words redeems it, she finds it, warning me that she might read in a halting voice.

She studies the Malayalam silently and explains that the poem is called "This Coming Friday," because "every Friday in Saudi Arabia people are executed and dismembered for their crimes."

Ya Allah!
At least now
punish me.
I did love him more
than I ever loved you
I found bliss in the scent of his perspiration
His perfect teeth became my necklace of prayer beads.
Chop off my arms that sort the treasures of his body
This coming Friday
go beyond the outskirts of the city
and on top of the hill
imprison me.

Pluck out my eyes
the eyes that did not have enough of his splendour.
Pluck out my heart
that missed a beat loving him.
Let blood flow from my bosom
like the fountain in the palace of the king.
I am a sinner, a fallen one.
I worshipped a mere human being.
My ears, listening to the music of my mate
did not properly hear the ten commandments coming from the sky
and in my ecstasy
I forgot every commandment.

I watch the Malayalam poetry flow though Kamala's mind, marvelling at her bilingual brilliance.

This Friday let it happen
my punishment.
Chop off my limbs that curled round him
like creepers around a tree
Remove my lips that kissed him
and went on kissing
this heart that loved
and was exhausted from loving
and afterwards let the remnants be wrapped up
the remnants of the sword sport
wrap them in white silk and bury them in the ground
Allah!
Oh kind one!
Do not any longer show me compassion
because I am Suraiya
a slave
who is asking only for punishment.

She finishes and tosses the poem to the side as if it has drained her dry. I stand silently beside the desk, moved by the extremity of her love, her translation feat, and the existence of this defiant poem.

I ride an auto rickshaw to the Ernakulam boat jetty, worried by a scene I can't forget: a commando is sitting at Kamala's feet, her foot resting on his thigh, his hand on her calf. He gazes up at her like an imploring suitor, and it seems to me he is massaging and stroking her calf with a sensuality beyond the call of respect and duty. It frightens me with its similarity to Winnie Mandela and her commandos – an isolated older woman hungry for affection, the proximity of lithe young male "protectors," the daily intimacy, covert sexuality, the shifting sands of power.

I board a two-rupee inter-island ferry to Willingdon Island, and the racket of the interior motor trumps my concern. I begin to notice the boat's plank floors, its hand-hewn struts, and the dark-haired women in red, yellow, purple, orange, pink, and gold-trimmed saris on the worn benches around me. Through the airy open sides I see the ocean-like vista of Vembanad Lake, and boys and young men standing outside on the bow, joking. The carved prow heads into the waves, the mainland recedes.

At Willingdon Island I leap onto the covered wood jetty and walk down Malabar Road, along the lake, to the excellently appointed Taj Malabar where Kamala has arranged for me to swim. I drag myself through the first laps, feeling suppleness and strength return as I swim. On the last length I decide to go to Calicut. Then I sit in a swing staring out at the water and the ferries chugging by.

I had forgotten how hot and bright day is in Kerala. In Kamala's house the blinds are permanently drawn, and fans whir to stir the air. Dark wood bookcases hold literary and humanitarian awards and heavy wood furniture is covered with dark upholstery. At Kamala's, in the best of times, time stops in the palm of her hand. Then, on the cool dark set, the poet entertains, or amuses herself with her guests. Other times, like last night and this afternoon, the drama spirals out of control. It unnerves me. But Kamala, who has loved play-acting since she was a girl, cares only that the drama plays.

"Would we go to Calicut in one car or two?" I ask, knowing Mr Abdulkhader, a *Chandrika* editor, is making the trip with her.

"One," she says.

"Policemen?"

"No, this death threat is nothing, Merrily. Writers in India get them all the time."

"You like the danger," I challenge. "I think you enjoy it."

"Yes, I do," she admits. "It's like a fragrance. The fragrance of danger."

"Come back to Canada with me. You can work there."

"I don't want to work. I worked every day since I was eighteen. I just want to live. Anyway," she adds fatalistically, "they'll kill me sometime. The only question is when."

I pray to every god there is that this is not true. And selfishly, since I am accompanying Kamala tomorrow, not on the way to Calicut.

The cement-block bedroom closes in, heat 32 degrees, no AC, now no power, therefore no fan. If I were smarter, I would flip the emergency switch, but I don't know there is one. Instead, I take shallow breaths. Every inhalation feels like it's dripping moisture back into my lungs, bronchi, alveoli. I want to run outside, gulp lighter air and let it dry my suffocating skin. I spend the night in the shower knowing I can't take this much longer but too depleted to plan beyond.

At 6 AM Mini rings the bell. I follow her downstairs and greet Kamala, who is securing her headscarf with bobby-pins. The door opens and the Imam interrupts to chant prayers.

Then, we wait for Abdulkhader, the *Chandrika* editor, and he, Kamala, and I squeeze into the back seat of the Ambassador. The spiffy policeman sits in front with the driver, and with AC on low, we leave the ragged outskirts of Cochin for the Malabar coast.

## ALWAYE, PERIYAR RIVER, ANGAMALI, CHALAKUDI

Someday I will drive the Malabar coast again. When I am not so tired. When Abdulkhader and I are not trying, impossibly, to keep our bodies apart. When Kamala's consciousness is not flowing so freely and there is less to scribble.

"I was seeped in misery and now I am verdant with adolescent dreams," she says. "I shall not be grounded by age, illness, widowhood. It's only that we should have confidence. I plan a little mischief, distribute myself to the cannibals, and grow stronger."

## THRISSUR

We stop at St Joseph's Convent where Kamala boarded when she was eight. "I was so scared, I could not sleep at night. My grandmother gave me a cushion and said, 'Call it Krishna, put it on your face and think of him, it will get rid of the night terrors.' I take it with me even now."

Through the window I see Malayali nuns in dark starched habits ushering a gaggle of children through high iron gates. The nuns are covered from head to toe, like Kamala.

## KUNNAMKULAM

We pass richly cultivated fields, traditional wood houses with second-storey verandahs, and a temple elephant en route to Guruvayur Temple.

"Malabar remained underdeveloped. The Malabaris are a softer people, more emotional."

## EDAPPALI, THE PONNANI RIVER

Kamala alternates between talking, legs crossed under her dress, and leaning back, splay-legged, sleeping. I crane my neck for glimpses of the countryside, a diversion from Kamala's interior journey. Sometimes her head lolls onto my shoulder and she rights it. Now her head is resting against the seat, mouth open, lifeless. It worries me because we have been driving four hours without a stop to stimulate the circulation. If Abdulkhader weren't here, I'd put my hand over her mouth to check her breathing. Finally, I feel the rise and fall of her chest against my arm.

I am cramped and tired. Abdulkhader sweats despite the AC. He tells me we will drive five and a half hours to Calicut; Kamala will speak at 5 PM; tomorrow we will drive three and a half hours to Kasaragod; she will speak again; we will sleep in Kasaragod and drive nine hours back to Cochin.

Really, it is too much. These men, and she is surrounded by men, use her without consideration. They hoist their shining star to reflect glory back on themselves.

### KOTTAKKAL

Kamala awakes and somehow dredges up a twinkle. "So, no one has killed us yet."

### CALICUT

We plough through the clogged outskirts of Calicut to the palm-lined entrance of the Taj Residency where Chief Editor Hanifa, flanked by liveried staff, waits with a 100-kilowatt smile. I retrieve my bags and crumpled pillow. Someone helps Kamala out of the car. She looks for me and waits until I come. Her feet are painfully swollen and she can hardly see. I crook my arm and hold it steady, parallel to the ground. She balances on my arm as on a railing, and we walk through the marble hall, past the gawking desk staff, into the elevator, and up to white sheets and room service.

Kamala bathes, I swim, and at 4:45 PM, Abdulkhader, the policeman, Kamala, and I are fully dressed and ready to be picked up for her 5 PM appearance. She wears a plum silk dress gifted by an admirer, and thick gold necklaces. "Gold makes me strong, gives me worth," she says, tightening her burqua to hide their immodest shine.

I too have been invited to speak and am busy working on my notes. To entertain herself, Kamala tells Abdulkhader my history: I am related to the Lindsays and the Fords through my maternal grandfather, I have a gold medal in swimming, and I am very wealthy but discreet.

An hour later we're still waiting, and Kamala realizes that the delay may jeopardize her 7 PM insulin shot. She reminds Abdulkhader that she needs insulin to live, and he promises she'll have a private room to administer the shot.

At 6:30 PM, our car collects us, drives along a main thoroughfare, and turns onto a narrow side-street leading to Calicut's largest auditorium, Tagore Centenary Hall. People are massed five deep outside the gates and lining the driveway to the auditorium. The car inches forward through the crowds. Men surge, contained by guards. Swells of covered women press, push, and shove, jockeying for a glimpse of Suraiya.

The instant Kamala opens the car door, she's mobbed by women trying to touch her. In the seconds before I realize I have to fight my way out of the car, we are separated. She is swept forward, and I am immobilized in a press of bodies. She arches back to find me, reaches out to me, but I can only move where the crowd moves, or be trampled. She calls to me, and finally the women see what she wants. Yelling and shoving, they form a cordon around me, pushing others aside and me forward until I am at Kamala's side. At the same moment the policeman reappears, and a giant human wave propels us to our seats.

Kamala sits centre stage flanked by the deputy mayor, city police commissioner, other prominent men, and me. The prominent women sit in the row behind, wearing saris, unlike their burqua-clad star. The paparazzi lean across the table, focus their 4 x 6s, and flash into Kamala's eyes. Thousands wait expectantly in the auditorium, and thousands more watch on TV monitors outside the hall.

Kamala's eyes close during the inaugural recitation of the Koran. Then, with a slow, deliberate delivery, more melodious than any I've heard in English, Hanifa welcomes the assembly. Two speakers follow, after which Hanifa graciously introduces me.

I stand and face more people than I have ever faced in my life. I'm not nervous because I'm in a state of extreme unreality. Jewish agnostic me stands at the mike in front of thousands of observant Muslims, but they don't know who I am. Only I know I'm here. It's the weirdest sensation. I'm invisible. I feel invincible. It's funny, an inside joke with myself. Also, vetted by Kamala, I too have something to preach.

"This speech will be strange but short," I say softly, distinctly, words translated as I speak. "I came to Kerala because I read the glorious poetry of Dr Suraiya. Suraiya is not only the star of Islam but a leading light of world literature."

This is greeted with the heady, exhilarating, utterly thrilling applause of thousands. For a moment I feel the seduction that Kamala must feel – the power to move masses, the warmth of their adoration, possibly even their love.

"I have been with Dr Suraiya four exhausting days," I continue, "and I am worried about her health. Suraiya suffers from cardiac disease, yet tomorrow she is scheduled to drive many more hours. No one would ask this of their own Amma. Please protect Suraiya, one of the greatest poets in the world."

There is polite applause, and I'm surprised there is even that. But I am rewarded by Kamala's appreciation and the look of astonishment on Hanifa's face.

Now, chief guest Kamala/Suraiya rises, face framed in black. Raising her arm in greeting, she floats toward centre stage.

A field of hands waves back at her.

When she reaches the mike, she faces the hall, lifting her arms to the sky and her eyes to the heavens. She appears enraptured.

"*Bismillah al rahman al rahim,* in the name of God, the compassionate, the merciful," she says ecstatically, "the words of the prophet are in me, this inner feeling takes me to God."

The audience appears mesmerized. Her tone is intimate, open, vulnerable. Her words enter her listeners' hearts and draw them close. The hospital director beside me hangs on every word, and seeing that I don't understand Malayalam, translates as she speaks:

"We should not allow dowries. It's actually buying the groom for money. When men demand and receive dowry, they are aiding and abetting an immoral act, just like male prostitutes."

Women giggle, the audience applauds, and Kamala's voice takes on strength.

"Your wife will tell you, you have been bought by us for fifteen lakhs. I plead with the young men of Kerala. You laugh at the poor male prostitutes. You, doctors, lawyers, don't become prostitutes too."

The doctor stops translating when he fears missing anything. Rhetoric is an admired art in India, and Kamala is a master. She segues into the words of the last prophet who said, if I remember Kabir correctly, that heaven is at the feet of the mother.

"It is not enough to distance oneself from society by saying, 'I have not committed any sin.' Allah will accept only good deeds. Only if we follow the path of love will we reach Allah."

The hall rocks with applause. The editor-in-charge proposes a vote of thanks. The finance manager presents a memento to Kamala/Suraiya, and the minute she sits, people leave in droves.

It's now 7:30, and Kamala's insulin shot is half an hour late. I appeal to the doctor to be taken to the promised private room. With Hanifa and Abdulkhader leading, we inch through crowds of women who thrust their heads onto Kamala's chest, grab her clothing, and smile in complicity when they connect, because now they too can claim, "I touched her in person. It was not a dream." I push more forcibly toward the room where she will inject herself, and we make it to the

folding chair in the centre. Finally she sits. We notice a smell but have no time to trace it. Kamala has taken out her syringe before we realize we are in a dirty toilet. The light is too weak for her to see. Afraid she will inject the insulin into an artery or a vein, she puts the syringe away.

"This is disgusting," she says.

There's no question: we have to go back to the hotel. Hanifa is reluctant to re-lease his chief guest, so Kamala agrees to return later. The policeman and I flank her though a gauntlet of clutching hands, the driver efficiently opens and shuts the car door, and suddenly we're released.

"I feel they are eating me," she sighs. "I feel their teeth when they kiss me."

We get to the hotel, Kamala administers her shot, and we order tomato soup and toast, the fastest items on the menu, so we can return to the hall.

"What a smelly room," Kamala says. "It stank of urine. So coarse. All this for a man. And now look."

"Yes," I agree, "it's a mess."

"And I didn't even get the man," she says sorrowfully.

And then the sadness of lost love pours forth – love tasted only in the words of others and only imagined in words. Love created from ashes, or bestowed on others. Love for a grandmother who could never have imagined, did not even know the words, could never be told what her injunction to "be a good wife" took from her granddaughter. Love that felt so perverted, so indecent, so sordid, she

> walked through streets beside
> The sea, where the barges
> Float, their undersides rotting and the garbage
> Rot, and the dead fish rot,
> And I smelt the smell of dying things and the
> Heavy smell of rotting
> Dead.

The rest of what she says etches itself on my mind but I write only phrases: "blue Krishna ... fleshy backside ... rape ... old men touching ... only love," be-cause Kamala is crying brokenly. I have never seen her cry before.

"How can I get out of it?" she sobs into the silence.

There is nothing to say. Nothing anyone can do. I would like to hold her but I move closer instead.

Then, she finds the loop, the evocation.

"'Soft as rain on the slanting wheat will be our mating,' he said. So gentle, so beautiful in Malayalam. He said, 'I will kiss your frail legs and make them stronger. I will kiss your sagging breasts. I love your weak parts. Don't worry about my weight,' he said, 'I'll be like an evening breeze hovering over the wheat fields.' Afterwards, I said I felt dirty, grimy. He said he would wash me. He took a towel and wet it and cleaned me. That was very tender. He said, 'Don't feel dirty, we will get married on the 12th, as soon as you become a Muslim.' I booked a room at the South Park Hotel and asked the Imam of Trivandrum to marry us. I had helped poor Muslim women and had sent them to him. I invited six or seven guests. Then I converted. And all hell broke loose."

She has stopped crying now. I look at her swollen feet and wonder how she plans to travel again tomorrow. I know I can't go any further: I've depleted my reserves. Apologizing, I excuse myself for being unable to continue to Kasaragod. Finally, Kamala realizes she is exhausted as well.

"I want to go home. Let's tell them I am unconscious," she suggests.

Before I can dial the doctor, Abdulkhader rings.

"She is almost unconscious," I say. "I'm calling the doctor."

"Let me speak to the driver," Abdulkhader demands.

I cover the phone. Kamala preps the driver.

"She is almost unconscious," the driver reports.

Fifteen minutes later, as Kamala sprawls in a chair chatting, we hear a knock on the door. I hustle her back to bed and lift her feet onto a pile of pillows. Six men stand in the corridor with gilt-wrapped gifts. They wait while the doctor examines her and to my great relief says Suraiya cannot drive to Kasaragod tomorrow.

Hanifa looks at me, confers with the others, and they push toward the door.

"But Suraiya is exhausted, almost unconscious," I say, Abdulkhader translating. "She can't receive all of you."

Still, they list toward the door, their presents like passports before them.

"She's sick," I shout, so immersed in the crisis scenario that I'm convinced if I don't stop them, they will drag my semi-conscious friend to Kasaragod. "None of you care about her," my voice breaks, my hands make fluttery gestures. I look, I am sure, unpredictable.

Chastened, or not up to dealing with a loopy woman, Hanifa reschedules the gift-giving for the morning. I wait until they are gone, collapse in my room, and call Kamala's mobile.

"I'm not answering the door because I think someone might come in," she says.

"They have gone. They'll be back at 8 AM tomorrow."

"Has Abdulkhader accepted?"

"Yes."

"I don't have to go tomorrow?" She sounds like a little girl, plaintive.

"No."

"Thank you, Merrily."

At eight the next morning, we report to the lobby and Hanifa breezes in, waving *Chandrika's* early edition like a prize. Kamala's hand darts out and pulls the front page close to her eyes. She scans the photos of herself and the crowd, sees the entire text of her speech, and makes a sound like a happy grunt. On cue, the Kasaragod proponents move in, until Kamala's nephew delivers the non-negotiable directive from her son.

"Amma's son says she must return home and take it easy," reports the eldest son of her eldest brother.

Since any good widow must obey her son, this cultural imperative sets us free. I collect the Asianet videos from reception and put my arm out for Kamala. She rises and no one stops her. Slowly, painstakingly, we walk through the ornate Taj doors into our pre-arranged car.

The long trip home is refreshed by a pit stop for cool, tender coconut water, and when we return, I find the AC still broken and the rooms not yet cleansed of the odour and belongings of the commandos. Luckily, I've heard of a good medium-range hotel minutes away by cab, and when I suggest that I move, Kamala is too tired to object. I pack my bag, cross the two bridges between Gandhi Nagar and downtown Ernakulam/Cochin, and register at the clean, efficient Metropolitan Hotel.

The room has two twin beds, a half-wall of windows, hand-crafted wood furniture, a writing desk, armchair, good lighting, and a safe feeling of anonymity. The AC has three working speeds, and the windows open and have screens. I call home to tell Arnie I have returned safely and give him my new numbers. I turn the AC to low and open the windows wide. The room is cool. I actually feel a breeze. I cuddle into bed, covered by a crisp white sheet and my soft, companionable Pashmina shawl.

# 15

## The Fear of the Year

I am awakened by the phone. On the line is a Das family confidant, just landed on one of his flying visits to Cochin. He asks if I want a lift to Kamala's and I say yes, because it's such an unusual call.

I'm hardly in the car before he begins his rapid-fire patter. Hunched, fidgeting in the far corner, eyes obscured by dark glasses, he gives me the party line on Kamala's conversion, the one I must follow, clarifying why I'm suddenly on his radar.

"Suraiya cannot leave Islam," he says categorically. "It would be an insult to the faith. These people believe in blood. They would wipe out not only her but the whole family, the entire brood. If they kill her, it will be all right, she's had a good life. She can even get out of it by committing suicide. But we are worried about her children's children, the little ones."

The briefing seems impersonal, something he's done before.

"Suraiya has become a cult figure. In mosques around the world, they say a prayer to her. She *must* be careful what she says. These 'boys' who come to her house have AK 47s and bombs. I know them."

He stops to see that I understand, and in that brief hiatus, his extremities do a jerky hand-feet jive of which he is seemingly unaware. And of course I understand what he wants. Like everyone close to Kamala, I am expected to stop her from speaking her mind.

"Sadiq Ali has been interrogated and has confessed to receiving one million dollars from Saudi Arabia to convince Kamala Das to convert, money he says he's given to charity."

"He never meant to marry her?" I ask incredulously.

"Never."

"But he was so clever about it."

"Not so clever. He is like a young boy who takes a girl from a good Hindu family and makes her pregnant, and then there are consequences."

"But he was clever about how he went about it."

"Yes," the friend agrees regretfully, "that he was."

I remind him that Kamala's eldest son supported Kamala's conversion, stood next to her during the conversion ceremony and on CNN.

"Publicly, he had to be wildly enthusiastic," the friend explains. "The other sons were not so enthusiastic, but now they are too. It's a question of survival."

The driver pulls into the driveway of Kamala's building. "The lawyer there is a Muslim League plant," cautions the friend. "They're all watching to see she behaves herself."

The friend greets Sulaiman, the lawyer, warmly, and so do I. During dinner Sulaiman worries that if Kamala admits she converted for love, it will insult the faith. "You cannot do just as you wish," he says to her, as if speaking to a child.

"You had a vision," the friend reminds Kamala, "a sign from God."

John, the driver, is summoned as witness to the vision of the red rolling sun. He testifies in the dining-room, holding the edge of his mundu, buck teeth protruding. "Bugs Bunny," Kamala calls him.

"Why would he lie?" Sulaiman asks rhetorically. "He is not of the faith."

"But isn't love one of the highest of human emotions?" I venture.

"Love of who? Not love of man, but love of God. All other loves are subservient to that," Sulaiman says, pointing and jabbing with a jolly giggle. "It is like a child who has faith in his parents and feels at peace. Or a woman knowing her husband will protect her, she is at peace."

"Yes, yes, well said," the friend exhorts.

"Islam means submission to God. Only then can you have peace," Sulaiman says.

"God showed her a vision, and that man is taking all the credit," the friend fumes. "It's like I fly to New York for business and make a deal, and my pilot takes all the credit. Someone should do something about him."

"No, no," Kamala pleads softly.

"He talked to her of Islam, taught her the prayers. That is his contribution," Sulaiman says. Then he leans toward me in a professorial manner and tells me what all good Muslims must do: "Believe in God. In the Prophet. In the Book. In prayer, fasting, pilgrimage to Mecca. Believe the Prophet is the last great Prophet." Sulaiman's exposition takes a long time. He makes very sure I understand that submission brings peace.

"Yes, yes, quite right," the friend choruses like a hallelujah.

Satisfied with his contribution, Sulaiman begins a six-minute fable. It is about the Prophet and his angel – only Sulaiman pronounces "angel" as "angle."

"The Prophet's angle was dying, and the Prophet wanted him to embrace Islam, not to make him a convert but so they could meet in heaven, not hell. But the angle was stubborn and didn't want to convert. The Prophet spoke and spoke, but only God could reveal the light, and God did not. So the angle died out of Islam."

A hysterical giggle froths in my chest. I suppress it because I know how serious this is. Which oddly, makes it funnier. First, the list of five things a good Muslim must do, now the dying angle, the point being the authenticity of Kamala's conversion. I do my best not to catch Kamala's eye. There's a dangerous twinkle there too.

"That man taught Suraiya about Islam, he showed her the prayers, but only God could show her the light," Sulaiman concludes.

"Yes, he did," says Kamala, "how to pray. The prayers."

"The proof is, the man is gone but her faith is strong, strong," says Sulaiman, punching the air.

"Right, right," the friend exhorts.

Sulaiman expounds for another ten minutes, during which Kamala and the friend leave the room and return. Now Sulaiman pauses, his eyes soften, and disarmingly, in his friendly old Sulaiman voice, he says to me, "Suppose my words mean something to you. If so, maybe you will love God because of them."

I remember Hanifa saying how good I'd look in purdah, and feel open arms beckoning me into the fold.

"Sulaiman is a real moderate, a real moderate," the friend emphasizes, so I know where we all stand.

Kamala starts talking about her speeches. About how she begins with praise to Allah. "I feel the light in my eyes, the limelight shining down, I fix them with my stare."

"But you can't see," I say.

"I can't see, but they see my eyes."

Sulaiman congratulates her on her anti-dowry speech published in *Chandrika*, and I report that it made the women behind me laugh, which makes Kamala more cheerful. Perhaps without me as mirror and interrogator, buoyed by honours, trips, hosannas, and her own imaginative powers, she will find ways to weather the storm.

"You see what we have to do," the family friend says as he drives me back to the hotel. "Not the man. God. A vision."

"She watched herself at dinner," I say defending Kamala.

"She better watch her mouth, or she'll get another one, six inches down. Any moment she could blow the whole thing apart."

"I think she knows what's going on. She's not stupid."

"No, she's not. She knows," he says angrily. "And if you write anything about this, no one will believe you. They'll say it's a Zionist plot. Zionists disparage Muslim leaders all the time."

I thought I knew what this self-appointed family protector wanted when we drove to Kamala's, but I don't know what he wants now.

Night washes over me, bestowing a solid, pill-free sleep. I shower while the downstairs restaurant prepares a package of veggie cutlets, yellow tadka dhal, roti, and masala fried fish to bring to Kamala's. The desk clerk orders a cab, and we drive across the canals to Kamala's apartment in Gandhi Nagar. This is the first day in weeks that I have felt physically normal. I am restricting my "prepared tea" intake, that addictive zap of "dust" tea cooked with milk and sugar, the Indian espresso. I have a space of my own and an escape route – auto to Ernakulam boat jetty, ferry to Willingdon Island, and the walk under the glorious mayflower trees along Malabar Road to the Taj pool. I spend part of each day swimming, writing poolside, eating light food, and shooing away the cheeky, persistent crows.

But I am discombobulated by colliding fact and fiction, by all there is to see that I don't see and don't understand. It's like getting older and slowly realizing how much there is to know that you don't know. Except this realization is happening too fast.

It is Friday, and Sulaiman calls Kamala to pray at the mosque. She considers accepting as a rehearsal for Qatar, but she has been avoiding praying in public for decades, "They'll all stare at me." She tells Sulaiman she is going to the doctor, and instead accompanies me to a jewellery store to buy sapphire and diamond earrings for my eldest daughter.

On this rare, unscheduled outing, she is like a schoolgirl. "What fun to be with you," she says in the back seat of the Ambassador. "I am free, more than free." She mentions another writer researching her biography with a more bibliographic approach than mine, and says she prefers that I write about her.

"What would like me to write?" I respond.

"Write about all of it, the conversion. Write the truth. What I did for love. I don't care about religion. Religion is like a garb, like this Muslim costume."

"But they may hurt you."

"I don't mind dying. Sadiq Ali has already killed me." She is talking through tears. "Warn your aunties I'm coming. Tell them my love story."

"You can tell them," I say, hoping she'll return to Canada.

"A sad story," she says. Then perks up. "Or a happy story. I can make it sad or happy, depending on the audience."

I know this is true, I've seen her do it. I try to distract her with talk of Shyamprasad's feature film *Agnisakshi* (Fire as witness), which Gita Krishnankutty screened for me at her house in Madras. One of Shyamprasad's first TV films was based on Kamala's story "A Summer Vacation," and she likes his work. But she finds this film, about a modern Brahmin woman alienated from her traditional family, too grim.

"I told him, 'Make a woman laugh, then make her cry, that is the secret of a good film. Not make her cry, cry, cry. What message is that for women today?'" She sketches a possible premise for a film she'd prefer – about a woman who plays games, makes mischief, and play-acts all her life, until one day the play-acting becomes too real.

I feel caught out. This was the very thought I had about Kamala. I can see the beginning of the film.

"And what is the ending?" I ask.

"There is no ending as yet. What is the ending, indeed?"

John negotiates the narrow streets, the Ambassador climbing sidewalks and honking past carts, autos, people, trucks, to the jeweller's gilt door where we enter

a showroom ringed with counters of glittering gold and walls draped with brilliant 24-carat displays. A salesman massages his colleague's back. Another polishes
a tray of hand-crafted bangles, fondling, almost caressing each piece.

Kamala, in gold-embroidered burqua and heavy gold and coral necklace,
heads familiarly up the staircase to the counters of precious stones. Diamonds
wink at us as we settle into upholstered chairs, and tailored salesmen swoop to
serve us. I hesitantly choose earrings with dark Ceylonese sapphires and diamonds, almost within my daughter's budget. The staff humours me, waiting for
Kamala, the real buyer. When I'm done, the owner's nephew smooths a fine white
cloth in front of her, and attendants hand him an array of choice diamond nose
rings to display. Kamala picks three, looks in the mirror, places each singly against
her nose, inserts her favourite, and with a rapidity that astounds me, buys it.

"Now I won't appear a pauper in front of the Amir's wife. I'll sparkle on stage
in Qatar."

Mustache bristling, the owner's nephew angles forward interrupting.
"Madam, why did you convert? We feel betrayed" – followed by further bombast
in Malayalam.

All business stops. Salesmen line up to stare at Kamala. Customers gawk from
their plush chairs. Kamala responds, and the nephew thrusts his face closer, his
staccato words like darts. "'Come back to Hinduism,'" she translates.

"Is he bothering you?" I ask. He seems so aggrieved.

"I am feeling sad. I'm a stupid fool," she says. "It's not his fault."

A jewel box with Kamala's purchase is placed on the counter. The nephew
persists, everyone watching. I want to leave.

"They're not being nice to you," I say.

"They're being nice," she answers.

"How?" I wonder.

"They have ordered coffee for me."

She smiles her bright, charming smile, the one that signals a resolve to forget
problems, insults, sadness.

I ask the nephew to please not push Kamala anymore, and tell him he's
making her sad. Reluctantly, he desists. When I mention that she will soon be
visiting me, he offers to be her secretary so he can get a US visa, and to pay his
ticket and hers.

"Certainly I would like a secretary to carry my bags," Kamala says, accepting his mobile number. He follows us down the marble steps, miming carrying bags, Kamala holding my arm and the golden banister, murmuring, "Lovely, lovely, my own secretary to carry my bags."

We wait inside the ornate doors for the car.

"Normally I am scared to go into a Hindu shop," Kamala says. "I did it only because you asked."

"Were you angry at him for pressuring you?" I ask.

"Not angry. He said, 'Come back to Hinduism. We are all so sad.'"

"What did you say?"

"'Won't the Muslims kill me like the Hindu fanatics? I am caught between the two.' 'We'll send our people to protect you,' he said. I told him I couldn't afford to feed them. He said, 'We'll pay.'"

"Great," I laugh, "Hindu guards and Muslim commandos can party at your house."

As we wait downstairs for the car, a first-floor salesman hails Kamala from the other end of the room. Other salesmen line up behind him, and business stops downstairs too. He raises his voice, "But madam, why did you leave your religion?"

Our car is idling on the curb outside, but they won't let Kamala go.

She responds in a full-bodied voice that carries throughout the glittering store. Only to herself does she say softly, "Sometimes I still say Krishna's name. Krishna is still with me."

"What did you say?" I ask as I help her down the steps. If it were me, I would not like others presuming they could control my life, nor would I tolerate their intrusive, incessant questioning.

"They said, 'Madam, why did you convert? We feel so betrayed.' I was just teasing them. I asked, 'Don't you know me? Don't you know my writings? Why would I do it except for love?' They said they guessed, but they weren't sure. 'Don't you love me?' I asked. 'Yes, we do,' they told me. I said, 'Why didn't you tell me? I would have gone with you.'"

On the way home Kamala tells me a caste law story her great-grandmother told her, about Ammu, a sixteen-year-old Nalapat girl, touched by a piece of material thrown by an untouchable:

And because Nayars were defiled by contact with untouchables, she was cast out. She hid in a field, and a Muslim found her there. He promised to look after her, took her home, and married her. Five years passed and her brother, learning of her fate, went in a palanquin to carry her off. He found his sister at the back of the house nursing a robust baby.

"Come with me now, the palanquin is waiting," he said.

"My husband is the life of my life, and I am his. I cannot leave him," Ammu answered.

"If you don't come, you will destroy the family honour," said her brother, unsheathing his dagger. And when he returned to Nalapat, the blade was dripping with blood.

"The Nalapat brother has killed his sister," said the villagers.

"See how I have avenged the family honour," boasted the brother. And then he buried his knife. But my great-grandmother told me that no Nalapat brother would kill his sister, and he must have plunged that dagger into a goat.

"The Nalapats were angry at me for telling the secret," Kamala tells me. "They want me to forget. But I find this story so moving. When I joined in my conversion, I said, 'As a Nalapat, I owe something to the Muslims.' Now I am making amends."

Kamala's elderly ex-neighbour from the Ambady Apartments, accompanied by the Ambady's sweeper lady, is waiting when we return. The old lady seats herself at Kamala's feet and holds her hand.

I sit on the settee, writing in my notebook. When I look up, I see Kamala crying. I leave the writing and perch on the table beside her chair. Kamala wipes her face with her chador. "She is the only one of her generation who comes to see me," she whispers. "The community has chucked me out. She is eighty years old, a Nayar woman like me."

Hunched in white khadi, the frail old widow murmurs like a stream over round stones, gently stroking Kamala's hand. Kamala cries silently, head framed in black against the chair back, face set in sadness, eyes closed. I hold her other hand. Her maidservant, Ammu, stands at the side, patting her shoulder. Kamala opens her eyes and I see our tableau of grief, the tragedy of her ostracization, and my place in the iconic frieze.

"Even her relatives would throw her out if she came to see me. It touches me, a beautiful gesture," Kamala says.

The gesture makes her remember all she's lost, and as her face becomes sadder, the old woman strokes, burbles, talks, until Kamala smiles, dimpling her tragic mask.

"She says she always remembers me wearing the amulet, a Hindu thing. She is looking for it now. She is saying that when her children see me on TV, they say how beautiful I look, how young."

"She's trying to cheer you up."

"Yes, she loves me," Kamala says, trying to regain her strength. "So many people love me."

Inching her stool closer, the old lady buries her head in Kamala's lap. She lies there, her neat, tight bun unmoving, until Kamala raises the silvery head between her hands. The old lady reaches forward too, cradling Kamala's face in her outstretched hands. Now they are looking directly into each other's eyes. As one, they lean forward, pulling closer to each other. The old lady's delicate skin touches the crown of Kamala's chador. Their foreheads meet.

"You are sweating," the old lady says when they draw back. "Because of this," she says, pointing to the chador.

Film producer Prakash and his young colleague, Winnie, the final visitors of the day, are a relief and are thus invited to dinner. Kamala does a riff on the proper male guardian to take to Qatar, "a very orthodox society with Friday executions." Kabir wants to go, but she has invited her son Chinnen so that she will feel comfortable uncovering her hair at night. Again I suggest a woman, saying I've discovered how much fun it is to travel with my women friends.

"Better to take a monkey," she responds, lifting her arms in leaping motions. "It will jump, and its long tail," she traces the tail in the air, "will be lovely."

Prakash, Winnie, and I crack up. The monkey's absurdist antics are a perfect ending to the day.

# 16

## A Pale Green Pond

People arrive to help Kamala practise her prayers and prepare for her trip to Qatar. She says they will work her hard there: state functions, public speeches, and the appearance at the mosque for which she's rehearsing her prayers. She has memorized thirty Arabic phrases, but with her Sadiq Ali hopes fading, can't seem to learn any more.

"I will say the opening prayer, and then I will lift up my eyes." She lifts her eyes and opens her arms wide in a gesture of exaltation, "I will say, 'Ya, Allah!'" She is on the settee, eyes beatifically ecstatic, arms to the heavens, framed in dramatic black purdah, the picture of faith intoning the call to God. "That will dazzle them."

We hug goodbye, each with separate travel plans, knowing we will be together again in a few weeks. Tomorrow Kamala flies to the Gulf, and I leave for a trip north along the Malabar coast to Nalapat, her ancestral home.

My driver, Jacob, and I hit the road with cars, trucks, rickshaws, and cows flying at us like obstacles in a video game. We take the fork to Punnayurkulam, Kamala's village, and drive along a road buttressed with bushes like English hedgerows. Everyone knows Madhavikutty, Kamala's Malayalam pen name, and they point us to an ancient wooden house with a red-tiled roof, the last traditional house on the grounds of the old estate. An old woman welcomes us hesitantly and with Jacob translating, describes the four-hundred-year-old Nalapat House that stood nearby, with its gate-house, portico used for classical dance performance, interior temple, outdoor snake shrine, bathhouse, cattle sheds, paddy-husking shed, and building for death rituals.

"You could stand in the middle of the courtyard and see the sky," the old woman says. "We could hear the air, the cooing of pigeons, see the lightning. The cross-ventilation made it so cool. We could see the stars."

Looking sad, she points east to remembered paddy fields, south to the familial burial grounds, west to the Arabian Sea. "I am very sorry the house is gone,"
she says, asking me to remember her to Kamala.

I photograph the overgrown swimming pond and the two-thousand-year-old
snake shrine with its corroded idols of Renuka and her father, Vasuki. Kamala's
poetry breathes life into the ruins, and I envisage myself and Kamala as children
playing in the water and drying ourselves in the Nalapat private bower.

O sea, I am happy swimming
Happy, happy, happy …
The only movement I know well
Is certainly the swim.
It comes naturally to me.
I had a house in Malabar
and a pale green pond,
I did all my growing there
In the bright summer months.
I swam about and floated,
And dived into the cold and green
I lay speckled green and gold
In all the hours of the sun …

Images of the Nalapat pond, sweet and full, erase my concerns about Kamala. I feel the presence of young Kamala, adored by her grandmother, carefree, floating, and the water buoys me too. Despite all our differences, I think this water-anointed childhood is an inheritance we share. From it, we have developed our taste for floating and swimming freely in an all-enveloping medium – like love.

Outside it's a blazing 33 degrees, and the old woman suggests we follow her inside, which has an immediate cooling effect. Jacob admires the squared roof beams, thick wood door jamb, strong bronze bolts, brass-studded door, and carved roof struts. Standing in the only extant Nalapat building, listening to Jacob lament the proliferation of concrete box housing, makes me realize that Kamala can't go home again. Her few remaining relatives here are angry with her, and the pre-independence village life she lived exists only in her stories. Her celebrated autobiographical trilogy has immortalized a vanished rural world, just as her contemporary stories reflect the tensions and turmoil buffeting southwest Indian Keralites in their transition from the old world to the new.

It is still true that Kerala has the highest literacy rate, highest life expectancy, and lowest maternal mortality in India, and South Asia's lowest infant mortality and highest women-to-man sex ratio. But the province also has India's highest unemployment rate, and the ruins of Nalapat reflect the fracturing effect on village life due to the exodus of farmers, craftsmen, and postgrad "remittance men" to the Gulf. Kerala now has India's largest consumption of liquor, highest suicide rate, and worst crime figures, including a steadily rising rate of crime against women.

As Kamala hurtles forward, the world of the last Nalapat dwellers disintegrates like the landscape around them.

I call Kamala the moment I return to Cochin. It's impossible to predict what happened in Qatar, and I can't wait to know how she did. Her report is like a geyser, and I write furiously.

"I had eighteen engagements, feet are swollen, health not good, but so exciting, of course, like a dream. They exalted me to such a position. More than ten thousand people, absolute slaves, bowed heads, a new cult. Now I know how fraudulent religious figures are. I am a remarkably successful fake.

"I was given a beautiful royal suite. Intruders were there, humanity all over. So much of embracing and kissing. Behind the perfume is the overpowering smell of their bodies. I soon learned to keep my legs apart so I didn't fall over, or else they would knock me over. My eyes are inflamed from constantly being in the light. Now I know how actresses feel. Someone should write about this, what happened to a poet. Now I am inhibited in my writing. I give you absolute liberty to write what you want. Let's have an interview."

I take a cab to her apartment as quickly as I can. She is glowing with energy. "I never believed I would become such a symbol, like Joan of Arc. Your friend didn't disappoint the audience. The women wept out of happiness because they felt I was talking about them. They fawned on me and cried. I did want love all my life, but I never bargained on this much love. I could burst like the dam breaking."

"Do you like it?" I ask.

"Something in me sure fattens on applause. I like it and I fear it, as if I would get washed away in the ocean. They don't know who I am. Quite often I think I'm a fraud. I want to tell them, but then they would send me home, game over. I wonder if I'm striking a pose because that's what they want, an absolutely sinless woman. One thing I am proud of, that I can love them all."

"What did you talk about?"

"One world. No visas. You are the axis of the world wherever you are. The minister of education asked me to discuss a blueprint for the next century. Imagine me deciding education for the next millennium. He was completely fooled."

"But in Montreal you spoke about education," I remind her.

"Then I had just started my career as a fake. I was not completely mature. Now I am a full fake. I think I have moved into the new role of the saint. Otherwise I was so notorious, now I am redeemed. Life has been a game for me. Who is the real me? Maybe I am a saint. So much of love going on within me. When I left Qatar, I was weeping. Great emotional investments were made, so many friends – even the men were weeping."

And then she says something I will need to transcribe and read over many times before I begin to think I understand. She says, "If I'm really a fake, as I expect I am, always wearing a mask, but never really a mask, it is the real me taking part in a masquerade as the real me. The nudity in the eyes is appalling, not of this mask but of my naked mask, this person with tears in my eyes begging for love, please love me, please love me."

I've heard Kamala compare the world she creates through writing to "shadow" and the external world to "substance," describing how both worlds can coexist within her. But these poignant identity shifts blur the distinction between "real" and "masquerade." She seems to be saying that her "naked mask," her vulnerable openness, is just another mask. Yet when she defines "naked mask," she says "*this* person with tears in *my* eyes." It seems that for her the real and the masked are indivisible.

But now I am trying to keep pace with the rush of her uncensored report from Qatar.

"What I do is look into a person's eyes, crawl into the person's mind, and see misery, darkness, suspicion, doubting, and then I must touch. With women I am permitted to hug, stroke the head, and you have to hold them long enough until they cry. Then they smile, and all is not lost. That is great *zakat* [compulsory giving of charity to the poor, one of the five pillars of the Islamic faith]. Better than clothes, money, gifts, is the *zakat* of love."

"Well, you've always been in the limelight," I say.

"Not this kind of glare. They say, 'You look like the moon coming out of the clouds. Suraiya came to show us a new way. This star has risen for us.' I'm taken as an old woman in my wheelchair, then suddenly I feel empowered. I lift my arms up, upturn my eyes and I pray, 'Brothers in Islam, brothers in Qatar, I have come to talk to you of a subject you probably don't take very seriously – love. The heart is a harsh terrain containing rough hillocks, the crusty cracked ground of a desert, and sandstones. Love is like the *zamzam* which Hajura saw after she ran from one hillock to another looking for water. Can't you hear the plaintive wail of her baby and the hiss of the *zamzam*?

"'*A hum dullillah,* all praise to God,' they all shouted back to me. It was like casting a spell.

"'Love is like the *zamzam*, that eternal spring which will not dry up.'

"'*A hum dullillah,*' they answered.

"'The naked face of Islam carries compassion. True power is in giving, not taking.'

"'*A hum dullillah …*'

"Everything I say, they all shout, 'All praise to God.' This community wants to hear. The TV quoted my sayings. They were posted on roadside billboards. I met all the writers. My words were immediately translated. When I was in Qatar, I always wanted to sing, it was bliss, and my prayer became a song. I was so charged with power that visit. Now Sadiq Ali will be sorry. I have more power than he. I was filled with pride and humbled because I didn't deserve it. But now this God is growing on me. Voices are beginning to speak through the silence.

"I have no regrets. It's delightful, Merrily, life is truly beautiful, it's a life in Technicolor, Panavision, Vistavision. Can you imagine the change from my old life to being a cult figure? I make a joke out of it so I can't be smug. I wished you'd been there, in the tenth row so no one would see you laugh. Merrily would say, 'Kamala's new stunt is fascinating. She's a real show woman.' I should have joined the circus."

Flying on the wings of adoration, she calls Sadiq Ali. He answers and immediately passes the phone to his first wife, who responds rudely and hangs up.

Kamala puts the phone back pensively. "A story I wrote came out last week in Malayalam. A sad love story about a love between a Muslim and Hindu. Perhaps they recognized Sadiq Ali, and that's why they are so unkind."

I ask her to translate the story so I can see how she managed to be subtle enough to publish a love story in a Muslim magazine and obvious enough to upset Sadiq Ali's family.

"Salim Ispahani was a guiding light of his community," she translates, her concentration visible only in the sub-speech movements of her lips.

> He would explain the technicalities of language to his followers. He would acquaint them with the commandments of Islam. In a voice as sweet as wild forest honey, he told the people who were guilty that God would forgive them. He was like a messenger from God.
>
> Salim Ispahani had very sturdy corded arms. He wore half-sleeved shirts so it was impossible not to notice that the muscles of his upper arms were as strong as a bison's shoulders. Probably that was the reason he was so prompt in lifting and carrying the lady poet who had come to inaugurate

the conference. He carried her to a stage decorated with garlands and sat her down on the stage with tenderness.

A slightly musky smell of perspiration lingered on her body and haunted her. She kept seeking the right words of thanks, but was silent. He was her son's age, and when she was free from his clasp, the freedom tasted bitter and she was surprised. For twenty-seven years she had observed celibacy, and persevered to belittle her body's needs. Now she was a widow, and the slight ecstasy her skin felt at his touch made her blush in shame.

Kamala translates all the repressed ardour of *An Incomplete Love Story*, which ends, "This is not a revolt against religion, or a plea for any religion. This is only a wailing. This is only a cry." And when she puts the magazine down, I see that she is actually crying. The phone call to Sadiq Ali has brought her crashing down from the heights of Qatar. She may have the adoration of thousands, but she still cannot have Sadiq Ali. Even though it makes no sense to her at all, she is beginning to realize that he is gone.

"Write my story," Kamala says the day before I leave. She tells me I am her close friend, one she can talk to without withholding, and she tells journalists that I have come close enough to her and learned enough about her to write a good book. She must also feel that I have grown to love her – her brilliant poetic sensibility, her playfulness, warmth, vulnerability, courage, and physical charisma. I have grown used to her mercurial nature, her need for love and assurance, her contradictions. I enjoy what she calls her "rustic" love of jewellery, and her female vanity. I am captivated, as are many, by her generous and total giving of self – stories, politics, flirtation, conversation, munificence – that metamorphoses her modest Cochin apartment into a grand, other-century salon.

She must sense that I secretly applaud her bold bid for love and her union with a potent soulmate – not fantasy or the blue god, but a flesh-and-blood lover who sang through her armoured resolve into her heart. Like Krishna in the *Gitagovinda* who worshipped every inch of Radha's body, even her feet, Sadiq Ali named and embraced all of Kamala, as her self. I know what it must mean to her. For decades her body was used by a husband who pretended she was someone else, and she felt "not there at all." Finally, someone thought only of her, and for the first time she could feel "this is my body. I am mating with somebody and he is mating with me. There was no shadow between us." With Sadiq Ali, as never before, she experienced "an identity that was lovable," the union she had longed for all her life. "Finally," she laughed, "I realized there *is* something like manna from heaven."

Kamala's consuming passion doesn't surprise me as much as it seems to surprise so many of her compatriots. Writer Jeanette Winterson in her beautiful book *The Passion* compared passion that comes late in life for the first time to the feeling of having a leopard in the house. It is wrought with devilish choices and hard to bear. Kamala told scholar J. Devika, "Physical love is intensely beautiful. It is not a gentle breeze; it is a veritable typhoon." She said that such passion requires a spiritual and emotional maturity "acquired slowly, after much effort."

And yet Kamala's love for Sadiq Ali is a potent mixture of many stages of love: the mature spirituality she describes; the haunting power of first love found late in life; and the thrilling excitement of fresh young love which I understood when she asked me to call Sadiq Ali and tell him she'd take him to Canada for treatment.

"I have some money in the bank. I'd pauperize myself to make him better."

"Why?" I asked.

"I want to be with him, to see him naked again."

I asked her why it was such a great thing to see Sadiq Ali naked, and she said she'd never seen a man naked before. I said she'd obviously seen her husband, and she said he disgusted her and she didn't care to look.

"But what is so special about seeing this man naked?" I persisted.

"I am an artist," she answered. "Before, I fantasized what they are like. To see the hair on his chest, the line of hair on his belly. So beautiful. I was bowled over – so that's how they are."

I tried to get my mind around the momentous effect of a naked man and understood more when I read Marguerite Duras's story about a young woman trapped in a monotonous country life. Inside the young woman's body is an amorphous hollow from which comes "an empty cry that was calling no one." When a young man enters her bereft life, the woman feels "a force has been growing I am powerless to resist, a thought has taken root there, in me, against me." With inexhaustible pleasure, like Kamala with Sadiq Ali, she thinks only of the young man's naked body.

But even understanding the cataclysmic effect on a great love poet of finally finding the love she longed for all her life, I can't predict the outcome of Kamala's sexual awakening and conversion, nor the ending of her story. Now that she is a Muslim, she has begun creating a role for herself in Islam, which she says "probably suits me." And if it doesn't now, I hope it ultimately will. She has formed a new political party based on love and preaches her own ecumenical brand of charity. Some visitors come to fête, admire, and adore her, others to use her. Today another delegation of mundu-clad, middle-aged men arrived from a Muslim orphanage/school/benefit society, flattering and entreating her to speak at an evening function three hours away. She declined because of ill health, but they persisted. She will probably go, since "this is what I have. I might as well give to this religion."

And, of course, Sadiq Ali is still not buried. An amusing young mimic appeared to say he had been to Sadiq Ali's home, and Sadiq Ali said he would come to Kamala and marry her secretly. I called the opportunistic kid a budding Rasputin for manipulating her aching need.

"I gave him two hundred rupees," Kamala said.

"Why?"

"Maybe it is true. I haven't given up hope." She smiles, shrugs.

I have known Kamala for five years now. Lived close to her in Canada and Cochin. I have a thousand typescript pages of our conversations, meetings, my journal, her books, columns, stories, and poems. "Write my story, because I no longer can," she repeats.

The task seems overwhelming. Yet I must see where this conversion leads her, see what I can through the smoke and the mirrors.

I swim for the last time in the Taj pool, run along Marine Drive to beat the fast-moving barge to the jetty, hop onto the ledge on the side of the boat, scramble into the hold, and head for the covered front, away from the noisy central engine. I find a lady to sit beside and look at the colourful saris, tired faces, animated conversations, the life flowing on the water to the next stop. On the horizon the sun hangs suspended in the sky, a gigantic fuchsia orb shot through with light. The boat pivots toward Ernakulam, and I twist to keep the glorious sight in view.

## FIVE

# The Laurentians, Montreal, 2000

This time
my friend Merrily
has got herself a bore
as houseguest
a love-struck woman …

# 17

## Gift of a Man

It's wonderful to have Kamala with me again, snuggled in under Auntie Katie's afghan on the screened-in porch. I'm glad she's come and that she'll be free of the haranguing she mentions so lightly – her son's plaint about her harming her grandchildren's marriage prospects, her in-laws' accusations of betrayal, her cousin's berating of her, "Why, at this age, do you need love? You're so old."

"That's precisely why I need love," she tells me. "I have no time to waste."

She soaks up my affection and tells me about her family, asks about mine. But these are just distractions. The topic she prefers is the hue of her lover's body, "tawny like the throat of a peacock," and "the tarnished copper of his phallus." Even though I appreciate her poetic descriptions, I think I've heard these paeans to Sadiq Ali before. Still, I so enjoy her company that I listen, smile, laugh, and Kamala responds:

This is what brought me here
priceless one
the laughing water
of your voice
and the way you have
of pulling out
like skeins of wool
one by one
my dismal memories
Folding each sorrow
and putting it away ...

But the Aunties are the real Laurentian draw, and Kamala can't wait to see them. After years sewing hats, making lampshades, and working as salesclerks in New York department stores, Auntie Sue winters with her electrician husband, Joe, in a Florida trailer park, and Auntie Katie lives in a co-op apartment in the Bronx. They migrate home every the spring for the summer gathering of the clan, as regular as the robins, herons, and Canada geese, and as soon as Kamala knows they're back, she asks to visit.

I wheel her to Auntie Katie's pathway, and she insists on walking the rest of the way alone. From her doorway Auntie Katie sees Kamala in an incomprehensible black outfit, hair hidden by her chador.

Katie,
pink as pastry
laid out at a children's party,
ageless and exquisite,
wept in my embrace
at the doorway of her home.

"It was such a shock. It hurt me so much," Auntie Katie tells me later. "I love that woman, and I felt so sad for her like that, with no hair. Then Cleo explained that she changed her religion but she still has her long beautiful hair, and that made me happy."

My old Jewish aunts embrace Kamala with all the familial love she feels she's lost, and we begin a routine of visits in their homes and ours. Kamala cuddles into the Aunties and tells them love stories. They hug her, marvel at her adventures, cheer for her.

"In her face she looks much better, much younger, softer," Auntie Katie says. "Love makes you feel younger, and it shows on your whole body. What is she, a Buddhist? I never saw that before."

Radiating enjoyment, black-etched Kamala sits between her white-haired co-conspirators, transporting them. She puts her arm around Sue, her head on Katie's shoulder, holds Sue's hand, and whispers mischievously. Sue giggles. Kamala laughs like a girl. Katie leans closer "to get all the dirt."

Auntie Katie spoke freely now
of the topics women fancied most,
of the love stories she read
avidly each day
to chase out the aloneness

"Here I can write," Kamala says, having flexed her poetry muscles with light, occasional poems. "It's the place egging me on. Here I am allowed to be whatever, not all curled up on myself like an insect. I spin here, you don't see the dance, it's a ballerina dance. What a lovely time I am having."

Auntie Sue calls Uncle Joe over, and looking expectantly at Kamala, asks her to read aloud the poem she's written for them. Happy to "give what I have to give," Kamala lifts the paper and reads directly to Sue.

Sue, light as a feather
has a springy gait
all her own ...
There is within her the warmth
of carnivals where children lark
and couples in love waltz half
the night away.

Auntie Sue stares at the paper speaking through Kamala's lips, rapt as a spectator at a magic show.

> It will be folly she thinks
> if I invite Joe now to dance with me
> he has screws in his pockets
> and nails in his mouth

Kamala almost bursts out laughing. Joe's screws amuse her profoundly. She stumbles over the last phrases, restraining herself. Now she has Joe's full attention.

> he is unaware of spiders
> climbing up his arms
> unaware of the fierce summer sun
> beating down on him
> Joe hammers
> he tightens the screws

The second screw does Kamala in. Her face scrunches, body rocks back, head unhinges, laugh lines ring her diamond-studded nose and lipsticked mouth, eyes close, and she forgets to hide her parted lips with her hand as she dissolves into mirth. Never have I seen her so openly joyful. Sue's eyes leave the magic paper to search Kamala's face, hoping for more. This is the first time Auntie Sue has appreciated poetry, and it's exalting. The final stanza bubbles through Kamala's laughter.

> and polishes well
> the polished ledges of his home.

The next day Kamala tells me, "I'm getting rid of my lawyer, Sulaiman. He makes bigoted statements like, 'You have to be a poet, or a Muslim. You can't be both.' I'd rather be a poet, but I can't say that."

A week later, she feels safe enough to be a real poet again, and expose her "essence."

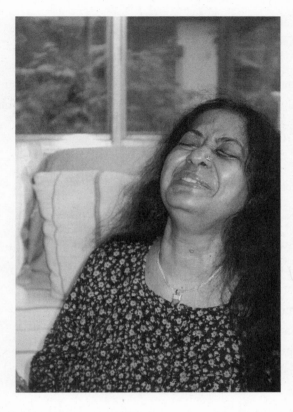

Among the maples
and the pine
among the cedar
and the birch
descends the hurricane
of my desire for you

I am so surprised by the force of Kamala's continuing passion for Sadiq Ali
that I ask to type the new poems, so I can read what she's feeling.

"Finally when I'm very old, I fall in love, really, truly, in love," she tells the
Aunties.

And even now the love remains palpable, alive
and the body lying disciplined

under the eiderdown trembles
recalling our last embrace ...

The next day Kamala sends me to find a perfect maple leaf, supposedly a gift for "a modestly demanding woman friend." She preserves it carefully. Typing that night, I see the leaf is not for a friend but for a lover.

I shall bequeath you
my heart, chilled and red
so like a maple leaf in autumn

"She's full of love, and I don't think she's getting enough," Auntie Sue tells me. "You can hear it in her voice, in the way she talks to you, in the way she writes."

a relic to remind you
of promises left unfulfilled
and a happiness dreamt of
but not realized.

With the Aunties' prompting, I notice that everything now reminds Kamala of sensuality and love.

"I remember being shattered by *Madame Bovary* and *Anna Karenina*," she tells me. "They are with me until death.

"Poet Laurence Hope had many lovers, including a lowly boatman," she says. "She wrote *The Garden of Kama*, erotic poems of flesh, blood, bangles, and charm bracelets. That is the poet I could identify with." She recites, savouring the words,

Pale hands I loved beside the Shalimar,
Where are you now? Who lies beneath your spell? ...
How the hot blood rushed wildly through the veins,
Beneath your touch, until you waved farewell.

"Malabari women are legendary beauties, supposedly great lovers," she tells the

Aunties. "Until about thirty years ago it was imperative for a Nayar woman to shave, or get women to come and remove all the hair, make it clean." She continues, describing the fine points of Nayar genital care. "Then they take a bit of turmeric, mix it, and rub it in. That is antiseptic. And invariably wash clean with water after urinating. When a Nayar woman waits for her husband at night, she is very clean and smells beautiful all over. Travellers from other places say if you sleep with a Nayar woman you will not want to go back to your own because they are so clean, like a cut fruit."

I look uncomfortably at my octogenarian Aunties and find them totally entranced. Even after writing *Our Future Selves*, my book on aging with its disproportionately long chapter on "Love and Sex," I have underestimated their interest in these matters. They love it when Kamala talks to them like "girls." So I tell them about the terrific hand-held "health aids" hooked on the wall of every decent toilet in Kerala. When you've finished eliminating, you detach the aid, elongate the extensible steel cord, position the small shower head, press the nozzle, and clean your genitals.

This leads Kamala to a further exegesis:

"This part is sacred to a woman, the core of her dynamism. How can you expect the man to hold onto you if you are a slattern or don't wash? What if your husband likes to smell you there between the legs? Or if you have a lover who is passionate, he will certainly poke his head in between your thighs. It's going to be a shock to the poor fellow, unless he is a western man who is not used to better smells. A beauty must not only look comely but must also smell good. Not the artificial smell of perfumes with an alcohol base, but the wholesome smell of a healthy body that reminds one of the tender leaves of the mango and of hay drying in the sun. Smell is very important in lovemaking, very, very important. It has an aphrodisiac effect."

The Aunties nod in agreement. They don't say much, but they know what Kamala's talking about and are ready for more.

"Beauty was a full-time job for upper-class feudal Malayali women," Kamala says, responding to their interest. "It meant rubbing medicated oils into the skin and washing them off an hour later with powdered lentils and turmeric. It meant cleansing the scalp with coconut milk and lime juice, and washing the hair with a viscous shampoo made by soaking hibiscus leaves in warm water and crushing them. It meant eating only curd, yellow plantains, and arrowroot pudding. Fried foods were not meant for beautiful girls."

Love and the Aunties seem to have unlocked Kamala's treasury of traditional Nayar health and beauty lore. I hadn't expected to amass more material, but I begin taking notes.

"For the body: grind papaya and *chole* to paste, mix with milk, and rub all over to delay wrinkles.

"For the face: Powder *moong dhal* [a green split bean] in a gritty fashion to make a scrub. It removes an invisible film or layer from the skin. In three days the skin is new.

"For the hair: Wealthy Nayar women wore their hair up in a topknot and sat on the porch waiting for their husbands to come at night. To scent their hair, they burnt incense in a loose, open basket and spread their hair open over the basket.

"To make a woman like a virgin, find white alum stone which barbers use to staunch bleeding. Put it in water for five minutes, no more. Use this for washing the genitals. It will tighten that portion. If an old woman wants to pass off as a virgin, she can."

Now we are all very alert.

"To tighten sagging breasts, pack the bodice with poppy leaves.

"To wean the baby, put jasmine flowers in the brassiere, and in one night the flowers stop lactation, the breasts are softer, smaller, no milk at all."

"For childbirth?" the Aunties ask.

"Ah, yes," Kamala continues. "Until the second half of the twentieth century, Malabari women in the wake of childbirth were confined to the inner rooms situated in the western wing of the house. Every day for ninety days, women came to give you a bath, wash your hair, give you a ceremonial massage. For half an hour they rubbed *dhanvantharam* oil all over your body, then raw turmeric to make it less dark and give you a good feeling. They used powdered *moong* to remove the oil and improve the new mother's colouring and skin texture. The *moong* was washed away with bright red water boiled with *thechhi* leaves. During the two hours in the bathroom tending to your needs, these women would tell stories tinged with sex details. One said a rich woman she knew stained her genitals with henna. It gives a deep orange tint, and they said this woman's husband was charmed by her tinted orifice.

"Malayali women who are not yet weaned away from the beauty traditions of their ancestors do all this. Chemicals do not figure on the cosmetics list," Kamala says, giving the Aunties a knowing look. "Without these things I would have been an old hag."

Once again I find myself scribbling haphazard quotes from everyone, about anything, on dinner napkins, scraps of paper, old bills, realizing despite myself that although I thought my research was complete, Kamala continues to catch me unawares. I thought her heart was broken. I thought she was devastated. But I forgot that she had written, "Like a phoenix I rose from the ashes of my past."

And I underestimated her resilience after other devastating "seasons."

The Aunties don't have my preconceptions. They see what there is to see. "She's all pent up with love," Auntie Sue says, trying to nudge open my mind. "She gets it from us women, but she's angling for a male. I don't know who's giving it to her, but he's not giving her enough."

"Sadiq Ali is being pressurized by the Muslim leaders to come back to me," Kamala tells me, less enthusiastically than I expect. "Muslim wives are having a very hard time. I don't want to be one of them. I don't want to be on Sadiq Ali's cross. The doctor is a better friend."

That night I type,

At night in sleep –
she is no poetry editor,
he is no surgeon –
only bodies cut off from
reality's membranes …

and finally realize that I am one Kamala-persona behind. Kamala may be broken-hearted, but she is also freshly in love. The poems I am typing are not for Sadiq Ali, they're for her new love, the doctor I met on my last visit to Cochin,

... this gift of a man
who is now my sustenance
the draught I thirsted for.

And although this love contains Kamala's usual mix of the sensual and the spiritual, there is a startling reversal in the hierarchy of their importance. Now love incarnate, not imaginary love, is pre-eminent. For the first time in her life Kamala unashamedly embraces an ordinary man as

the sole raiment
for my nudity, both my body's
and my soul's.

"Sixty-five years in a fraudulent life is like having a priceless instrument with some chord left untouched," she tells me. "This is like running out of a nunnery. This is the real me. Sadiq Ali reminded me there was a woman waiting to be fulfilled before I say good-bye."

The Aunties arrive early the next day with home-baked cookies and hand-knit slippers, happy to see Kamala again. Last year she said she could make her story happy or sad, depending on the listener, and she enthrals the Aunties with a mixture of both. They identify with her. They too have had good times and hard times, and they feel the same need for love. They want to protect her, and they can't get enough of her stories.

I leave them talking and go to meet my walking buddies. We hike the mountain trail over part of the lower Laurentian shield, then take a forest path through the valley to the wild, glacial lake where we swim. It seems a ritual as divine to us as Kamala's prayers, blessed by the grace of a heron in flight, sunlight on lily pads, the exaltation of the spring snow melt. It makes me think that perhaps for us being at one with a natural world greater than ourselves is our truest spiritual connection.

When I return, Kamala quizzes me: who went, who did what, who was naked, what about mixed nudity? I explain the community's unwritten rules of decorum and describe the meditative rhythm of the swim, the silky feel of the water, the silence and grandeur, and my dawning realization that, for Canadians, nature is their spirituality. I have no idea what she makes of it all, until one day she asks for felt pens and paper and begins to draw. She fills a sketch pad, and I look at the drawings and grin.

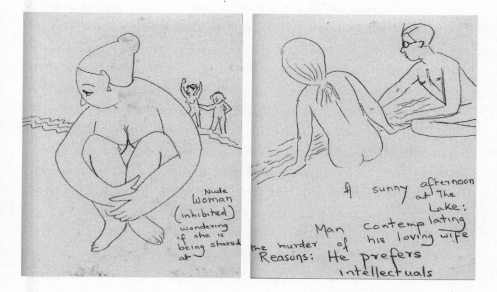

Where do these quirky drawings come from? What have I missed? The drawings provide the perceptual jolt of Kamala's tropes and confirm the impossibility of fathoming her mind. As does the following exchange that greets me when the Aunties leave and we sit down for lunch:

"The doctor tells me I need an ointment before he can enter me, or it will bruise and hurt," Kamala says. "He asked if I have any ointment, and I said, 'Detol.' He said, 'This is inappropriate.'"

I remember a list of "ointments" in the excellent self-help book, *Our Bodies Growing Older*, and the brand, KY Jelly, from adolescent jokes. I offer to buy her some.

"Really?" she asks, impressed by my gumption.

"I won't tell them it's for you," I promise. "How many?"

"One will be fine."

Then Kerala's most loved and reviled wild woman says, "After age sixteen, no man has entered. It has remained a closed cave" – claiming her husband's later impotence necessitated artificial insemination. She seems to be saying she is almost a virgin. She has never said this before.

"Sadiq Ali?" I ask.

"He left something on my skirt."

I spend a moment considering this as the ultimate, ironic confession of the love queen of Malabar, then quickly recall Kamala's repeated descriptions of rape and her earthy descriptions of intercourse with "the lion." I remind myself that for fear of reprisals, and to prove her "purity," she has spent a lifetime hiding, dissimulating, and spreading disinformation about her sexual history. It is difficult to separate sexual fact from fiction in Kamala's life, and critics still argue about whether the men in *My Story* are imagined or real. She once called Iqbal Kaur one of her favourite critics, and Kaur emphasized Kamala's deep-rooted Nayar "concept of Purity." When Kamala told the Aunties about Nayar women, she extolled the charm of their clean personal hygiene and made it clear that although they made a career of charming men, they would never "dirty" themselves by sleeping simultaneously with two men.

She propagates a morality based on love and mocks mindless convention, but she draws on traditionally based standards of purity to maintain her dignity and self-respect. As she wrote in notes to herself, "I speak for the cause of female emancipation, attack the hypocrisy of conventional morality, but seek fulfilment within the nest of traditional values."

Or, as she told researcher Purnendu Chatterjee, "I do not like to be a branded cattle of Nalapat morality, yet I have the seeds of orthodoxy instilled in me by my grandmother and great-grandmother. So, I could not break away from my family. I had love affairs. Everything was not fictionalization, but I had to keep within some limits."

If she has cold feet about what she's told me, either because she has exaggerated or admitted too much sexually, then propounding another, more socially acceptable story would be totally in character. And she does it well: telling me I'm her only guru in sex, asking the location of the urinary opening, querying whether it's in front or behind the vagina, expressing her fears that if she allowed intercourse, her lover might put his penis in the urinary part. It gives me pause, as it's meant to.

"Isn't it remarkable you don't know more about sex?" I ask.

"It happens in all the best of Hindu homes," she says, justifying her situation as culturally normal.

Then I remind myself that in the five years I've known Kamala, she's been a Krishna lover, a proselytizing celibate, reclusive widow, star convert, awakened sensualist, and now an almost-virgin. As she often says, "I am my greatest creation." And as she told the interviewer P.P. Raveendran, "Reality is very drab, as drab as white *khaddar* – I try to perfect my life by adding things which may not really have happened."

But her latest incarnation with its combination of spirituality and sexual stirrings may test the limits of her adaptability. "I still pray to Hindu gods too," she tells me. "I'm all mixed up. In India I said, 'Oh, Shiva, Shiva, what is this?' and a Muslim leader said, "You are exclaiming to Shiva.' I quickly twisted, not wanting another civil court case. 'Let me praise Allah in this way. All names belong to him.' Another time I was praising Mohan Lal, our greatest actor, saying we should be proud of this man with stricken eyes, he should play opposite Anna Magnani, and Lal said, 'Bless me, Mother, touch my head and bless me.' I touched his head as the Hindus do, replying, 'May the Guruvayur God give you fortune and fame.' 'Madam, you are calling on a Hindu god,' said a Muslim filmmaker.

"I've invented myself as a character, now I'm stuck with it, as if I'm possessed by her. I belong to you, Madame Frankenstein," she says with frighteningly prescience.

Then she leavens the darkness as she always tries to do, with whatever she can find to celebrate. "Yet I dreamt Krishna was taking me in a chariot, and I looked over and it was the doctor. Krishna did not serve me as a man, it was a fantasy. Now I don't have to imagine, I have a man. My arms ache with his weight."

# 18

## The Depth of Sequestered Pools

Today I leave Merrily's home …
Here I was the owner of my time
each tranquil hour my own

The Aunties and Joe arrive bearing pre-parting gifts, and I snap the photos everyone wants to have.

"Sit on Joe's lap," Kamala urges Auntie Sue. "It will make a good picture."

To my surprise, eighty-three-year-old Auntie Sue hops up, plunks herself on Joe's thigh, slings an arm around his neck, and smiles like she belongs there. Joe looks bemused but willing. It's a great picture.

Auntie Katie holds Kamala's hands. "I hope I'll be able to see you next year," she says.

"You and I are riding the tightrope, we are on the trapeze," Kamala smiles.

"Take better care of yourself and have a good love life," Auntie Katie urges. "I feel so sad because I don't know when I'll see her again," she whispers to me. "I approve that she's in love, but I don't approve how he acts toward her. He snuggles her but doesn't have sex with her. I'm ninety-one, but if I have a man holding me and making love to me, I want him to go the limit. Still, he makes her feel loved."

"You'll be taking the plane soon," Auntie Sue says to Kamala.

"It is called the plane to loneliness."

Auntie Sue hugs her. "Don't do anything harsh. Do it slow and sweet."

Kamala walks her "Canadian family" to the door. When we're alone, I raise her feet to the stool of her favourite chair, where she can look out at the trees.

"Merrily, you have such an effect on my life," she says, in a remarkable echo of what I have been thinking about her. Without Kamala I would never have had the confidence to press for an agreement formalizing my arrangement with Arnie. Or have appreciated Auntie Katie's sublimated artistry or Dad's spiritual world, or questioned whether there is a price to pay for sexual liberty. I wouldn't know the beauty of hennaed hands in motion, or have read *Karma Cola*, Gita Mehta's sharp, absurdist satire about Westerners and spiritualism in India, or Ginu Kumani's *Junglee Girl*, R.K. Narayan's *Malgudi Days*, or Amitav Ghosh's *The Shadow Lines*, which I didn't want to end. Knowing Kamala makes me care about her poetry, its roots, and its rebellion. Which involves her mother's poetry. Which makes me interested in Balamani Amma's spiritual, scholarly poems. Which necessitated Sulu's introduction to *puja* (Hindu devotional practices). Which requires books to understand what Sulu began. Which reminds me of Kamala's love for Krishna. Which leads to David L. Haberman's anthropological pilgrimage, *Journey through the Twelve Forests: An Encounter with Krishna*, and meanders into the gloriously erotic lyric cantos of *The Gitagovinda of Jayadeva: Love Song of the Dark Lord*.

Bits of the world Kamala has opened to me flash through my mind as I wait, wondering what she is going to say next. I know she has reassessed the stereotypes she had about western families after meeting ours. But how have I affected her life?

"Even the fact that Sadiq Ali touched me and I didn't feel so outraged that I committed suicide," she says in answer to my questioning expression. "The part that occurred to me after knowing you is that the life choices I would have considered a sin, you are draping yourself in as a mantle. I even felt so superior. I think truth is so startling.

"Sadiq Ali said, 'We are two rivers flowing side by side. Can you feel the rush?' Sex was so powerful but tender, not like my husband. It's an art, like a concert, the beginning, crescendo, diminuendo, the loud roar of a padlocked door being opened, you feel you're being adored – the hands, the mouth – it's a worship rite, such ecstasy. I'm glad I had it once in my life. I liked it."

"An orthodox Hindu woman with a Muslim man," I tease about her double transgression.

"I lost caste immediately. I allowed it. I even loved the experience. Each cell in me trying out, celebrating the body. I thought, I must tell Merrily the change that has been wrought within me – internally, not externally. Externally I don't even lift my hem. I'm not even assessing the pros and cons of this new attitude. I think God is saying, 'Be happy in your body too' – that must come from being here."

Arnie and I push Kamala's wheelchair to the departure area and join the line of passengers requiring assistance. We wait for the stewardess, as people on our left line up, press forward, show papers, and stride through the embarkation gate. Other passengers wheel past us, pushed by their children.

"Reading Isadora Duncan at thirteen and Oscar Wilde at fourteen can mess you up," Kamala says out of the blue, thinking perhaps of the constraints awaiting her at home. Then she withdraws into silence, head and body covered in black, conserving the energy she will need for the long return journey, a small, contained figure indistinguishable from the other Muslim ladies waiting to board the flight. No stranger could imagine the person underneath that purdah. Or how this frail, nondescript person could inspire sensible Phyllis, my dad's wife, to say, "She's so powerful she wraps herself around your heart and sucks you into her aura."

Kamala says the permission to be happy in her body must have come from knowing me, but she was comfortable in her body and her psyche for the fifteen years she lived with her grandmother in Nalapat. She has always been less prudish about body parts and functions than most Westerners, and when accused of obscenity for painting nudes, she asked how something totally natural could be obscene. Long before she knew me, she wrote of the hypocrisy of sex without love and the propriety of sex when there is love. I don't think she ever completely bought the de facto "sin" of non-marital sex – her Nayar matrilineal culture sanctioned non-legal sexual arrangements for women, and her new morality condemned sex in a loveless marriage. It's just that with me, in Quebec, she experiences a culture in which women's sexual desire is acceptable and normal.

I think Isadora Duncan and Oscar Wilde messed Kamala up because she took them to heart in a powerfully inhibited society with such a repressed culture of concealment that the poet Vijay Lakshmi thought Kamala would have been much happier living somewhere else. And recently, when an interviewer asked Kamala what she would change if she could relive her life, she said, "I would not like to be born in Kerala. Kerala gives me a feeling of claustrophobia." I think knowing me reinforced her impulse to act on what she already believed, because she saw me living with a man outside of marriage and the sky wasn't falling in.

I hug Kamala one last time before the steward turns her wheelchair toward the embarkation door. Supposedly she cut this visit short to prepare her fledgling political party for the elections, but I now suspect she's returning to celebrate her body. I watch her go, and when I imagine her flying from Montreal, to Europe, to Delhi, to Cochin, I worry about sending her off alone. I hope she'll feel secure, and that she'll be well received when she returns. I watch intently as she's wheeled past the gaggle crowding the gate, past the airport guard, the mouth of the hallway, and I leap about frantically when she turns once, softly, to wave.

# SIX

# Cochin, 2003

Suraiya
you are no longer alone

# 19

## A Touch of Moonlight

Kamala and I have been apart for almost three years, our longest separation since we met, and in that time Muslim fanatics bombed the World Trade Center and the United States invaded Afghanistan. In our monthly phone conversations I hear the toll these events are taking on her spirits and her life. Finally, two years after 9/11, Arnie takes me to the airport and I go through security, awash in conflicting sensations of anticipation and loss. I want to see Kamala to buoy and reassure her with my friendship. But I'm scared of how changed she sounds, and this time I dread the long journey alone. As soon as I'm seated in the waiting area, I read the notes of our phone calls to remind me why I have to go.

I read that Christian women started descending on Kamala immediately after 9/11, "preaching about the Holy Ghost and Jesus Christ, trying to scare me into conversion." She told me that Muslims were so frightened at being branded terrorists and wild animals that they were powdering their faces and shaving their beards. She said that as soon as she was named recipient of the Ezhuthachan Book Prize, Kerala's highest literary honour, Hindu fanatics threatened to bomb the hall. "I'll invest in huge earrings that dangle, henna on my palms, to give me confidence. They can't squash me out," she said defiantly. To forget her circumstances, she often spoke of kinder times and places, "your dad, his crinkled eyes, his smile. I'm cradling your family in my memory.

"Don't cut off now, Merrily. I like to hear your voice, it suits me."

One day I called her and no one answered. I called and called.

"I was at Sulu's because my blood sugar was rising," she said when I reached her. "I had a heart infarction returning from Bahrain. I'm trying to hide myself in the bedroom, the fanatics are out to get me, I have given a visitor's list to the guard. I hold onto my God, a large God, shapeless like an ocean, formless, a mantle like a guardian that covers me with heat, cold, breezes, moonlight. I want something which will make deep indentations on my soul – giving alms, holding a free medical camp for the poor, prayer, attempts at prayer – not close enough to God, but reaching out."

As I was preparing to go to her, she told me she had fallen off her office chair and had to crawl to the phone to call her maid. "In the morning there is chest pain, palpitations. When I step out of bed, I fall."

She scared me so much I thought she was going to die.

"Everyone comes to laugh at me, angry still. But there is something not tattered in me that you can blow up into something big. We'll go to the beach, watch the light, the rain. You will have to come here. So much has happened in my country."

I find a public phone booth outside the waiting area and dial a friend in New York to buck me up. I'm worried about how or if I can help Kamala, about days of disorienting travel, and I ache with the craziness of leaving a life and love that comforts me. Yet I can't know Kamala's situation from afar or be of real use unless I go to her.

My friend's energy and encouragement assuage the airport depersonalization. The plane lifts off, and I watch Montreal's skyline recede until it is too small to see. Then I let go of all doubt and flow into the long, wide sweep of the St Lawrence River, its robes of white, mist in its curves, sun on the cloud tops.

I am flying east to Kamala, into the light.

Kamala lies on a white bedspread, propped on embroidered pillowcases, looking younger, thinner, and more vulnerable after her illness. She greets me warmly but seems distracted and subdued, unlike our playful visitor to Quebec. She gestures to her newly painted pastel bedroom. "This is my sanctuary. This is where I pray." I notice that pale wood cabinets have replaced her dark metal lockers and the blinds are open to the light. She tells me that when she is alone, her bedroom is converted into a desert with date palms, little sandstorms, no longer a bedroom but Arabia where the Prophet was born, and she lies on her bed and talks with the Formless One.

"I was praying in my room and felt bathed in moonlight," she tells me. "Yet when I opened the window, the night was pitch black. The light was Allah's light."

Sometimes pilgrims come asking to pray in the room where she's had these visions, and several nights ago, she says, "Archangels, or spirits wearing earrings like chandeliers flew around me glowing like moon-lit clouds, their earrings jingling. They were like white Madera flowers aglow in the hour of dusk."

Then she stops, leaving me speechless. Sensing my incredulity, she assures me that her Imam told her she is not crazy, but rather, since angels really exist for Islamic believers, she is blessed.

Even so, this is a disconcerting reunion, especially for someone like me brought up to believe in the common humanity and equality of all, "the brotherhood of man," not God and the archangels. On the other hand, spirituality has always been part of Kamala's life: her grandmother was a devotee of Krishna; the Nalapat women chanted mantras, tended the gods, and performed daily religious rituals; and unmarried aunt Ammalu composed devotional poems to Krishna. When Kamala was deathly ill as a child, she felt the healing presence of Krishna, and during childbirth, chanting the Gayatri mantra helped her through. As a celibate, she "loved chanting mantras, keeping myself clean in body and mind." I remind myself it is in character for her to take each new incarnation to its outer limit. And seeing angels, as did Blake and Milton before her, is not such a stretch for a poet used to playing with Krishna and listening for the sound of the mystical Saraswati River. Yet I feel a major change in Kamala. She seems present but not-present in a way that's unusual for her, more peaceful, as if something invisible to me is palpable to her.

I excuse myself and take a cab to the Metropolitan Hotel to unpack before dinner. The desk clerk welcomes me – "Madam, you are back" – and sends my bags to my usual room where everything is consolingly exactly as I left it. With a pleasant sense of familiarity, I open the curtains, unlatch the windows, put my tape recorder in the top drawer and my files on the desk. The largest file contains the English translation of *Sasneham Suraiya* (With love, Suraiya), Kamala's post-conversion journal. She gave it to me when I arrived, and since she seems to be somewhere I've never been, I lie on the bed and read, hoping the diary may bring me closer to her. I read: "When America declared war against Afghanistan, my close friends abroad sent me messages saying I must flee to Paris or Quebec to be less vulnerable. What am I to tell them? My safety is in Islam. Even if I say so in so many words , they will not and cannot fully understand or acknowledge my conviction. I am afraid if the war lingers on, my friends may turn into enemies. The disappearance of love is the inevitable result of all terrorism."

I close the book, wanting to assure Kamala of my continuing love, and at the same time acknowledging her insight about my concern that she might be swayed by Islamic fundamentalists. After 9/11, fear, hatred, and anger turned to paranoia in the West, and even as a secular Canadian I had to struggle against being influenced by enflaming propaganda and profiling. As Islam's star convert, Kamala was under much greater communal pressure than I, a lightning rod for polarized fundamentalists. I couldn't imagine how she could withstand or moderate such wild, fanatic passions.

I return to her apartment for dinner in time to overhear her describing her recent speaking tour to Qatar, one of many such visits to the Gulf States of Bahrain, Muscat, Dubai, Sharjah, and Abu Dhabi. It seems a good opportunity to learn more about how she navigates the religious shoals, and I ask how she addresses the thousands who flock to hear her.

"I tell them the story of God commanding Ibrahim to take his son up to the hills and kill him, to prove his love for Him," she says, "and how instead Ibrahim sacrificed a goat. And I say that I cannot sacrifice anything. If Islam says, 'Sacrifice your son,' I do not think that I own these boys, or even a goat, because these things belong to Allah. So I say, 'Allah, why are you asking me to give such gifts to you, they are all yours, including my poor wasted aging body, all yours. I am like a well that grows when you take the soil out and that is enough for me, Allah, I have accepted you, just as you have accepted me.' This is what I say."

This convoluted, non-violent message reassures me and reminds me of the clever way Kamala manoeuvred Suliaman, her lawyer, into driving more carefully when she was in the car. First she admired his profile, then told him she could admire it best if he looked straight ahead at the road instead of turning sideways to talk to her. She explained to me that she had figured out how not to hurt Sulaiman and also how not to be hurt herself. She has accomplished a similar feat in her speeches in the Gulf. By praising Allah's guardianship of all life, including hers, she negates the need for sacrifice or killing in the name of God, and so declares her submission to the fundamentalists without hurting herself or her beliefs.

On the other hand, she has been quoted saying, "All mosques should be de-stroyed. All mosques, temples, churches. And Muslims shouldn't eat meat." Which may explain why she now receives death threats from Muslim extremists as well as Hindu extremists, and why she has a new security system.

To protect herself, she has a guard in the hallway outside the apartment door who questions visitors and has a gun. He leaves at 5 PM. She has a rapid response security system, "forty seconds max," says Monu, which relies on Kalyani, the maid, calling Command Central. Tomorrow Monu will teach Kalyani how to dial. The phone is monitored against death threats by a computer programmed to respond to words such as "kill." Kamala thought all the calls were monitored, but now that she knows there's a trigger, she plans to set it off immediately. She keeps a loaded rifle on the shelf beside her bed. Her semi-blindness is not a problem, as Kalyani knows how to shoot and has already shot a hole in the wall. After 5 PM a wizened old man with a flashlight takes over the watch. He stands beside my waiting cab at the unfinished entrance columns, saluting with his flashlight as I leave.

I don't know whether to laugh or lose heart. It seems that God and the extremists have taken over Kamala's life. I hope there is still space for me.

Back in the hotel, I reopen Kamala's post-conversion book. As I read, I am appalled by the volume of hate mail and abusive calls she received for exercising her constitutional right "to profess, practice and propagate religion of one's choice." So crushing is this persecution that she likens her sense of loneliness and abandonment to the devastation after a storm – "Birds' nests lying damaged with the eggs broken. Big trees fallen with the naked roots exposed. A homeless cat moaning from the roof of a floating hut, its sound reminding hearers of their own utter loneliness. Who will take up the responsibility of a homeless cat? The Master of the Earth took me up and embraced me."

As I read further, I see that all too soon after her conversion, Kamala felt "alien" to her ancestors, "cast out," devastatingly alone. What sustained her then and now was her God. She could "wear his tenderness like an armor" and walk with her head raised high, "my natural gait." When she turned to him, she no longer felt alone. Vulnerable though she was and is, "Devotion covers my nakedness."

She asks, "Who am I? The mind that goes on asking but never gets any reply shudders like a fish left gasping on the shore. My pride is the raised head of a

cobra. I hear its incessant hiss and feel guilty and ashamed." Struggling to maintain her dignity in the face of adversity as she had done all her life, she writes,
"My pride is born out of my possession of Him."

The next day, admitting to Kamala that I am spiritually challenged, I ask her to
help me understand more about her relationship with God.

"I have given myself to God," she says. "I think I've changed during the past
year and a half. Sometimes the love for him is so much that I sit alone and cry out
of so much of happiness."

Then, seeing the incomprehension on my face, she tells me one of her grandmother's children's parables, to help me along:

There was a chap called Baputty who was considered to be mad. He lived
on a beach called Mokeri with nut trees, flowers, white sand, crabs that walk
backward, and the frothy sea. Every morning the fishermen would go to
the sea with their nets, their little narrow boats, and Baputty would tell his
mother, "Amma, don't worry, I will bring the Golden Fish for you and all
our problems will be over."

And his mother would say, "Oh, my son is mad."

But one day he came home at midnight and said, "Mother, I have got
the Golden Fish."

And she said, "Where?"

"Here, see how it glitters? See the eyes, they're like emeralds, they shine."

"Baputty, you are mad," she said and went to sleep.

In the morning, the fishermen came to Baputty and said, "Let's all go
fishing."

"No,' said Baputty, "I will not fish again. I have got the fish."

"Where?" they asked.

"Here. Here's the fish."

"Come along, Baputty," they scoffed, "where is your boat, where are
your nets?"

"I threw them all away," Baputty answered. "I don't want them because
I have found what I have been looking for these many years. After getting
the Golden Fish, why would I go out to the sea again?" And he was happy.

"I am like that," Kamala says. "I went out searching for God for many years and finally I found a God who is real and available to me, and therefore I don't need any religions anymore. I don't even really need the religion of Islam, now that God has made me his dwelling place. And I dwell in him too, so we don't know who houses whom."

I thank her for the story and excuse my difficulty in following her. "It's just that, except for being close to nature, I have no experience myself …"

"It's no use trying to believe what others say," Kamala cuts in. "You have to experience it yourself. It's like childbirth, you can't define it. What is the feeling when the child is coming out and there is pain and the pain suddenly ceases and the child slips along the thigh, that feeling? You created life. It's like that. You've created God. You can't explain to anyone. And besides, they'll think it's lunacy. When Baputty talked about the Golden Fish, poor fellow, he was called a lunatic. And many people in my home state call me 'the mad one' – 'she keeps changing names, religions.'"

"Did anyone else except Baputty see the Golden Fish?" I ask.

"Only he saw it. That's why I can't take it out and show it to you. I can't show you Allah, because he's everywhere."

The last house is yours, my Master
And like the fragrance of flowers, you embrace me.

The redesigned Taj pool opens onto an oceanic view. The wall between the spa and Kerala's all-embracing waters is gone, and at the end of each lap I see fishing boats, yachts, kids net-fishing.

Around the pool are the unusual local plants and well-tended international physiques. I rest my arms on the end ledge, my body weightless. Beside me a young businessman from Brussels chats up a bikinied American girl.

I think about Kamala finding her refuge in God and wonder if Dr Hussain, her current suitor, or my being here are any use at all. I dangle a bit longer, then swim with additional aesthetic pleasure to the end of the new infinity pool. I swim until the sun sets on the horizon of Vembanad Lake.

When I return, Kamala is lying on her bed, AC on, TV on, or just her mind on. She has diarrhoea from her maidservant Kalyani's use of tap water, it's weakened her. I report that I have it too. Mine confirms Kamala's fears: "She's killing me." I hurry out to buy crates of mineral water, choosing toxic levels of chemicals in bottles over bacterial infection from taps. Washing and rewashing her hands, Kamala lectures illiterate Kalyani on the dangers of microscopic germs.

The phone rings with another reminder about Kamala's speaking engagement in Muscat. "She can't walk to the next apartment, and they want her to come to Muscat," Kalyani laughs. Kamala ties up her hair up so it can be quickly covered for Muslim visitors. The phone rings again, and Kamala's photographer friend, K.C. George, answers the call, a demand that she attend the launch of the Arabic edition of *Ya Allah*.

"I don't want to go," she tells George. "I have become so different from what I was three years ago. I do not want to be an exhibit on a stand confronting an ocean of men." She wraps her arms around herself. "My physical presence is withdrawn."

The phone rings and it's my turn to pick it up. M.R.V. Nambyar, Kamala's husband's old friend, asks after my "esteemed daughter," who is passing through after meeting Indian colleagues, and congratulates me on having made the journey to

India "at your age." When I hang up, Kamala insists I call back to say that a Saudi prince has proposed to her. "That will impress him."

"If the prince has proposed, it is because of the glamour," Nambyar says when I give him the news. "No one should be interested in Kamala at her age. We should all think of her as *Noble Mother*," he intones.

"Why do you do this?" I ask Kamala.

"Because it distracts from the pain in my legs," she says.

Nambyar calls back three times, scolding Kamala because I haven't visited him. "I'm an old man. I'll be dead next time Merrily comes."

Kamala says to me, "Tell him 'Kamala is almost crying because I haven't gone to visit you, but I have stomach pains – you know, women's problems.'"

"I understand," says Nambyar scuttling backwards when I mention women's problems. "Your daughter, your responsibilities."

Kamala lies down and invites me to lie beside her. Hand flicking, she tells me how she touches Hussain. Turning sideways, she faces me, her face soft and beautiful, eyes dark, lips full. She describes how she holds Hussain, how she knows how to hold him, how she plays with his hair, his nipples, calling him "little boy." His wife puts the grandchildren on the bed between them, allowing sex only as a duty. She says he washes his face, hands, and feet five times a day before prayers, and showers before touching her. He is clean, or she would never touch him with her mouth.

Now I am totally unnerved. It is beyond me to reconcile the archangels and the sex.

# 20

## You Embrace Me

A Kumar Gandharva raga rolls out the open door of Kamala's guest apartment into the hallway, drawing me in. Kamala is in the immaculate, sweet-smelling bedroom, selecting choice linens to make her suitor's bed. Shadowing Ammu, she smooths sheets, plumps pillows, arranging the aesthetics of the boudoir. "Hussain loves this room," she says.

I wait for her in the main room of the apartment until she settles into the chair closest to the tape deck. Her eyes close and as the raga plays, she starts to talk – about Kumar Gandharva, "the celestial being" who sang "Malhar," the rain raga, to her and when they met again, said "I always sing for you"; about her amazement at the change in Hussain from "a soft, dark shadow falling on me" to a virile suitor. "Why?" she asked him.

"The power of your eyes, your face," he answered.

She lounges as if she has no bones in her body, visualizing the raga flowing through her, "rain getting thicker and thicker, falling over huts, vast fields, streams forming, distant thunder." Hussain likes to see her with her hair down, adorned in gold and jewels. She likes to lie in the dark cuddled into him. She can hardly believe the waves of desire and the youthful energy flowing through her. "Hear the grandeur of his voice," she says, mingling music and longing so that I'm not sure if she's talking about the singer or her lover. "After knowing him, I've never admired anyone else … I really love that man."

Later we move to the office and Kamala sits behind her desk, a salmon-pink chador draped softly around her face. Dr Hussain arrives, freshly scrubbed, a large, boyish man in his fifties, and sits languidly in the chair at the side of the desk. I sit across from Kamala, preparing to record her new story. She opens the magazine to "Paritoshikam" (A gift). I raise the mike to her lips and Hussain leans forward, all looseness gone, to face her.

"This is the first time I write about Hussain," she says, taking a deep breath. "'Before prayers, he wets his hand and strokes his hair,'" she translates.

Often have I buried my face in that damp hair and the familiar scent of his skin I take in with greed. The fragrance of his lips and the comeliness of his body have defeated me.

Hussain's eyes hold Kamala's face, his tall, strong body immobile. When he was eighteen, Kamala was thirty and already a famous writer. Her love poetry and much-photographed beauty made her a national sex symbol, and like many others, he has never forgotten her writing. In *My Story*, he read things that caused him "a lot of commotions," and her poems "transplanted" him into her longings.

Kamala enunciates lightly, caressingly. Her words stroke, enter, fix him rapt to her lips, her breath, his hoped-for immortality.

Perhaps our souls resemble the little flames you put in earthen pots and float on the waters of the Ganges. Perhaps our souls are like that. Dissimilar, perhaps, and yet on the horizon we might blend with each other and with the great radiance that is our creator's, destined to meet once in Paradise, and fated to share again and again this love that we are sharing now.

Kamala and Hussain gaze at each other as if they are alone. He smiles, beholden, vulnerable, hardly believing this is happening to him. I feel awkward and fascinated, like a voyeur. First the verbal seduction and now this high-tension buzz, as intimate as sex. I mumble praise for the story.

"It brought criticism," Kamala says. "They say I'm a woman who's going astray, swearing by Allah but wrapped up in the beauty of a man's body. But when a cyclone removes the ceiling, leaves you bare, all trees gone, how can you not talk about it? A writer bears witness to all aspects of life experience. I watch, I watch, I watch, and I am watching within myself."

Hussain straightens himself, takes a breath, and leans forward, elbows on the desk, face in his hands, obviously moved. On his smooth skin is the blush of the newly anointed.

"I do not have your learning, or your culture," he says, addressing Kamala, "and you write this beautiful story about me. It is hard to believe." He speaks tenderly, almost formally, praising her writing, her charity, her learning. "I am just an ordinary man. Yet you take this ordinary man and make him great. That is why I love you so much."

It seems like a momentous moment, and even though I feel like an interloper, I want to applaud. Yet Kamala is calm and unfazed. Perhaps she expected Hussain's homage, his reciprocal *paritoshikam*. Perhaps she set it up. Only later will I remember that when I was still in Canada, she had said, "I want Hussain to tell me in your presence that he loves me. Something I must leave behind."

I will never know what might have happened next, because the phone rings and Kamala answers. It gives me time to think of some of the men she has loved – her noble Brahmin lover, the unsatisfying selfish Lion, her pleasant Italian suitor, cowardly Sadiq Ali, and now Dr Hussain. None has given Kamala the physical and spiritual communion she longs for, but each has received the fullness of her love. As poet Balan Chullikkad says, "Kamala always mentally elopes with love itself to another world, always in love with love itself. She writes about love, always wanted to be loved, tries to live her maximum love, and to establish a religion of love."

"It is a marriage, really," she replies when I ask her about Hussain. "We have exchanged rings, cloth, had a Nayar marriage [the bridegroom ties a *tali*, a thread, around the bride's neck and presents her with an expensive cloth]. I don't feel anything illicit. Without Hussain, I could not have withstood Sadiq Ali's betrayal."

She opens her wardrobe and shows me the fine white *mundu* that Hussain wore at their private Nayar wedding. They "prayed and paid" at the temple, she says, and were also "married" privately between themselves at the mosque – "it is enough for me." But she wants their marriage known.

Two men from a cooperative bank in Alleppey, a coastal city north of Cochin, are waiting attentively when we re-enter the receiving room. They represent a trust that provides interest-free loans, and rather than appear in person, Kamala has made a fundraising cassette for them.

"What message have you sent?" I ask, trying to keep in touch with her public statements. The men offer to play the Malayalam cassette, and I listen to Kamala's musical, unusually declamatory delivery.

"Don't give money to political organizations, give to orphans, poor people," she translates. "From the rock of your heart, let compassion flow out to the distressed. Interest will come as merit, you will go to heaven, be the richest.

"Say to yourself, this whole world belongs to God – the earth, the moon, you are a citizen of the world. Learn Arabic, learn French, bring up your children to be world citizens.

"Don't give too much importance to religion, this frightens me. Muslims are associated with Jihad, terrorism, but Jihad really means fighting the evil within you. Jealousy, suspicion, hate – this is the darkness within. This is what you are fighting. This is the word of God.

"May I wish you my greetings. May God save you," says Kamala Suraiya, concluding her sermon.

She tells me her poems are sung in the Gulf, her book of personal prayers is in its third edition. She is designated as a "preacher" in her Abu Dhabi visa, and her burning mission is to find a solution to the war of religions. "I'm fighting like a cat that's in pain," she tells me, "physical pain, mental pain, not spiritual. Spiritually I'm flying like a pennant in the wind, flaming free within the burqua."

With Kamala balancing gracefully and lightly on the arms of her maidservants Ammu and Kalyani, we walk down the hall, back to the guest apartment. The doctor is gone, replaced by two large trunks and five satchels to be sorted for Delhi's Nehru Museum and Library, "an honour," Kamala tells me. I lift armfuls of paper from the trunks and hand first drafts of stories, handwritten poems, and letters to her, relieved to be doing something I understand. Kamala scans perfunctorily, lingering only over photographs that remind her of people, places, kindness, play. I discover a yellowing 1975 scrapbook with handwritten text and old photos secured by triangular black corners, souvenir of Kamala's famed Bombay salon, "my club, the Bahutantrika, which in Sanskrit means a many-stringed instrument that produces lovely music."

I show her the scrapbook, and she conjures up the large hall of her sprawling Bombay Bank quarters filled with poets, actors, playwrights, dancers, singers, writers, musicians. "All were welcome, all with talent and all who loved talented people." She presided over hours of plays, dance, classical singing, and open-mike poetry and introduced young artists to those who could help them. She sees the photo of dancer Geeta Nair, and her hands flow gracefully into the nerve-etched movements of Manipuri dance. "Of course, I was also supposed to learn Kathak dance, but my father with his unerring South Indian puritanism decided that no girl after puberty should continue dancing. No fear," she laughs, "our Bahutantrika club motto was, 'Shed your inhibitions with your shoes at the door.'"

I laugh easily with her, realizing now that my playful friend is back how much I've missed her. I'd like to stay with her here in the past, ignoring the bodiless, formless one. Fortunately the Bahutantrika club story is not over.

"By 1976, Prime Minister Indira Gandhi's Emergency Act was entrenched, and it became almost impossible for me to hold the conferences," she says, explaining that Gandhi had responded to the movement against corruption and inflation by suspending the constitution and arresting opponents. "Nobody was allowed to criticize the government, and yet some of the younger poets in my group began to write lines opposing Mrs Gandhi. Some were associated with the Naxalites [armed Indian Maoists], thin boys, you saw them in the libraries, and at our conferences they read out the poems they had written criticizing the Emergency Act.

"The government sent in detectives, plain-clothes men posing as artists, to listen to proceedings. Then the prime minister's secretary phoned my father, who was chairman of the Press Club of India, president of the Indian and Eastern Newspaper Society, a very important journalist, and told him that his daughter was to be put in jail. My father scolded me, pleaded with me, and warned that if I continued with this organization, I would harm the interests of my brothers, sister, parents. He ordered me to sign a document, an apology. But I could not obey. Having tasted freedom, I was not willing to give it up for any Emergency. I didn't want to produce the literature of slaves.

"So, they raided my house, just messed it up. I had gone out with my son to buy ice cream, and when I came back, the place was swarming with policemen. I was afraid all this would hurt my husband, and yet there was no way I could back out. Then my husband was asked to go on leave from the Reserve Bank because of me. He went into his room and closed the door. Finally he said, 'I can't bring myself to say no to you. You are doing the right thing, but I dread the repercussions.' The police stayed posted, surveying. A government doctor asked to examine me, but I had heard rumours that an opposition leader had died due to kidney failure from injections in prison. For safety, I took my child out of school. I told the children, 'You will be angry at me now but proud later.' Eleven months my husband was without pay. I said, 'Don't worry, we'll sell jewellery.' Finally we were selling utensils. There was trouble, a lot of trouble within our home."

Kamala is interrupted by the maidservants, and my mind flits from Emergency to scrapbook to steamer trunks, to all the unpredictable ways I discover her past. I am thinking how frequently certain patterns like courage and reinvention recur, when I see that her attention is decidedly wandering. I hurriedly box the files about her work as chairman of the Forestry Board, chairperson of the Committee on Environmental Education, officer of the Kerala Council for Child Welfare. I add her notes about being saved from arrest during the Emergency by Achyutha Menon, the chief minister of Kerala, who made her a state guest, assured Prime Minister Gandhi she would be guarded like a prisoner, and sent her off with her nine-year-old son and a security guard, in cars and boats, from one government guest house to another, scouting sites for tourist complexes.

"I never submitted to Indira Gandhi's demands," Kamala says, "and when the Emergency was lifted and Prime Minister Desai came in, garlands were thrown on me as a victim of the Emergency, and my husband was made chief of the Agricultural Finance Corporation."

I rifle quickly through Madhava Das's meticulous business files and find the foreign rights contract that Kamala really wants, the proof she expects will give her bushels of unpaid rupees to give away. She hands the contract to the security guard, asks him to make five copies, then lies down to rest.

That evening Kamala is livelier and more engaged than when I first arrived. She sounds more like herself, talking non-stop, embellishing old stories for her dinner guests, and telling new ones like the long story about her teenage son tormenting the liberal columnist Krishna Raj, the editor of the *Economic and Political Weekly*. She begins the story and immediately wants to phone Krishna Raj. Then she recalls something she's done wrong.

"I better read *The Upanishads* [a Hindu holy book]," she says.

"*The Koran*," her son Monu corrects, worried his mother will offend her new religion and cause more trouble.

"Ah, yes," she smiles ruefully. "Islam is certainly discipline. A Muslim woman can't paint nudes. She can't write love poems. Let's scrap them all, all religions. Then I'll take this off" – she touches her chador – "and wear an ochre sari and jump up and down."

"You just heard her say, 'Let's scrap all religions *except* Islam,'" Monu admonishes, slipping in an Islamic caveat.

I assure him that's what I heard. He tells me to remember "the light," and reminds me that Kamala is the hope for bringing together the warring faiths.

That night I read Kamala's poetry, not her prose. I copy part of "Terror," written during the 1976 Emergency, because it reminds me that I have not done justice to her social and political poetry, and because it speaks to me now in our post-9/11 state of fear and heightened emotion. I think, once again

Cowardice wardens us night and day
... the sky
is taut like the face of a drum. We
go round and round singing the national
nursery rhymes ...

On the last morning before the end of this perplexing visit, Kamala says she is ready to hear what I have written for the book. We lie side by side in her bedroom, and I take out the manuscript. This is the first time I'm reading it to her and I'm beyond nervous. The style will be a surprise, not necessarily a convivial one, and Kamala will have to confront the publication of her intimate life.

I start the reading with a description of our first meeting. Kamala laughs and says "that's true" when she hears apt quotes, and changes Das's designation from "cousin," to "relative." When I read about her marriage at fifteen, she says she was born in 1934 but her father changed the date to 1932 because she was too young to be married off legally. I read for over an hour. It seems I am holding her interest, but she hasn't pronounced herself.

"Shall I read more?"

"Yes, read on."

I begin the conversion chapter and am soon describing her visit to Sadiq Ali's home overlooking the river. When I read "I was almost asleep when Sadiq Ali climbed in beside me," she jerks upright.

"You can't say that. It will get him arrested. Rape is a criminal act. I haven't told my children of the assault. He assaulted me or I would not have let him. Soften the rape. Say Sadiq Ali's touch may have released sexual energy lying dormant for years. Rape is a criminal act."

This is what I was dreading. "Write the truth," she said, but there was always the chance she'd be unhappy. She has pulled the first thread. When I finish reading, will it all unravel?

"Can I read the rest of the scene?"

"Yes, why not?"

"I was almost asleep when Sadiq Ali climbed in beside me," I read, "holding me, breathing softly, whispering endearments, kissing my face, breasts ... and when he entered me, it was the first time I had ever experienced what it was like to feel a man from the inside." The next day, she told Sadiq Ali, "I feel sullied."

"I come from a very conservative background," Kamala comments. "I didn't want it to be illicit."

I take this as encouragement and read for another half-hour, then wait.

"It's such a beautiful story, but they will arrest him," Kamala says, distressed.

I try to imagine ways of complying with her request to write the story of her conversion without including the sensuality and the passion. I could offer as a pretext that she was fed up with Hindu hypocrisy, or was seeking exaltation, or that her restless writer's spirit sought experimentation. But although each is relevant, it doesn't work. "Readers won't really understand your conversion without this scene," I say.

"That is true."

"Can I read more?"

"Yes."

I read the whole chapter, Kamala silent, me fighting despair.

"Such poetry, humour," she says when I finish. "Like a prayer wheel, you have everything in it. You have reconstructed me. Such strength in the writing, Merrily. I didn't know."

"What about Sadiq Ali?" I ask.

Her face clouds. "I don't know."

"Can we change his name?"

"Yes. Let's change the names. And that of my solid doctor friend. Otherwise you must wait, and then remember I'm laughing from Paradise at Sadiq Ali's discomfort, his wives' discomfort."

The hotel sends a taxi to Kamala's gate to pick me up for the last time this visit. The cab drives past the familiar landmarks between Kamala's house and the hotel – the market, water tanks, State Institute of Training for Women, Rajiv Gandhi Stadium, the billboards for banks, mobiles, radio stations, underwear – and I imagine Kamala cutting a swath though past and present, pushing boundaries and taking risks. Even within the confines of conversion, she manages to write what she sees and to love defiantly. And even if I don't know what will happen to her next, as the cab crosses the final bridge into downtown Cochin, I know that she has given me her blessing for what I *have* written, the blessing I hoped for as her friend.

# SEVEN

# Cochin, 2004

The last breath
exhaled
is the last poem
released

# Exhaltations

I am home for less than a year when it becomes apparent that I must return to Kerala as quickly as possible. Kamala has been sicker than at any time I have known her, and our phone conversations carry a current of illness and grief. In the fall she needed high-tech medical tests and stayed with her son in Bangalore. Sick enough to think she had cancer, she watched the newly rich drink vodka and whisky, "forever planning to buy islands, beaches, and palaces," and hid from the "creeping, ambitious" publicist hussling contacts for the "Corporate Guru." Mostly she was alone,

> Burrowing …
> Beyond the skin

Beyond the bones and the marrow
To the nadir of life
The hot, dark cellar
Of loneliness …

We kept in touch throughout, and I tried to raise her spirits, reminding her of all who love her, of who she is.

Then a *Mathubhumi* journalist found her. "I've thrown off the purdah," she told him, escalating the already palpable household tension.

"Recant," demanded her older sons, dreading more trouble and trying to scare her. "They will inject a bubble in your veins and kill you instantly, they will harm the grandchildren."

"It was not Islam but religion I renounced," Kamala protested, feeling misunderstood, hurt, and betrayed by children who had become

stranger-foes who carried
in their scabbards
sharpened steel-words …

"The mind has its own limbs, and they're all folded up," she confided sadly.

She moved to a friend's house and her mysterious illness was diagnosed at last – "a slow case of arsenic poisoning," she told me. "They found it even in my hair. A servant said that Kalyani used to put brown powder in my coffee. Hindu fanatics may have asked her to do it."

Kalyani was paid off, and Kamala returned home. Then she summoned me.

I enter Kamala's familiar sitting-room and see a swarm of seven young men with cameras, booms, lights, reflectors, and a still camera flashing like a strobe. Kamala sits stoically in her rosewood chair, looking weaker than ever. The camera points at her fixedly. It shoots our warm greetings, our asides, and her engaging riffs, which take flight and oddly peter out. The director approaches Kamala's feet and crouches. He sounds like he's wheedling. "The love affairs in *My Story*, are they really true?" he presses.

A Nikon flashes, searing Kamala's eyes for days to come.

"The greatest love of my life was my grandmother," she answers. "She loved me so much."

"Then tell us about your childhood," the cameraman prods.

"I'm so bored with all that," she looks away, looks at them. "It is enough," she says. "It is finished."

She undoes her burqua, lets down her hair, and warns the filmmakers not to film her uncovered head because it's dangerous for her. Her maidservant helps her stand and pivot toward her room. Supported like the aging Gandhi, she walks slowly away as the cameraman leaps up and switches on the camera behind her back. I run forward to block the lens.

As soon as I've settled into my hotel room and stopped moving, I wonder what I'm doing here. Besides the usual phone calls, visitors, and media, Kamala has an uninvited foreign visitor in attendance, Dr Hussain and Monu about to arrive, plus my current travelling companion, Elizabeth, and me. I came because Kamala was ill, but I can't imagine how we can connect profoundly in the midst of so many people. Perhaps, although I'm not looking forward to it, I should ask if we can discuss her publication concerns. Even though we have a legal agreement authorizing me to write about her life, I feel morally bound to understand what she wants published, what not, and when.

As Janet Malcolm wrote in *The Journalist and the Murderer*, there are potentially disastrous pitfalls in writing about a living person, particularly when there is a conflict between the author's story and the story the subject expects. I had hoped to avoid these pitfalls by writing *with* Kamala. But Kamala doesn't write long form non-fiction and says she isn't up to it. She calls me her "biographer" publicly now and often asks me to record for the future, "because you are my biographer." I dread the possibility of conflict, but ultimately I may have to decide:

What needs be published so that Kamala's life and work can be fully appreciated and understood?

Will publishing these "truths" cause Kamala harm?

Is the trouble now worth the truth for generations to come?

And am I asking these questions so I can publish a saleable book, or because I truly believe that if readers discover the life Kamala really lived, they will, as her professor friend Sarada told me, "understand her better and love her even more in intensity than we are doing now"?

When we first met, Kamala and I made a pact to be honest with each other. In our third meeting, she graphically described the excruciatingly painful, legitimized, repetitive, marital rape that permanently affected her life and work. "Publish and be damned," she said when I asked if I could print what she had said. More marital disclosures followed, and on our fourth meeting I asked her for formal permission to write about her.

"Merrily, what a question to ask your dearest friend," she answered. "I love you very much, Merrily, and I want you to write about me and clear the misconceptions that my countrymen have regarding me."

"So, Kamala, just to understand, you're happy if I write these …"

"Of course you can write these things, which have been given to you as personal confessions because I trust you and have faith in your love for me. That's enough, Merrily. That gives you permission to write anything you want about me. I will accept."

Yesterday, when the documentary crew asked Kamala when the "biography" would be published, she surprised me by saying, "After my death." When they asked again, she repeated, "After my death."

I *do* have to talk to her.

Meanwhile, I take pleasure in beginning my simple, satisfying Cochin routine: papaya, curd, and ready-made tea for breakfast, mid-morning auto rickshaw to Kamala's, buy vegetables for the cooks, lunch together, ferry to Willingdon Island to swim, and late afternoon visit and early dinner with Kamala.

I can't stop staring at her this evening. Hussain has come, and she sits beside him looking like a sunburst – red lips, red headband, bright pink housedress. She has been saying things to me like "The life is draining out of me. Sometimes I think the light is not worth the candle." And when I look sad, she says, "But don't worry, Merrily, you will still have memories, like tentacles." Her metamorphosis tonight is astounding. She is radiating pheromones.

Vishalam serves a succession of South Indian dishes, and we begin a discussion about language. I recall Kamala saying that she's never heard a crude word for intercourse in Malayalam.

"People speak Malayalam differently depending on their place and caste," she explains, "fisher folk, city people, north of Kerala, south. I learned Malayalam at Nalapat from my uncle the philosopher, and from the women of Nalapat."

I tell her that Balan Chullikkad said she was the first Malayalam writer "to make a rainbow" of the city idiom written in standard Malayalam and the local rural dialect written as it is pronounced. She agrees, saying she used both idioms in her stories because she learned her Malayalam from her grand-uncle's translation of *Les Miserables* and also from hearing the servants speak. "I connect the two because I watched the city through a villager's eyes." She says that as an adolescent she loved the Sanskrit plays of Kalidasa, "whose classic *Shakuntalam* cast a spell on Goethe so that Goethe too employed a narrator and a chorus in the writing of *Faust.*" And she also loved Bhasa, the great playwright who wrote *Swapnavasavadattam* (The dream). "Such a beautiful story it is," she says, covering her heart with her hand. "It gives me goosebumps."

"That is not a poetic word," admonishes Dr Hussain, surprising me with this interruption. "Why do you want to confuse it with animals?"

"But you eat animals, Sachee," Kamala laughs, miming stuffing her mouth. "A goose, a goat …"

"It is not appropriate," Hussain persists.

"My husband used to say 'horipulation,'" Kamala deflects. "He always used words from the dictionary." Then to make Hussain happy, she drops "goosebumps" and says that she knows a good story when it produces "that feeling on my skin."

"Go wash your face so Merrily and Elizabeth can kiss you," Kamala instructs Hussain when he's finished eating. "He is very clean," she assures us.

At this, Elizabeth who is over-stimulated by the food and the vast unknown, flips. "She's cast a spell on me," she whispers urgently. "I don't know what world I'm in."

Hussain looks mortified, and I assure Kamala we don't want to kiss Dr Hussain. "He's yours," I say.

"Ah, private property," she agrees, having succeeded in connecting us all together anyway.

I don't want to write anything new or collect more material, and for a while I don't. Then I find myself scrambling for writing implements with my fingers sopped in sauce, scribbling names of publishers I agree to chase and descriptions of visitors like Srinivasan, a Chaplinesque actor whose grim face makes Kamala laugh. I buy a hardcover notebook that I can feel and extract quickly from my backpack. Illness has heightened Kamala's sense of mortality. It's made her more determined to speak truth as she sees it, and me more eager to write it down.

"We make our own path, picking up revelations along the way," she says, having felt the thrill of her Islamic honeymoon fade to a life-long prospect of prescribed behaviour. "Wait for your own revelations, don't go to the Hindus, Muslims, Christians. Religion cost me too much, cost me dearly. If there are voices to be heard, I will hear them myself."

She tells me that even in Kerala, which prides itself on religious coexistence, she is still being attacked from both sides. The Hindu Sangh Parivar, an association of Hindu nationalist organizations, protests her ownership of the snake shrine on her own ancestral property at Nalapat because she is a Muslim. The Muslims are "disgusted" with her because she speaks against their practices and clergy, refusing to support sectarian politics she finds unpalatable. "They feel they are losing their grip on me." She sounds increasingly fed up with fundamentalism of all stripes, culturally sanctioned male superiority, religious interference in her writing and painting, and discourteous behaviour like that of thirty-two-year-old Rahman who doesn't rise when she, an elder, enters the room. She is particularly disillusioned by the behaviour of an esteemed friend who, while hiring teachers for a new Muslim school, "wrings money from their very poor families," forcing them to sell everything so their sons can train as teachers and earn a minimal eight thousand rupees a month.

"How can I be friends with someone so avaricious?" she asks.

Her dislike of organized religion is so much more pronounced than on my last visit that I wonder if any beliefs remain to comfort her.

"Yes," she answers. "A concept of God. A presence in my room. I'm not alone. I visualize a shower of moonlight falling on someone in prayer. It is a soothing exercise. I feel bathed in light, and I know there is a God."

It's easy for me to accept her distrust of organized religion, any religion, but harder to empathize with her faith. Yet as we talk, I realize that being thrust into the spiritual limelight propelled her on a profound spiritual journey. Unwilling to hurt or insult other Muslims, she remained a Muslim and created a personal god that commentators associate with the Sufi strain of Islam, a point of convergence for Hindu and Islamic mysticism. I ask her why she is compared to the mystic poet, Raabia, an eighth-century Muslim woman, and why her recent poetry is linked to Sufism.

"Direct contact with God, like talking to your lover – it's as private as that," she answers. "God is within your bloodstream. You have every right to talk to your God. I've burnt my bridges here, burnt my bridges back to Hinduism. I've made my own book, my own personal prayers. There is a kind of seeking. Maybe it is God, maybe it is ourselves."

But Sufis believe that the human soul belongs to the spiritual world and is forever seeking to merge with God, to reunite with its source. That human love is just a stepping stone to dissolve in the Divine. Yet Kamala still longs to touch Dr Hussain and inhale his scent. She wants him to kneel at her feet and put his head in her lap so she can play with his hair and bring him close to her.

"Desire is like an evening wick lit at night at the snake shrine," she tells me. "If you look out, you see the wick burning till dawn. If you don't have this, all the lights are out, and all you do is age. Hussain brought his wife here. She looked at me and told her husband, 'There is such a luminous glow, it's because she has seen God.' She doesn't know it's because I've seen her husband naked in the shower. It's a spiritual thing too, Merrily. We are phallus worshippers, we Hindus. I don't think God could give me a feeling like that."

Last year she was so anguished by the conflict between sacred and human love that she wrote, "Oh! Allah, put an end to my eternal craving to be loved, the intense hunger. Train me to free myself from all bodily desires. Oh! Allah! Forgive me! Behind this glowing face of mine burn not only the sacred lamps of devotion, but the fire of love."

It is meaningless, then, to ask how she could reconcile these loves, since the conflict still exists. But unless she's making shocking paradoxical utterances to stimulate thought, it seems a good time to ask how she can give herself totally to God and to Hussain too. "How do you do it?" I finally ask.

"Because there is some legitimacy about passion brought on by excessive love. I cannot think of it as anything illegitimate. I'm wedded to him. God has given him to me as a reward for becoming a good Muslim. I feel purer with him."

I wish her sweet dreams and close the door remembering how she marvels and delights in Hussain – the stirrings she feels and never felt before when she sees him fumble with his belt, the throbbing between her legs when he holds her, the thrill of lying on top of him, rubbing as if she has a spot of eczema and enjoying the itch. Feeling "purer" with Hussain must have something to do with abilities beyond my ken, like her identification with Krishna's sacred love games, or her capacity to give herself wholeheartedly to a worthy truth.

# 22

# A Cloudburst of Intense Fantasy

Beyond the lip of the infinity pool, ephemeral as a dolphin's arc, a massive shape manifests, then slowly reabsorbs into the waters of Vembanad Lake. "Look!" Elizabeth stops me mid-lap. "A submarine."

We swim more laps in the soupy afternoon water and hang at the edge of the pool. A battleship steams across the horizon, a frigate, and another warship on training exercises from the HQ of Southern Naval Command. As the sun sets, round wooden fishing boats, refurbished Chinese junks, sailing ships, and ferries take back the water.

Chugging home on the ferry to Cochin, we pass barges, huge container ships, geared vessels with sculptural cranes, a police launch, and the giant metal chutes, conveyors, and loading booms that front the storage sheds along the shoreline of Willingdon Island. Salman Rushdie's *The Moor's Last Sigh* is set in Cochin, one of the world's oldest, most cosmopolitan trading centres, and Amitav Ghosh's *In an Antique Land* evokes Cochin's twelfth-century trading height at a time when Jews, Arabs, Hindus, and Muslims found modes of accommodation, and difference didn't necessarily mean conflict. "Kerala was introduced to Europe from the first century AD," Balan once reminded me, "so an international sensibility was part of Kamala's inheritance."

When I return, Kamala is alone at her bedroom mirror fumbling with her eye drops, too agitated to get the fluid in.

"Rahman just brought this doctor of nature medicine here," she says in a rush, "about sixty-six, white goatee, an arrogant man. He said, 'Remove your maidservants, I'll bring three women related to me.' He started calling my maidservants names – crook, thief, prostitute. He told them, 'I have every right to enter the bedroom. I treat her,' and he entered the bedroom. My seventy-eight-year-old Nayar maidservant Ponnamma said, 'No, in our culture, men don't enter the bedroom.' Again he called the maidservants prostitutes. Ponnamma bent down and grabbed him by the throat, saying, 'I am not your wife.'

"Now Rahman calls so the doctor can come back. I am a Nayar woman," she says covered in black purdah. "Hindu law forbids this. I have a code of ethics. I have adopted their God, God is so ambiguous, so vague, it's okay. I don't mind the scarf, I'll wear it. But not these men walking into the bedroom."

Rahman arrives on the heels of the phone call in his white Imam's dress.

Kamala sits in her chair, swollen feet covered by a clean, white cloth. "He is a father now," she says, being gracious. So I congratulate Rahman on his paternity and on having been to the Haj, the pilgrimage to Mecca that every good Muslim hopes to undertake. Rahman smiles proudly.

"He brought me holy ZamZam water," Kamala acknowledges. Then, courtesies over, she tells Rahman she will not have the old doctor back.

"Maybe Rahman would like to see the pictures we took during Dr Hussain's visit," I chirp to lighten the mood. Kamala likes the pictures because she thinks we all look so happy, and because in close-up she can see Dr Hussain's admiring gaze.

I hand Rahman the pictures and leave to do some filing. When I return, Kamala is gone. I find her inert black form on her new pink bedcovers.

"Did Rahman like the pictures?" I ask.

"He said I look well bred when I wear the purdah," she says listlessly, not looking at me. At first I don't get it. Then I realize that the photos I so blithely gave Rahman show Kamala with her hair uncovered in front of Dr Hussain, and therefore Rahman has implied that she is not well bred.

She lies on her side, without makeup or jewellery, hair down and swept back, features hard-etched by this new affront.

I sit silently by her side, feeling responsible and seething with anger at this hideous situation in which Rahman can insult Kamala with impunity, she has to swallow it, and I'm made to feel guilty for what I consider nothing. I stew in bilious juices, wishing I could make Kamala feel better, until she opens her eyes and changes the subject. She soon regains her composure, and since there is no hiding this drastic change from cult adoration to petty insult, I ask what she makes of her experience of Islam now.

She answers the question as if it's been on her mind, saying she thinks she picked up "rudiments" that were good for her – not the rudiments of religion, since no religion appealed to her, but the fact that she could worship "an invisible God."

"If I have to love a God and accept him as my owner, I have to see that he is set free first. He's no longer a Muslim, or a Hindu, or a Christian," she says, making it clear she's made this conversion her own. "I create my own God, it's only God and me. I think I've become stronger for that."

Yet sometimes she says she is a Hindu *and* a Muslim. She learned the Hindu mantras, kept the idols, chanted particular mantras for each god, and that knowledge remains within her, along with her early Christian and recent Islamic training. I wonder which of them comforts her most and ask what she turns to when she's sad or lonely or scared.

"I turn to the man I love," she says to my astonishment. "I try to dial his number. It's not enough having a God. I want a man's touch. So I tell him, 'I'm lonely, when can I see you?' That's the ultimate discovery. I think even when I'm about to depart for another world, I will try to phone him. I will not speak words to God."

"That's an amazing thing to say, Kamala."

"That's the truth. I don't want to be a sham in front of you. I would like his words in my ear, to be brave, because when I go, I go alone, but he must send me. I don't romanticize God. It's not enough for me. I need the voice of the man I love saying, 'Goodbye, be strong, and I'll say you're the bravest girl I've come across.'"

She rolls onto her back, barely moving, waiting for the next question. I can't say anything. I remember being with her in the Ambassador, inching across the bridge to Matancherry, Kamala almost in a trance as she looked out across the water. Then, like petals opening, she said, "Maybe death is like this, a journey over a bridge with water on either side. No stillness. Stillness is frightening. There is movement. You travel like this. You must go leagues and leagues before you shrink into an embryo and end up in someone's womb." It was the first death concept I'd ever found comforting, and I remember then, as I do again now, silently thanking her for the thought, that

There is a love greater than all you know
that awaits you where the red road finally ends
its patience proverbial ...
Its embrace is truth and it erases
even the soul's ancient indentations so that
some unknown womb shall begin to convulse
to welcome your restructured perfection.

Still, I feel like crying for the lonely end that Kamala faces, that we all face, and because she tries so hard to be the strongest, bravest girl.

Then the phone rings and she reaches for it, responding with a lightness that defies sadness, pain, and death itself. Two more calls transform her mood, while mine remains moved by her poignant declaration of the primacy of human love. Phrases she has used to describe her concept of God come back to me – "a kind of seeking ... your own God ... energy within ... all soul inseparable from the body... maybe God, maybe ourselves." And I remember her telling me that creating her own God was "like childbirth," the same metaphor she used to describe creating a poem. "Anything beautiful is God, " she said, "I can't think of God separate from the beauty of creation."

I think I am beginning to comprehend this new God that Kamala has created, a God I can envisage. When I think about it in my own way, her God lives at the Back Lake, in a great poem, in the joy in my young granddaughters' eyes.

"But if Hussain were a good Muslim as he claims, he would conduct a Nikah [an official marriage] ceremony with me," Kamala says when she puts down the phone. "If he doesn't, I may not go to Paradise. I was slated for Paradise, Merrily. I make only one request of Allah: If you are there, there must be a Paradise, don't leave me in the middle limbo, take me up to Paradise."

I suggest again that legalizing her arrangement with Hussain may not be a wise decision if she hopes to leave an inheritance for her grandchildren. As her legal husband, Hussain might inherit all her possessions and money.

"But would he keep it?" she asks incredulously. "Won't he give it to the grand-children?"

I remind her that when we talked together about her acts of charity, Hussain said, "Who can resist free money?"

"But I'm glad," she sidesteps adroitly. "If I had known only my husband, I would never have known this physical part. I can't live without someone to hold me, even if he's only a marionette. I say, 'What a beautiful shape you have. What a king. Like an animal, what a beautiful body you have.' I don't refer to his weakness, I pamper him. Desdemona loved a Moor, and she walked in a state of grace. I make Hussain feel like a great brute of a man, a morsel for a woman. It's not as if I'm destroying the morality of ancient India."

Ponnamma sings in the background, soothing us as we talk. She lives a metre from a famous Shiva temple and worships Lord Shiva. Every night she lights a lamp and from 6 to 7 PM sings in praise of Shiva.

*Namashivaya.*

The handle of a circular bronze mirror lies imbedded in a large bowl of rice on a pedestal in the receiving room where we sit. It represents a goddess who bestows prosperity. "The goddess has a birthright to be in my room," Kamala says.

*Valkannati.*

Above the entrance of every door are carved rosewood lintels from Kamala's ancestral home.

*Nalapat.*

Kamala's high black headdress is decorated with the iridescent green rococo costume jewellery I brought from Montreal.

*Purdah.*

"He puts his head on my knee. I stroke him. He's like a dog: if he had ticks, I'd remove them."

*The ordinary one.*

Kamala rummages in her cupboard to find me a parting gift. She pulls out a silk brocade dress, pressing it upon me. I protest – the dress is obviously meant for awards, state functions, grand halls. Kamala insists, "You're the only one I can talk to. I trust you. I feel I'm talking to the future, confiding in history."

I settle my bill, give gratuities to the hotel staff, count the bags loaded into Jacob's Ambassador, and calculate four hours with Kamala before leaving.

The phone rings as soon as I open her door. A friend says there's a documentary on Kamala's life right now on TV. We catch a photo montage of guileless young Kamala, followed by a lyrical if maudlin chronology of Kamala, "a slave to love," writing "in the language of the soul, like music that is not heard by most people."

The phone rings again. Kamala's brother announces that a film based on her story, *Nashtapettah Neelambari* (The lost Neelambari) is on another channel, and I tease her about Kamala-Kamala TV.

"It's International Women's Day," she says, and concentrates on providing an English voice-over.

"A girl living in Madurai falls in love with her Brahmin music teacher," she translates over the images. "One day she falls into the temple tank, and her teacher carries her out. It is the first time she touches a male body. Soon after, just as she is learning the Neelambari, her father stops her music lessons. He sends her away to Madras and marries off the music teacher. The girl becomes a doctor and marries too. Years pass, and when her second husband dies, she feels she absolutely must see her teacher. But he is dead and she cannot even see his body because he is a Brahmin. She walks past the temple and hears the music of the Neelambari. It is dusk. Someone is teaching the tune to another girl."

I have forgotten the time, but Kamala notices it is getting late. "She feels everything is lost," she says, shutting off the television. "A sad story, also beautiful. Merrily, we must eat."

As soon as we sit, she tells me she has been thinking about my warning that Hussain might stake a claim to her estate should they marry. "I can't have that, upset my children," she says. "So I guess you and I exchanged roles. I told him, 'I'll be happy being your concubine, and it won't cost you one paise.' There is no legitimacy or illegitimacy in love. When I visited you, I put marriage in your mind. Now you have given me sane advice not to marry. I am not Muslim enough this year to believe in Paradise. Last year,

> I thought I would
> learn from Islam
> a clean way
> to compromise –
> I did not.

I am hard as a nail
on the cross


"There is no Paradise," she says resolutely to me now. "There is only this life."

Vishalam and Ammu hover, Ponnamma fills my plate. Ammu says that next year I should wear a sari. Dye my hair too. I stuff myself with okra, mango curry, kichadi, curd and puffy Kerala rice. It is food I could eat forever. Kamala tries to give me a pair of her beautiful gold bangles, desisting only when I invoke her granddaughters.

"You're leaving a very lonely friend," she says.

"I'll see you next year," I promise, hoping she will have the strength to continue making her own path through the minefields. I tell her I find her brave – to break free of religion, create her own God, write daringly despite censorship – and that she's my most courageous friend.

"Frankly, Merrily, I don't want to die a coward," she says, as if she's stuck with an immutable genetic trait. "All my life, enemies emerge out of the woodwork. If I lose my nerve and succumb to political or social pressures, it's better you strangle me. In my culture, honour is to keep your dignity until you die."

I nod, letting her know I've figured this out.

"The book will be ready?" she asks.

"Yes," I say.


The maidservants accompany me to the road, insisting on lugging my bags. Ponnamma is barefoot and has trouble descending the stairs. She leans heavily on the railing but won't give up my backpack. Tears catch me as I leave Kamala's apartment, sobs as I open the cab door. Ponnamma mimes gestures of talking on a telephone, I mime, yes. And as the car pulls away, I look back at Ammu, Vishalam, Ponnamma, until I can't see them anymore.

## EIGHT

# Cochin, Punnayurkulam, 2005

also her nature, the urge to fly, and the endless
pathways of the sky

# 23

## That Close to Me

I finish the last page of *The Love Queen of Malabar*, and fly – London, Frankfurt, Dubai, and finally to Cochin. I am carrying with me a memory stick, pencils, sharpener, cellotape, the manuscript, and an ambitious plan. If I read to Kamala two hours a day for ten days, we can cover the text. Kamala can rest while I read, and I will note her reactions. If there are problems, we will decide together how to handle them. The record of this process will be the epilogue: the final word.

Kamala puts down her pen the moment I enter her office and shuts her note-book. She says she is writing a new Malayalam novel, and announces, "I am tired of being Suraiya. I want to be Madhavikutty again." She tells me she's enjoying the writing and that it makes her feel she is becoming her "own self."

I stand there grinning. This is the Kamala to whom I relate most easily – the writer I first met through her books and later watched blossom anew in the Laurentians at the pine desk my father built. Her poems were the heartbeat of our conversations, and her memoirs brought me close to the child and the young woman I missed in real time. Kamala once gave me a handwritten Quillmark notebook, some phrases underlined, some not, from her 1985 US lecture tour. I read them as her artist's manifesto:

My poems epitomize the dilemma of the modern Indian woman who tries to free herself domestically from the bondage sanctioned by the past.

My forms are direct expressions of an autobiographical voice. But that – individual voice also asks to be read symbolically ...

A woman writer takes herself apart and recreates a new identity. For this transformation we have first to locate alternatives, search for the roots of a self-hood to create a transformed self.

I like to see Kamala writing. In Suresh Kohli's documentary, *Kamala Das: An Introduction*, novelist Namita Gokhale described how Kamala's serious writing had been hijacked and diminished by a press that sensationalized her life rather than celebrating her literary stature. But prurient, moralistic critiques never stopped her. No matter what ulterior agendas she faces, writing reinforces her self. Seeing her write makes me think that she is tapping into what she calls her "invisible soul," and her mind, the lean greyhound of her poems, is awakening and leaping up once again.

She smiles and summons her maidservants Vishalam and Ammu, a most responsive welcoming committee. Everyone seems surprised I'm not fatter, although my shape hasn't changed since I started visiting ten years ago. I am surprised at how regal Kamala looks. She is dressed in light colours, and her topknot, tied in black cloth, is covered by a chador rising high above her forehead like a crown, with flowing white folds. The maidservants help her to the drawing-room, and I see it too is lighter – pale yellow upholstery, white tiled floors, open screen windows, and soft blue walls. Kamala sits in the sitting-room with me, but she clearly hasn't left her novel behind. She's bursting with it. She tells me that the hero, named Sadiq Ali like the pseudonym of her lover, is the chief trustee of a hospital. He falls in love, "finding Paradise right here, not there," then is seemingly found charred to death in his car. The heroine, Annasuraiya, a Hindu classical singer, is devastated by the tragic loss of her lover.

Kamala says she is growing into the character of Annasuraiya and doesn't know what to do with her. Drawing on her own experience, she says, "At nights, to cope better, she enters little dreams, seeing his shoulder, his back." Kamala also loves her creation, Sadiq Ali, "one of the best men I know," and regrets having killed him off. "How will I resurrect him?" Things are somewhat uncertain. "How will it end?"

Kamala's food consecrates my homecoming. My fingers mush morsels of dry curries, wet curries, curd, rice, and my thumb shovels it in, as she reports on the British documentary crew that just left, the Italian critic coming, a untraceable Australian poet friend, and Bombay where "I was so alive it was like a hundred people in me, like worms in a can." I ask about her mother's funeral, and she says Dr Hussain carried her, her hair loose, wearing a white sari, up the stairs for the twenty-one gun salute, and the Muslim magazines decried the photos. She tells me that when she was on television she said, "The last word is not the Koran, the last word will be spoken by the last man on earth," and that the threats began again. So now the watchman is wary of bearded Muslims in white headgear instead of Hindus with stripes of sacred ash. Finally, she insists I meet J. Devika, whose work I've read and who, she said, interviewed her brilliantly. And also Jayaraj, the talented filmmaker developing a film from one of her stories.

Then, John the driver arrives with the daily pile of mail, the phone rings with TV producers promising they'll take only five minutes, fans call and coo, Shrinivasan downloads the email, neighbours visit to arrange a building association meeting, Kamala lies down for her afternoon rest, I leave to swim, and everything is once again as I remember it.

The next day I arrive early, with great seriousness of purpose. Luckily there are no visitors. I sit on the chair near the head of Kamala's bed and begin to read the chapter entitled "The Stranger and I."

"Who is he, what stranger?" Kamala asks, and I explain that I've used the titles of her poems out of context to introduce the chapters and section headings of the book.

I resume reading and she listens quietly until manuscript page 7, when I can't take her silence anymore.

"How are you doing?" I ask.

"I'm enjoying. I'm amused." And after I read excerpts from her poems "Composition" and "Loud Posters," she says, "It's like chewing on good sugarcane. What a troubled, turbulent time, my youth."

At the mention of her husband's overdraft, she choruses, "About six thousand rupees, poor chap."

And adds, "What a slave driver," when I read how he made her work.

"That's gracious for all this messing up," she comments, hearing her husband's dying words of thanks. "Don't bring out the depth of his cruelty. I protected him for the sake of the children. They don't know."

When I read the poem suggesting that her husband tried to make her forget "her nature, the urge to fly, and the endless pathways of the sky," she says, "I'm hearing this as a reader, and I'm crying for Kamala Das. At that time, when I was young, strong, radiant, I would have liked to have a better life."

By page 16, when her early relationship with her husband is sketchily introduced, she erupts, "This book should show truth, like the store that sells knives – the glitter, the gleam, and the violence. Tell the truth, Merrily. Allow me to be as truthful as possible."

At page 19, I pause.

"So far it's so interesting. Such a good book," Kamala encourages.

"Riveting," she says at page 25. "Without Saint John giving publicity, Christ would be nothing. You are my Saint John."

At page 40, we are called to lunch. "I trust you with my secrets because I was burdened with them," Kamala says.


By the next day Kamala has figured out how to save Sadiq Ali, the Muslim hero of her novel who was car-bombed by fanatics for loving the Hindu singer Annasuraiya. It is the mechanic, not Sadiq Ali, who has been burnt to death. But Sadiq Ali has been badly injured and is wandering the roads not knowing who he is. He has lost his memory. Meanwhile, Annasuraiya thinks Sadiq Ali is dead.

I read briefly from my manuscript before Kamala interrupts to tell me that Dr Hussain has cancelled his promised visit, "some distant hospital, something to be amputated, I haven't seen him in months." She says that he wants me to use his real name in the book, but his wife has become her friend and the children love her too. She says she's worried about the effect of publication on his family.

I suggest that changing his name won't make any difference to the story and read her a reference to "the surgeon," asking if we should change his profession too.

"Change his name but not his profession," she decides. She checks with Hussain, reciting the poetry being considered for the book – "his large hands/ accustomed to scalpels/ turning gentle/ and precise/ in a different rite" – and he agrees too.

I am gearing up to read again when Kamala suddenly insists I call Mangoo, a childhood friend of hers. Yesterday her comments were flattering and over the top. Today she seems distracted, bored, looking to leaven the scene. She invites Mangoo to visit and greets her old schoolmate in Malayalam, "lips palpitating with Dravidian polysyllables that bubbled forth," as British travel writer Geoffrey Moorhouse wrote about a Malayalam speaker. Then, laughingly, in English, she says, "Did you hear how Merrily said 'Malayalam'? 'Mál a yál am, Mál a yál am," she mimics, syllables thumping.

Mangoo leans toward me gently. "You know there are no accents on syllables in Malayalam," he says as if to a recalcitrant child.

I am always captivated by Kamala's English-speaking voice with its bell-like enunciation, music, and sweetness. But her Malayalam persona is another world, glimpsed only in translation and from critics such as K. Satchidanandan, who explained how Kamala redefined the very genre of Malayalam prose and "gave it singing nerves." Another writer wanted me to understand that "Malayalam is the land of the heart for the masses."

Kamala and Mangoo are waiting for me to say something.

"Malayalam," I say burbling like a Canadian brook.

"Remember our school song?" Kamala asks Mangoo with a wicked gleam. They sing,

Rule, Britannia! Britannia, rule the waves;
Britons never shall be slaves,
The nations not so blest as thee,
Shall in their turns to tyrants fall;

While thou shalt flourish great and free,
The dread and envy of them all.

Then days pass without a mention of my manuscript, and I'm not sure what
Kamala wants to do about it. It squats in my backpack like a fat, hooded toad
while she devotes her energy to her own work. She tells me that a law of gravity
pulls her back to the past and that her way of dealing with it is to write about it,
"put it away, frame the whole thing," as she is so cheerfully doing now. I can't
help but admire her life-long capacity to rebound, renew, reinvent – to be, as she
says, "a tough survivor." As her mother Balamani Amma wrote when Kamala was
ill and suffering but still writing poems, "Your power of turning worms into but-
terflies/ Comforts me."

Finally I understand that Kamala hasn't time to hear my entire manuscript,
and I suggest reading her the problematic parts. "Yes, at least I should hear the
tricky parts," she acknowledges. Yet there seems a coolness about the whole
endeavour. I worry about reading difficult passages out of context. I don't know
what she worries about, but more days pass and neither of us interrupts the
steady flow of visitors, the daily exigencies, mealtime, her rest, my swim, to confront the uncomfortable question of what to do. When I bring up specifics like
the cruelty of her early marriage, she describes again how painful it was, more
details, more pain, and then she mentions her sons.

Flummoxed, I email my friend Linda who has read the manuscript.

Kamala was flattering the first days I read to her.

Today, Hussain cancelled his visit and she seemed distracted and bored.
She wants to play, not confront uncomfortable questions. And this has become, ultimately, someone else's book.

On the other hand, Kamala voluntarily told me about her Italian lover,
admitting afterwards she tells me these truths because she needs to unbur-
den herself. It will require great bravery in this traditional, conservative
society for her to sanction publication of what I have written. Sometimes
I wonder if she secretly wants me to take the responsibility – and the rap.

Every day is different, up and down like a rollercoaster.

Linda responds immediately. She says I am probably right about Kamala wanting me to take responsibility and therefore maybe I'm the one, not Kamala, who cares about having her informed consent and "blessing." Linda relieves the pressure by suggesting that we don't have to finalize everything during this visit.

I return to find Kamala finishing another instalment of her novel. Characters multiply like rabbits, and side-stories disintegrate and reintegrate. Annasuraiya has transcended her grief through singing and become "a goddess of music." And wandering, amnesiac Sadiq Ali is on a pilgrimage with a busload of Hindus going to sacred Mount Kailash.

"And then?" I ask.

"Ah," Kamala teases, as if she knows.

Since manuscript reading is out but action is a possibility, I lobby for a visit to Punnayurkulam, Kamala's ancestral home. She hasn't been back since her conversion, when local fanatics threatened to stone her to death if she appeared. She is worried the villagers will treat her badly, even spit on her; still, she is tempted to go. She says she would like to see for herself what remains of her land, her trees, the snake shrine and its sacred grove.

Hari, my scholar friend, meets me at my hotel, aware that I came seeking publishing guidance from Kamala. I admit that the subject has been so difficult that we haven't really talked. "Western audiences won't judge Kamala for her sexual disclosures, but I can't fathom this society's response," I tell him.

He asks me which parts I think might cause Kamala trouble.

The problem is, I'm not sure. And I don't know how much trouble, from whom, and what quantity Kamala is ready to take. Her attacks on organized religion are problematic, as is the cruelty of her early marriage, her husband's hidden sexuality, the physicality of her "affairs," her "duty" as a "social asset," and her post–Sadiq Ali sensuality and sexuality.

Hari suggests that the difficult revelations about her husband could be balanced by emphasizing the positive aspects Kamala has mentioned, such as "he didn't beat me, never used bad language, never raised his voice, never ill-treated me publicly, always spoke well of me, was my most constant supporter, didn't cause me embarrassment. I never had to worry about that." Hari thinks that Kamala's sexual disclosures are the most damaging to her.

"If she had sex, it would jeopardize feminist admiration," he warns. "Malayali readers would not expect it to this degree. The moment you mention intercourse, it's finished."

"How do I talk about sexuality without intercourse?"

"Tone it down," he advises. "See how Kamala handled the sexuality in *My Story* and in her poems. Make sure it is not sensational."

"What will Kamala do if the fallout is more poisonous than for *My Story*?" I ask.

"It will be," he answers.

"But Kamala doesn't seem worried about herself," I say. "She worries about her children, and the families of Sadiq Ali and Hussain. I press her for comments on specific passages and details, but it doesn't work. Nothing she's told me is sensational for me, so I wish she would tell me what she wants. I wish I could talk to her."

Hari considers silently. "You are trying to talk across orbits," he suggests hesitantly. "Hers is poetic, yours is something else. The imaginative levels are very different. Do you know what I mean?"

Whether I do or not, what he says clicks. "How are you going to enter her orbit?" he asks.

I don't yet know. I leave him with my manuscript and hop in an auto rickshaw to Gandhi Nagar, mind humming.


A Malayali journalist sits across the office desk from Kamala, tape recorder spinning between them. Kamala tells me he has travelled hours from the countryside where he lives with his parents for whom, to provide subsistence, she has bought a strong, young cow. He is a non-practising Muslim who edits the new instalments of Kamala's novel and delivers them to *Mathrubhumi* for serialization.

She waves me to the chair adjoining his.

"What kind of book is she writing?" he asks Kamala.

"It's up to her," Kamala says. "We're free, our minds are free."

He asks me when Kamala and I first met, if I like Kamala's poetry, why I chose to write about her, and settles in like everybody else who asks for only five minutes. I put my tape recorder beside his and, heeding Hari, try to find a new way in.

"The thing that worries me," I admit to Kamala, "is that this society seems very inhibited and also hypocritical. You get attacked while politicians rape and get away with it. So it's one thing for us to be very honest with each other and trust one another. Then there's the society that – "

Kamala picks up, "– is false. Really and truly, it's so difficult because it's like going to a masquerade. The rapists will pretend to be very moral, religious, spiritual leaders. And many of those who interview me will be sly and burdened with prejudice. Whatever I utter will be misinterpreted. And they'll use it as a weapon to beat me, calm me down."

"I worry that what you say to me, which I don't judge, may cause you trouble when it comes back to this society."

"I don't think it can affect me because my children know me. The earlier secrets like my marriage with him, play it down. Don't make me out to be a very tragic figure, because I wasn't," she says, nuancing the one-dimensional view. "Within the tragic fabric that was my life, I had lots of enjoyment and fun."

"And how about this society: do you care what they think?" I ask. "Let's say this book comes out and it's like *My Story*?"

"It's worse, of course."

"Because in *My Story* you were very ..."

"Guarded."

"I could make the good parts about your marriage bigger."

"No, no, that's why I've turned against this arranged marriage business. Isn't life decided by how you first get to know of sex? If I had not been treated this way when I was so young ... the bitterness remains."

"So how will you cope?"

"There will be trouble from members of my community, the Muslims. Because a good Muslim woman is not supposed to feel any desire for her mate. She should not respond to love. So that kind of goodness I loathe."

"And how about the conservative Hindu community?"

"That is okay. I don't belong there, so now they have no right over me. It's okay. I won't get out of the house. Anyway, I'm not allowed to get out."

For some reason, this still isn't enough for me. This has never happened with my writing before, but I keep hoping that Kamala will take or share editorial responsibility – relieve me of the sole burden of it. Perhaps it's the length and intimacy of our friendship and the protective role I've assumed. Or the persistence of my original co-writing impulse. Whatever it is, I can't seem to leave it alone. "So you are not worried about the larger community?" I ask again.

"What can they do? They can refuse to bury me near the mosque, that's all. So don't bury me there. I'll get myself cremated."

"Anyway, you belong at Nalapat House," I insist, distracted for a moment from my editorial dilemmas.

"I don't care. After death you can have the bloody carcass. I think I will leave it to the Nehru Museum. You can go dump it there. When life is out, who's bothered about the poor body? If the Muslims want one bone, they can take it. Hindus take another bone. Christians take the head. It doesn't make a difference to me."

The journalist asks a question which I request that Kamala translate.

"He asked how I saw the conversion, what is my attitude?"

"Did he ask you why you converted?"

"No. He knows. Everybody knows that it was not purely religious. It was because I really hoped to become somebody's wife. But they made it out to be a big joke. They didn't make a joke out of the prophet Mohammed marrying a widow of sixty-six, but they made a joke when I fell in love with a man who provoked me to become a Muslim, saying he would look after me. And later, when he backed out, people thought I was the biggest fool in Kerala. But it gave me a good chance to know the mind of the average local male Muslim, and I can warn others they cannot respond to you because they think of a woman as a sex object, something like a toilet commode, it's very functional."

"So, should I care about your society, you? How much should I censor?" I ask, like a kid scratching a bite.

"It's not important," Kamala says, and that clinches it, for now.

# 24

# The Place of Quiet Happiness

K.P. Pavitra, an attractive, well-dressed reporter for *Mathrubhumi*, waits with her photographer in the sitting room, having seen Kamala and me on television.

"It is Merrily's desire to see Punnayurkulam with me," Kamala announces, pre-empting the interview. "Tomorrow my friends are going transport me there."

"We're going?" I ask.

"I'll take Ammu and Vishalam. No Nalapat woman travels without two maidservants. John will come too." She tells the journalist that she's rented a van, reserved the Casino Hotel for lunch, assigned the host's role to the rich new owner of Nalapat, and advised her sons, who will send Sudhaker, the senior manager of the *Times of India*, as their envoy. There is an urgency about this homecoming, a now-or-never momentum.

Delighted with her scoop – Madhavikutty's first visit back to Nalapat in eight years – Pavitra moves closer to me. "Why did you choose to write about Kamala?"

"Because she's a fascinating person," I say, thinking: because she still surprises me; because her writing gives me goosebumps: because her vast reservoir of East, West, esoteric, recondite, traditional, modern baggage and lore gives her unfathomable scope; because it's instructive to discover meaning or reason in behaviour, pronouncements, and choices that appear arbitrary and contradictory; because her tumultuous mixed and unmixed, oriental, occidental, city, rural, unique poetic narrative makes her an adventure to comprehend.

"What do you think Merrily is writing about you?" Pravita asks Kamala.

Kamala says something in Malayalam. In English, she repeats her disclaimer, "It's her book. It's up to her."

Then the photographer asks me to pose on the armrest of Kamala's chair. Not wanting to appear larger or too prominent, I sit on the stool nearby.

Early the next day, my brother, on vacation in Kerala, awakes on a houseboat in the backwaters of Alleppey to the shouts of villagers waving a newspaper at him from shore. He walks down the ramp and joins a barefoot couple pointing excitedly at the front page.

On the left, Hyman sees an illustration of half-naked Shiva with his trident, cobra, leopardskin, and beads, floating cross-legged in the snowy mountain tops. On the right, separated from Shiva by swirls of Malayalam, he sees Kamala swaddled in flowing pink robes, and his sister, Merrily.

Hyman and his houseboat crew have just withstood a semi-hurricane in the middle of Lake Vembanad, where the crew entreated him not to make them anchor. He can't read the headline announcing that tomorrow at 11 AM "The Love Queen of Malabar returns to Punnayurkulam." He doesn't know that Kamala is quoted talking about my book, saying, "This book contains elements of my *atmamsam* [my soul.]" But here's his sister on the front page of a newspaper he doesn't know is *Mathrubhumi*. He thanks the villagers, whips out his digital camera, and takes a picture of the thing.

Kamala's entourage readies the vehicles for the trip to Punnayurkulam, and she emerges from her building wearing gold, diamonds, a black burqua, white-fringed chador, and a cellphone around her neck. She is supported by Ammu and Vishalam in their finest saris, and shielded from the sun by John holding a colourful parasol selected to brighten her attire. "I'm going to the place where Nalapat stood, the place of thinking, the place of quiet happiness," she says softly, stopping momentarily to accommodate the *Kerala Times* photographer while I hustle by with pillows so that she can rest.

"This bridge was built because we had a chief minister who had to go to Guruvayur Temple once a month," she indicates as we cross the first body of water. She doesn't rest but soaks in the familiar landmarks – marble quarries, Kottapuram tollbooth, the signs to Hussain's hometown a short detour away.

"Hussain said, 'Come to me for breakfast.' I told him, 'Don't order me. I don't want to be a Muslim doormat.' I gave 80 per cent of my energy to the one I loved. Now I think I should have kept it for my work."

She sits upright, stimulated by landscape and memory. As we pass the signs for the temple at Guruvayur, she says, "Sadiq Ali spoke chaste Malayalam, not coarse banter. He took the business of conversation very seriously, like gardening, tending a sapling, each thought … I used to think love was a fragile thing, like the fleshy petal of a magnolia. I had not anticipated it could hurt, the wounds …"

Out the window I see a parade of bedecked elephants and men blowing horns, beating drums, balancing and twisting storey-high, shiny plastic extravaganzas. I stare at this boisterous, blazing warm-up to Shivratri, the great night of Shiva's grace, swivelling my head as we pass.

Kamala glances over. "I am not allowed to go to the temple," she says distantly, "Christians are allowed. I would pollute."

We stop because she says she wants chewing gum. John rushes over from the accompanying car to confer with our van, our driver rushes back with him to the car, our driver takes the lead in the gum hunt, and gets lost. Finally we reach the Casino Hotel, all wilted except for Kamala. She eats specially prepared vegetarian dishes in a room reserved for her, Ammu, and Vishalam, who are shy initially, then proud to be eating alongside their mistress.

"Everyone is calling," Kamala tells us when we reassemble. "They say the television has been there in the hot sun since 10 AM." She changes vehicles and sits in the back of Sudhaker's car. I sit in front.

"I love these red-tiled houses," she says on the road to her village. "Nalapat didn't have paint, it was red tiles and white walls, because when you paint you use lime from the mollusk shells, which makes it not vegetarian.

"I feel a pain within that I will see the place without the house, without the trees," she says. "Actually, I am planning to build a mud cottage, AC in the bedroom, with an inner courtyard, and go there and hide out. If I win an award, I'll buy back the land, get someone like my grandmother there, resurrect this. But how can you resurrect love? There's no dummy for that. Turn right at the statue of the Virgin Mary," she tells Sudhaker, pointing ahead. "Also the *altara* [the sacred Banyan tree in its protective embankment] marks the road to the village."

Young scouts on bikes spot us at the turnoff to Nalapat. They check the window for Kamala, their Madhavikutty, wheel around and pedal ahead.

"My grandmother would think I betrayed her. We were staunch Hindus," Kamala says quietly. "My mother's sister wanted to meet me even after I became a Muslim, but her son told me, 'Don't come here or I'll get you killed.' Now he's changed his mind."

We follow the cyclists along narrow byways through tightly packed homes, to a razed, open field. Sudhaker slows the car. Ahead is a wide, thick, agitated, frightening (to me), mostly male scrum. The entire village, every local and national newspaper and TV channel, are there – *Mathrubhumi, Times of India, The Hindu, Indian Express,* India Vision, Jeevan TV, Asianet, Kairali TV. They lurch toward us like a human tsunami.

"Stop," I shout to Sudhaker.

"No," says Kamala.

I watch warily as Sudhaker drives slowly toward the crowd.

"I think the television crew would like to see me cry," Kamala says. "Merrily, see that I don't, make me laugh." As we drive closer, she says, "I could cover my eyes with my sunglasses so they wouldn't know my feelings." The scrum parts, and the car enters a wall of people. "Put your arm around Vishalam, and they'll mistake her for me," Kamala laughs. "Such fun. What a life. Considering all, I've had a lovely life."

"Do you want to drive through it?" Sudhaker asks, facing the remains of Nalapat.

"No, I'll get too sentimental." Kamala looks around hastily. "I don't recognize this desert of a place."

Sudhaker brakes and opens her door. In the time it takes me to get to their side of the car, she is seated in her wheelchair, holding court on the small piece of land she still owns. Protected by a parasol, her hennaed hands dancing and the Sonys, Leicas, and Nikons flashing, she entertains the hundreds of villagers who have come to see her.

Lakshmi, who raised young Kamala, pushes through the crowd and grabs her hand. Kamala holds her hands close. "I see you remember me, Lakshmi," Kamala says.

"How could I ever forget you, little one?" Lakshmi answers.

I hear someone in the crowd say that "Aami" – Kamala's childhood name – "has come like the blossoming of the neermathalam tree," and another villager say it scalds his heart to see her in a wheelchair. I look beyond the crowd. The co-conut grove where I met Parukutty in 2000 is gone. I search for the snake grove and see newly buffed snake idols displayed on cement in a clear-cut field.

Kamala fortunately does not dwell on naked idols, missing trees, or the granite steps left like ancient relics in rows of newly planted banana trees. She smiles with pleasure at the tentative approach of Urmila Teacher, a grey-haired school friend in widow's whites, and opens her arms in welcome. The old friend places her hand on Kamala's shoulder and with poignant tenderness bends until her forehead and Kamala's touch.

Then Kamala's chair is on the move, and she's beckoning to me. With the journalists following, we squeeze into the modern bungalow of Sukumaran, the new owner of Nalapat. Facing media four rows deep, Kamala holds court elegantly and effortlessly like the professional she is.

"Why did you choose here to visit?" someone asks.

"My journey began here. I love this place, every grain of sand. I had thought of never returning to Punnayurkulam because people here said bad things when I became a Muslim. But all that is over. The wounds Punnayurkulam inflicted on my heart have healed."

"Is this your last visit?

"I shall not come back to Punnayurkulam in human form. I yearn to be a bird in my next life. I shall return as a kingfisher seeking the scent of the neermathalam, hovering above the ponds."

The prodigal daughter shares herself generously for thirty minutes, then signals to us that she is done. Quick as roadies, we pack up and head home.

"How was it?" Kamala asks in the car.

"Amma, they're loving you," Sudhaker says.

"How did you feel?" I ask her.

"I liked it. I was awed. Somehow I didn't think anyone would remember me. Now, I'll take a bath, and what a bath that will be. Many people have touched me. I want to wash off all that."

The next day I notice a new, intricate, Escher-like religious painting on Kamala's bedroom wall. She says it's the Sri Chakra, her favourite Hindu painting, recently welcomed back into her life. "You can't tell lies or eat meat with the Chakra in the room," she tells me.

I remind her that she keeps saying she doesn't believe in any religion.

"Yes, only those who fatten on it praise it," she says evoking a cacophony of strident voices sermonizing. "But spirituality is a separate entity, a kind of silence within the blood that is sacred to me." She says she has faith in a personal, symbiotic relationship between a believer and God, "like that of Siamese twins. So, if you take from me what I think is to be my God, I don't exist. And without that adoration, without that relationship to the worshipper, the devotee, God cannot exist either."

That night Kamala's non-dogmatic, non-religious concept of God settles comfortably in my mind, and I find the Post-it I put in *The Old Playhouse and Other Poems* years ago. The page contains Kamala's poem "The Inheritance," written when she was in her thirties. Rereading it confirms for me her prescient horror of religious fundamentalism. Her words reverberate through time as she comes full cycle, back to herself.

> This then was our only inheritance, this ancient
> Virus that we nurtured in the soul so
> That when at sundown, the muezzin's high wail sounded from
> The mosque, the chapel bells announced the angelus, and
> From the temple rose the brahmin's assonant chant, we
> Walked with hearts grown scabrous with hate, illogical,
> And chose not to believe – what we perhaps vaguely sensed –
> That it was only our fathers' lunacy speaking,
> In three different tones, babbling: Slay them who do not
> Believe, or better still, disembowel their young ones
> And scatter on the streets the meagre innards. Oh God,
> Blessed be your fair name, blessed be the religion
> Purified in the unbeliever's blood, blessed be
> Our sacred city, blessed be its incarnadined glory …

The savage irony leaves me wondering if Kamala's feelings about religion have changed from the time she wrote "The Inheritance" to now.

"I was very angry when I was thirty," she tells me when I call to ask. "I called religion 'lunacy,' and thought it a diseased gene passed from blood to blood. It's still very unpleasant. I don't respect it, and now I don't even find it relevant. But I feel I've progressed, because I don't hate. I see religion to be a fake. So, if someone comes as a monk, a *sanyasi*, and I know he is a fraud, I accept him as Mr Fraud and offer him a cup of tea. I am not angry any longer."

The next day Kamala tells me the end of her novel, the wrapping-up of this last hard season of her life.

Amnesiac Sadiq Ali, now a Hindu pilgrim, enters the sanctum sanctorum of Hindu religion, the temple containing the Shiva lingam. In the temple, he hears the voice of Annasuraiya singing sacred *bhajans*, and instantly he remembers the past. Kamala says that usually at this peak of religion, the soul takes over, but when Sadiq Ali hears Annasuraiya's voice, he remembers the body. "Once you go to the peaks of religions, religion thins out and you have no religion, only yourself." Trembling in fear because he has gate-crashed a Hindu temple, Sadiq Ali falls at the feet of his teacher, asking forgiveness.

"What do you want to do?" asks his teacher.

"I want a second chance," Sadiq Ali says.

The teacher understands his feelings. He advises Sadiq Ali to take the early bus and meet Annasuraiya halfway. "Don't tell anyone. Go and live by the banks of the river together."

I clap my hands at the end of the story, which I interpret to be Kamala's own, reclaimed.

"I've sent a Muslim in ochre robes on the best Hindu pilgrimages, and nothing bad happens," Kamala says, pleased. "I have to prove to people that these things can be changed. And I've revived human love. Maybe happiness, maybe unhappiness, but they're happy together."

It seems she is using art to overcome fundamentalism and fear, the perfect ending for us both.

I try to organize a going-away party, but Kamala swings into action and invites everyone we've seen this past visit – Mangoo and his wife, my brother Hyman recently returned from sightseeing, Minnie, a family friend, poets Balan and Vijaya, David from Montreal, my middle daughter, Cleo, and her husband, and two young women visiting from the American College in Madurai. The cooks prepare all day and set out a feast served in shiny Tiffin-carriers. Kamala asks Balan to recite, and he performs his poem in a Malayalam form called *cholluka*, a mix of singing and reciting so captivating and tender that almost all breathing stops. And then talk bubbles up among the young students, and Kamala takes off, vignettes flying in wild bursts of "Merrily, you should kiss Mangoo," and "Has Hyman kissed Minnie?" – whipping up a froth, remembering gay soirees and Lady Ottoline Morrell "who gave parties and fell in love," all the Delhi, Bombay, Calcutta parties she ever hosted, this one party.

When the guests leave, she sits in her chair, lamenting her foolishness and enjoying every last drop of charm, flirtation, humour, fun, because there's no permanence in happiness. "It's like a bird cry, and then it's off from one branch to another, from one tree to another. If it alights, take pride in that moment, because it will go away." With my leave-taking tempered by my daughter's continuing presence in Cochin, I bend to hug Kamala goodbye. She encircles me with her arms, hugs back, pushes me away, and examines me carefully.

"I'll call. I'll see you next year," I say.

She watches soberly as I back out, blur. "I realized today you were leaving, and it seems to me I am still waiting for you to come," she says.

A taxi picks me up and negotiates its way through supine cows, heavy and slow from the bounty of the dumpsters beside the road. My brother meets me for a Kingfisher in the bar and describes his five-day Munnar-to-Allepey tourist junket. I listen, thinking it might be fun to be a tourist in Kerala, thinking of the jolts of uncertainty, shots of humility, flashes of insight, innumerable shades of black and white, the glorious friendship I would have missed.

As soon as I'm back in Canada, I call Kamala to learn how she's resolved the end of her novel. Now that I'm home, all I can think of is how much I don't know, how the best of Kamala's work is in her poems and the Malayalam stories I can't read, questioning if this is the best I can do and if it's enough, no matter how much has eluded me. I tell her that the reunion scene between Sadiq Ali and Annasuraiya seems the perfect ending for her book, and mine – Kamala triumphing over age, illness, and adversity, with her pen.

She says a man came, a Pentecostal, and banged on her head, shouting, "Jesus, save this daughter of yours," giving her a throbbing headache that still persists. She says more people are beginning to hate her, complaining that at her age spirituality suits her better than writing a novel. Rahman, her Imam, thinks her fictional lovers should not meet, and when she tells him she hopes to reform the Muslims' idea of love, he is shocked. Sometimes when she writes in Malayalam, she can't find a word and consults the dictionary. "I wanted the Malayali word for 'clitoris,' and I found a beautiful word, *bhagashisnika*. So I wrote about the centre of a woman's body, the *bhagashisnika*. I'll write those words even if I get killed for it, because I want Malayalis to know what love is like." As for the translation I requested of the end scene, "There is no reunion as yet. I am thinking of killing the woman in an avalanche within ten miles of the reunion. It seems a bit childish if they reunite."

"Ahh," I moan.

"I know you would prefer they meet," she says.

"It's your book," I say adamantly. "Only you decide what you write."

"That's true," she agrees. "And beautiful dreams might reveal the ending of the story," she says for us both.

Kamala suffers another diabetic crisis, and I wait several long weeks until we are able to speak again. She is in pain, her head still throbbing from Pentecostal salvation. She says her daughter-in-law and grandchildren are visiting, her new full-time maidservant provides security, and a seventy-five-year-old prince is offering to take her to London for treatment.

"I guess you haven't finished the novel," I say.

"It's not ended. Nothing ends in the last chapter. We end, legs thrashing, breath ending, but the story will never end. The characters stay where they are, like they're frozen."

"And Sadiq Ali and Annasuraiya – what happens to them?"

"They could not spend a night together. They recognize each other, but an avalanche descends, a snowstorm. They are kept apart. But it doesn't end because their longing goes on, remains in other people like a candle snuffed out and another one lit. Only names change, situations, destinations. We stop writing, someone else continues. No story ever ends."

# Epilogue

First I will strip myself of clothes and ornaments. Then I will peel off this light
brown skin and shatter my bones. I hope at last you will be able to see my
homeless, orphan, intensely beautiful soul, deep within the bone, deep down
under, beneath even the marrow ... will you be able to love me, will you be able
to love me someday when I am stripped naked of this body ...

*Ente Katha* (Malayalam version of *My Story*)

Kamala Das died on 31 May 2009, two years after leaving Cochin to live near the
family of her youngest son, Jaisurya, in the large industrial city of Pune. Her body
was washed by her two closest daughters-in-law and flown to her home state of
Kerala. Thousands of mourners of all ages paid homage, weeping and placing
flowers on her hearse during her funeral procession. The proceedings were covered live on television, and the procession stopped at public halls in Thrissur,
Cochin, Alleppey, Kollam, and Trivandrum.

Kamala Das's funeral at the Palayam Mosque in Trivandrum reflected her
ecumenical spirit: admirers of all faiths attended the service, party leaders spoke
personally and non-politically, and for the first time in India, women stood at
the graveside in a Muslim service. She was buried in a grove on the grounds of
the mosque, adjoining a temple, near a church. Her son Jaisurya planted neermathalam saplings, like those from her family's snake shrine, to flower with the
scent of jasmine by her graveside.

Before she died, Kamala Das gave her ancestral land in Punnayurkulam to the
Kerala Sahitya Akademi, the "guardian angel" of Malayalan literature.

# Acknowledgments

My bond with Kamala is greater than I can express. She shared her life with me and entrusted me with her history, her confidences, carte blanche use of her work, and the responsibility of writing about the life she had revealed. In attempting to do so, I was blessed with wonderful friends and allies whose intelligence and knowledge pepper the pages.

Ellen Coon brought Kamala and me together, and without her this book might never have begun. Linda Gaboriau was my first substantive editor and Ann Charney my final exigent editor: no writer could wish for more vital encouragement or perceptive guidance than I had from these two friends. As well, I greatly appreciate the formative comments provided by readers of various drafts, notably Nora Burkey, Harold Crooks, Brian Fawcett, Guy Lawson, Carol Lazare, Medrie McPhee, Joy Portugal, Don Sedgwick, Rebecca Taichman, and Noah Weisbord. Nicole Winstanley was my agent when the writing began. Her continuing support and friendship brightened the difficult times, and when much needed, Ed Carson and Susan Golomb added a welcome boost. This book is a work of literary non-fiction, a challenging form to market in recessive times, and I applaud publisher Philip Cercone's commitment to writing he believes in, which delivered the book to press.

I have also benefited greatly from the insights of other writers close to Kamala Das, especially Balan Chullikkad, who knows Kamala's writer's soul, Suresh Kohli, who has documented Kamala's life and her profound connection to her readers, as well as Vijaya Lakshmi and Meena Alexander, who were influenced by her life and work. Many scholars have studied Kamala's writing, and I am particularly grateful to J. Devika for her original analysis of the well-spring and evolution of Kamala's sexuality and her translation from *Ente Katha*, B. Hariharan for his cross-cultural appreciation of Kamala and his generous help to me, Savithri Shanker de Tourreil for her Malayalam/English translations and Nayar expertise, S.C Harrex and Vincent O'Sullivan for their early championing of Kamala's writing internationally, K. Satchidanandan for his excellent exegesis on Kamala's Malayalam prose, Paul Love, Premila Paul, and Jessie Furvin for welcoming me to the Kamala Das Archive, SCILET, American College, Madurai, and to Iqbal Kaur, Irshad Ahmed, P.P. Raveendran, K. Radha, and Devinder Kohli for their contributions to Kamala lore.

Elizabeth Klinck was my intrepid researcher and dear travel buddy, literally and figuratively, for the long haul. Colette Lebeuf created the first Kerala research file, S.D. von Wolff contributed later, and Alasdair Gillis, Brian Sanderson, and Steven Legari patiently transcribed lengthy conversations, stories, and poems. And when the manuscript was accepted for publication, the MQUP editorial and production team led by Joan McGilvray and Susanne McAdam surpassed their reputation as "ace."

On my visits to Kerala, I was welcomed and logistically aided by Gita Krishnankutty in Chennai and Steven Roessler in Delhi. Mr Sitaraman took excellent care of all travel arrangements on my first trips to India. I am grateful to them for smoothing my journey. On home turf, Marian Hebb elegantly negotiated all legal conundrums, and I laud her mind and appreciate her support. Angie Kaye braved the first foray with me, and the swimming ladies, Jocelyne Clarke, Hila Feil, Joan Russell, and Frances Samuels, helped keep me in shape.

Ted Riccardi and Riva Heft facilitated Kamala's inaugural visit to Canada, which was financed by the Canada Council of the Arts, Shastri Indo-Canadian Institute, Canadian Department of Foreign Affairs, Indo-US Subcommission on Education and Culture, Concordia University, Canadian Department of Foreign Affairs, the Writers Union of Canada, the Federation of English Language Writers of Quebec, and the South Asian Women's Centre. Andrew Arkin was the patron of Kamala's next visit to Canada and the United States, and he is remembered with love. A Canada Council grant gave me a year to write free of care.

I would like to acknowledge my daughter Cleo's close separate friendship with Kamala, and her advice, that which I followed and that which I did not. My thanks to my daughter Anna for welcoming Kamala and caring for her, to my daughter Kim for her unqualified acceptance of my writing, and to my father, Sydney Weisbord, his wife, Phyllis Amber, my brother, Hyman Weisbord, and

Kamala's dear friend, Gwen Troncin, for their belief in my work. I thank Kamala's children Monu Nalapat and Chinnan Das for their kindness to me, and Kamala's youngest son, Jaisurya Das, and her daughter-in-law, Devi, for their overflowing love and understanding of Kamala, which included a warm acceptance of me.

At Kamala's request and my discretion, I have changed names that are irrelevant to understanding Kamala and her work, and maintained those that are. The name to be writ large is that of Kamala's maidservant Ammu from Kumbalam, who accompanied Kamala to Pune, cared for her, spoke Malayalam with her, and kept her company until her death.

I am blessed by Arnie Gelbart's support and conviction that I should write free of censorship, including his. For this, the ultimate generosity, I thank him.

# Bibliography

## WORKS BY KAMALA DAS IN ENGLISH

Das, Kamala. *Summer in Calcutta*. New Delhi: Rajinder Paul, 1965. Reprint, Kottayam India: DC Books 2004.

– *The Descendants*. Calcutta: Writers Workshop, 1967.

– *The Old Playhouse and Other Poems*. Madras: Orient Longman. 1973. Reprint, London: Sangam 1986.

– *My Story*. Jullundur, Punjab: Sterling 1976; London and New York: Quartet 1978. Reprint, Kottayam: DC Books 2004; New Delhi: HarperCollins India 2010.

– *Alphabet of Lust*. New Delhi: Orient Longham 1977.

– *A Doll for the Child Prostitute*. New Delhi: India Paperbacks 1977.

– *Collected Poems*. Trivandrum, India: Kamala Das 1984.

– "Running away from Home." *Indian Literary Review* 3, no. 3 (October) 1985.

– *The Best of Kamala Das*. Kozhikode: Bodhi Publishing House 1991.

– *Padmavati, the Harlot, and Other Stories*. New Delhi: Sterling Publishers 1992.

– *The Sandal Trees and Other Stories*. Translated from the Malayalam by V.C. Harris and C.K. Mohamed Ummer. Hyderabad: Disha Books 1995; London: Sangam, 1995.

– *Kamala Das: A Collage*. One-act plays compiled by Arun Kuckreja. New Delhi: Vidya Prakashan Mandir 1984.

– "My Instinct, My Guru." *Indian Literature* 33, no. 5 (September-October) 1990.

– *The Path of the Columnist* (as Dr Kamala Suraiya). Calicut: Olive Publications 2000.

– *Only the Soul Knows How to Sing: Selections from Kamala Das*. Kottayam: DC Books 1996.

– *A Childhood in Malabar: A Memoir*. Translated by Gita Krishnankutty. New Delhi and New York: Penguin 2003.

– *Ya Allah* (as Surayya). Kozhikode, Kerala: Islamic Publishing House 2003 (quoted from unpublished translation by Kamala Das).

– and Pritish Nandy. *Tonight This Savage Rite: The Love Poems of Kamala Das and Pritish Nandy*. New Delhi: Arnold Heinemann 1979.


## WORKS BY KAMALA DAS IN MALAYALAM AS MADHAVIKUTTY

This bibliography is based on Leena Chandran's compilation of works by Madhavikutty published in *Bhashaposhini* 33, no. 1 (July 2009): 28–31.


*Mathilukal* (The walls: short story). Kozhikode: Mathrubhumi 1955.

*Pathu Kathakal* (Ten stories). Kottayam: Sahthiya Pracharna Sahakarana Sangam 1958.

*Naricheerukal Parakkumpol* (short stories). Eranakulam: Sahithya Parishad 1960.

*Tharishu Nilam* (Wasteland: short stories). Eranakulam: Sahithya Parishad 1962.

*Ente Snehitha Aruna* (My friend Aruna: short stories). Thrissur: Current 1963.

*Chuvanna Pavada* (Red skirt: short stories). Thrissur: Current 1964.

*Pakshiyude Manam* (The scent of the bird: short stories). Thrissur: Current 1964.

*Thanuppu* (The cold: short stories). Thrissur: Current 1967.

*Rajavinte Prema Bhajanam* (The king's lover: short stories). Thrissur: Current 1969.

*Premathinte Vilapa Kavyam* (Requiem for love). Thrissur: Current 1971.

*Ente Katha* (My story: autobiography). Thrissur: Current 1973.

*Madhavikuttyude Munnu Novelukal* (Three novels of Madhavikutty). Kottayam: Sahithya Pracharana Sahakarana Sangam 1977.

*Manasi* (novel). Thiruvananthapuram: Prabhatham 1978.

*Madhavikuttyude Kathakal* (Short stories of Madhavikutty). Kottayam: DC Books 1982.

*Irupathionnam Noottandileku* (Towards the twenty-first century: articles). Kottayam: Sahthiya Pravartaka Sahakarana Sangam 1984.

*Ente Kavitha* (My poems: translations from English). Panthalam: Pusthaka Prasadhaka Sangam 1985.

*Ente Cheru Kathakal* (My short stories, 2 vols.). Kozhikode: Mathrubhumi 1985.

*Bhayam Ente Nishavasthram* (My nightdress fear: essays). Kozhikode: Mathrubhumi 1986.

*Balyakala Smaranakal* (Childhood reminiscences: memoirs). Kottayam: DC Books 1987.

*Chandana Maranga* (The sandal trees). Kottayam: Current 1988.

*Manomi* (novel). Thrissur: Current 1988.

*Kadal Mayuram* (novel). Kottayam: Current 1989.

*Varshangalkku Munpu* (Many years ago: memoirs). Thrissur: Current 1989.

*Palaayanam* (Exodus: short stories). Thrissur: Current 1990.

*Kamaladasinte Thiranjedutha Kavithakal* (Selected poems of Kamala Das: translation from English). Kozhikode: Mulberry 1991.

*Swathandrya Senaniyude Makal* (The freedom-fighter's daughter: short stories). Kozhikode: Poorna 1991.

*Diarykkuruppukal* (Diary notes). Kottayam: Current 1992.

*Nirmathalam Poothakalam* (When the pomegranate bloomed: memoirs). Kottyam: DC Books 1993.

*Ennennum Thara* (Always Thara: novelette).Thiruvananthapuram: Neruda 1994.

*Kamaladasinte Pranaya Kavithakal* (Love poems of Kamala Das: translations from English). Thrissur: Megha 1994.

*Nashtappetta Nilambari* (short stories). Kasargode: Kalakshethram 1994.

*Chekkerunna Pakshikal* (short stories). Kottayam: DC Books 1996.

*Ottayadippatha* (Narrow lane: memoirs). Kottayam: DC Books 1997.

*Madhavikuttyude Premakathakal* (Love stories of Madhavikutty). Kozhikode: Olive 1998.

*Amavasy* (novel written in collaboration with K.L. Mohanavarma). Kottayam: DC Books 1999.

Ente Pathakal (essays).Thiruvananthapuram: Prabath 1999.

Veendum Chila Kathakal (short stories). Thiruvananthapuram: Prabath1999.

*Kavadam* (The door: written in collaboration with Nalapat Sulochana. Kottayam: DC Books 2000.

*Madhavikuttyude Pranaya Novelukal* (The love novels of Madhavikutty). Kozhikode: Olive 2000.

*Surayya Padunnu* (Surayya sings: poems). Thiruvananthapuram: Prabhath 2001.

*Snehathinte Swargavathilukal*. Kozhikkode: Pappilon 2001.

*Hamsadhwani* (short stories). Kozhikode: Pappilon 2001.

*Januamma Paranja Katha* (short stories). Thrissur: Current 2002.

*Parithoshikam* (The gift: short stories). Kozhikode: Pappilon 2002.

*Malayalathinte Suvarnakathakal: Madhavikutty*. Thrissur: Green 2002.

*Ente Priyapetta Kathakal. Kottayam*: DC Books 2003.

*Madhavikkuttyude Kathakal* (Complete collection of stories). Kottayam: DC Books 2003.

*Unmakathakal*. Nooranadu: Unma 2004.

*Nilavinte mattorizha* (poems). Kozhikode: Mathrubhumi 2004.

*Peeditharute Kathakal* (Stories of the oppressed). Thiruvananthapuram: Prabhat 2004.

*Madhuvidhuvinu Shesham* (After the honeymoon). Alappuzha: Fabien 2004.

*Madhavikkuttyude Sthreekal* (Madhavikutty's women: short stories). Kozhikode: Mathrubhoomi 2004.

*Vandikkalakal* (novel). Kozhikode: Mathrubhoomi 2005.

*Madhavikutty: Pranayathinte Album* (Madhavikutty's album of love). Kozhikode: Olive 2005.

*Pattinte Ulachil* (short stories). Kozhikode: Poorna 2006.

*Madhavikuttyude Novelukal*. Kottayam: DC Books 2006.

*Vakkilammavan* (short stories). Kannoor: Kairali 2006.

*Anuraginiyude Padachalanagal Kozhikode*: Haritham 2007.

*Ente Jivithamkondithramathram* (Kurippukal). Kottayam: DC Books 2007.

*Budhanilavu* (essays). Kozhikode: Poorna 2007.

*Vishadam Pookkunna Marangal* (memoirs). Thrissur: Scenario 2007.

*Nirmathalathinte Pookkal* (The pomegranate flowers: stories). Thiruvananthapuram: Priyadarshini 2009.

*Sasneham* (With love). Kozhikode: Islamic Publishing House 2009.

*Kerala Sancharam* (travelogue). Kottayam: DC Books 2009.

## ABOUT KAMALA DAS

Ahmed, Irshad G. *Kamala Das: The Poetic Pilgrimage*. New Delhi: Creative Books 2005.

De Souza, Eunice. *Nine Women Poets*. Delhi: Oxford University Press 1997.

Devika, J. "Beauty, More Beauty: A Tribute to Madhavikutty." Kafilia.org, 1 June 2009.

Harrex, S.C., and Vincent O'Sullivan, eds. *Kamala Das: A Selection, with Essays on Her Work*. CRNLE Writers Series 1. Adelaide: Centre for Research in the New Literatures in English 1986.

Kaur, Iqbal, ed. *Perspectives on Kamala Das's Prose*. New Delhi: Intellectual 1995.

Kohli, Devindra. *Kamala Das*. New Delhi: Arnold-Heinemann 1975.

Radha, K. *Kamala Das*. vol. 8, *Kerala Writers in English*, Madras: Macmillan India 1986.

Raveendran, P.P. "Of Masks and Memories: An Interview with Kamala Das." *Indian Literature: Sahitya Akademi Literary Bi-Monthly* 36, no. 3 (May-June 1993).

"Text as History, History as Text: A Reading of Kamala Das's Anamalai Poems." *Journal of Commonwealth Literature* 29, no. 2 (1994).

Satchidanandan, K. "Beyond the Body." *Frontline* 26, no. 13 (20 June–3 July 2009).

Weisbord, Merrily. "Kamala Das: Indian Poet and Writer." *The Times* (online), 13 June 2009.

Zacharia, Paul. *Tehelka Magazine* 6, no. 23 (13 June 2009).

## ADDITIONAL READING

Canetti, Elias. *The Secret Heart of the Clock*. New York: Farrar Straus Giroux 1989.

Cather, Willa. *My Mortal Enemy*. Toronto: Macmillan Canada 1926.

Chullikad, Balachandran. *Poems by Balachandran Chullikad*. New Delhi: Sanskriti Pratisthan.

de Tourreil, Savithri Shanker. "Nayars of Kerala and Matriliny Revisited." *Societies of Peace: Matriarchies Past, Present and Future*. Toronto: Inanna Publications and Education 2009.

Devika, J. "Housewife, Sex Worker and Reformer." *Economic and Political Weekly* (Mumbai), 29 April 2006.

Duras, Marguerite. *Emily S.* New York: Pantheon Books 1989.

Frater, Alexander. *Chasing the Monsoon*. New Delhi: Penguin India 1991.

Ghosh, Amitav. *In an Antique Land*. New York: Vintage 1994.

Hope, Laurence. *The Garden of Kama and Other Love Lyrics of India*. London: William Heinemann 1917.

Kakar, Sudhir, ed. *Indian Love Stories*. New Delhi: Roli Books 1999.

Lakshmi Holmstrom, ed. *The Inner Courtyard: Stories by Indian Women*. Toronto: Virago Press 1990.

Malcolm, Janet. *The Journalist and the Murderer*. London: Granta Books 2004.

Manolokan Group. *Crime 57*. Calicut: Manolokan Group Publishing 2000.

Mehta, Gita. *Karma Cola: Marketing the Mystic East*. New York: Simon and Schuster 1979.

Miller, Barbara Stoler, ed. and trans. *The Gita Govinda of Jayadeva: Love Songs of the Dark Lord*. New Delhi: Motilal Banardsidass 2003.

Moorhouse, Geoffrey. *Om: An Indian Pilgrimage*. London: Hodder and Stoughton 1993.

Nair, Anita, ed. *Where the Rain Is Born: Writings about Kerala*. New Delhi: Penguin Books India 2002.

Paniker, K. Ayyappa, ed. *Malayalam Short Stories*. New Delhi: Vikas Publishing House 1981.

Paz, Octavio. *In Light of India*. India: HarperCollins 2000.

Raveendran, P.P. "Of Masks and Memories: An Interview with Kamala Das." *Indian Literature* 36, no. 3. New Delhi: Sahitya Akademi 1993.

Rushdie, Salman. *The Moor's Last Sigh*. New York: Pantheon Books 1996.

Singh, Khuswant, ed. *Our Favourite Indian Stories*. Neelam Kumar, Mumbai: Jaico Publishing House 2005.

Winterson, Jeanette. *The Passion*. Toronto: Vintage Canada 2000.